OXFORD MEDIEVAL TEXTS

General Editors

C. N. L. BROOKE   D. E. GREENWAY
M. WINTERBOTTOM

THE DEEDS OF THE FRANKS AND THE

OTHER PILGRIMS TO JERUSALEM

THE DEEDS
OF THE FRANKS
AND THE OTHER
PILGRIMS TO JERUSALEM

EDITED BY

ROSALIND HILL

CLARENDON PRESS · OXFORD

Oxford University Press, Walton Street, Oxford OX2 6DP

OXFORD   LONDON   GLASGOW
NEW YORK   TORONTO   MELBOURNE   WELLINGTON
KUALA LUMPUR   SINGAPORE   JAKARTA   HONG KONG   TOKYO
DELHI   BOMBAY   CALCUTTA   MADRAS   KARACHI
NAIROBI   DAR ES SALAAM   CAPE TOWN

ISBN 0 19 822209 2

Published in the United States
by Oxford University Press, New York

First published in Nelson's Medieval Texts Series, 1962
Reprinted as an Oxford Medieval Text 1972, 1979

*Printed in Great Britain by
Weatherby Woolnough,
Wellingborough, Northants*

CONTENTS

Preface   vii

Introduction   ix

    I   The Book   ix

    II   The Author   xi

    III   The Translation   xvii

    IV   The Crusade   xx

    V   Manuscript and Editions   xxxviii

Select Bibliography   xliii

Latin Text   *verso* 1-103

English Translation   *recto* 1-103

Index   107

MAPS

The Route from Durazzo to Constantinople   xxviii

The Route from Constantinople to Antioch   xxx

The City of Antioch in 1098   xxxii

The Route from Antioch to Jerusalem   xxxv

PREFACE

In this edition of the *Gesta Francorum* I am responsible for the translation, the notes to the text and the historical introduction. The Latin text and the critical apparatus are the work of a better hand than mine, that of Professor Roger Mynors, with whom I am honoured to be associated.

I am most grateful to the custodians of the MSS in the Vatican Library, in the libraries in Madrid, Berlin and at Corpus Christi College, Cambridge, for their kindness and ready help. My debt to earlier editions of the work, and especially to those of Hagenmeyer, Bréhier and Lees, will be clearly apparent. I should like to express my gratitude also to Professor Galbraith for his unfailing encouragement, to Professor Brooke who rescued the work when I had almost abandoned it and generously gave much time to editing it, to Professor Wormald for his help with palaeography, to Professor Du Boulay for his advice about forms of address in a modern army, and to Miss Elsie Simkins for her care in typing. My knowledge of the text I owe to two people, the late Mrs Agnes Leys and Miss Nancy Miller, both of them teachers to whom my debt is beyond repayment.

The idea of translating the work into English took shape when I read the letters written during the Second World War by my brother Gray Hill. Had he returned, my understanding of the crusaders' strategy and tactics would have been greater.

Rosalind Hill

INTRODUCTION

I

THE BOOK

The *Gesta Francorum et aliorum Hierosolimitanorum* is a history of the First Crusade, beginning with the Council of Clermont in November 1095 and ending with the battle of Ascalon in August 1099. It is divided into ten books, of which the first nine appear to have been composed before the Author (whose name is unknown) left Antioch in November 1098, and the tenth, which is the longest, at Jerusalem, not later than the beginning of 1101, and probably fairly soon after the battle of Ascalon. In 1101 Ekkehard, later abbot of Aura, went to Jerusalem on pilgrimage and saw there 'a little book' in which were described the adventures of the crusaders during the three years preceding 'the joyful victory of the taking of Jerusalem'.[1] About 1106 Robert, a monk of Rheims, was ordered by his abbot to re-write 'a history' (*unam historiam*) which the abbot thought unsatisfactory because it was rough in style and contained no full description of the Council of Clermont.[2] Baudri, later archbishop of Dol, in his *Historia Jerusalem* written in 1108, also mentions 'a little book' which, according to him, was anonymous and very rustic and unpolished in style, so that he felt himself called upon to re-write it.[3] This little book cannot have been the *Historia Francorum* of Raymond of Agiles, which announces the author's name in the preface and which is written in a style which even an archbishop could hardly have called rustic. Besly, in the seventeenth century, assumed that it was the *Historia de Hiero-*

[1] *R.H.C. Hist. Occ.*, v, 21
[2] *R.H.C. Hist. Occ.*, iii, 722
[3] *R.H.C. Hist. Occ.*, iv, 10

solymitano Itinere of the priest Peter Tudebod of Civray.[1] This opinion was generally held until the middle of the nineteenth century, when independent research in France and Germany restored the primacy of the *Gesta* as the 'little book'. The introduction to Hagenmeyer's edition of the text (1890)[2] deals with the problem in full, and gives conclusive reasons for thinking that the *Gesta* is the source from which nearly all the other historians of the First Crusade have borrowed.[3]

Tudebod's work and the anonymous *Historia Belli Sacri* are both examples of early and quite innocent plagiarism. Both authors make full use of the text of the *Gesta* without acknowledgment, but this was an accepted practice of the time and regarded as showing respect for the earlier author rather than as stealing his work. Tudebod had himself taken part in the Crusade and probably wrote before 1111. He adds to the text some information of his own, such as the account of Yaghi Siyan's massacre of his prisoners,[4] which does not occur in the *Gesta*. The anonymous author must have finished his book not earlier than 1130, since he adds material covering the period after the Crusade and mentions the death of Bohemond II of Antioch. He makes use of Tudebod and of Raymond of Agiles.

The *Gesta* was used, although not extensively, by two other writers who took part in the Crusade, Raymond of Agiles, a priest and canon of Le Puy, who followed Count Raymond of Toulouse, and Fulcher of Chartres, chaplain to Baldwin who became the first king of Jerusalem. While Hagenmeyer attempts

---

[1] For Tudebod, see *R.H.C. Hist. Occ.*, III, 3-117

[2] H. Hagenmeyer, *Anonymi Gesta Francorum*, pp. 39-92

[3] Some modern historians (A. C. Krey in 'A neglected passage in the Gesta', *The Crusades and other historical essays presented to Dana C. Munro*, ed. L. J. Paetow, pp. 57-76, and C. Cahen, *La Syrie du Nord*) assume that the work was edited and circulated in the West after 1105 in support of Bohemond's claim to the principality of Antioch. This may well be true, but it cannot be proved from the MSS. The *Gesta* is not entirely favourable to Bohemond. It shows, for example, that the Author deliberately left his service in the autumn of 1098, when it became clear that he would not go on to Jerusalem. See *The Crusades and other Historical Essays presented to D. C. Munro*, ed. L. J. Paetow, pp. 57-79.   [4] *P.L.*, CLV, 785-6

to press the similarities rather too far (since, after all, there are only a limited number of words which can be used to describe the same event) he does establish the fact that both these authors had access to the text of the *Gesta*.[1] The book also had some influence—either in its original form or through immediate borrowers—on most of the twelfth-century histories of the Crusade written by western Europeans, Guibert of Nogent, Ralph of Caen, Hugh of Fleury, Robert of St Rémi, Fulco and Gilo of Paris, Albert of Aix and William of Tyre.[2] It was also used in more general histories, such as those written by Ordericus Vitalis and William of Malmesbury. Its influence upon the historical writing of the time can therefore hardly be overestimated, and its 'rustic and unpolished style' has stood the test of time far better than the more complicated prose of those who tried to improve it.

II

THE AUTHOR

Of the Anonymous Author of the *Gesta* we know absolutely nothing except what he has revealed in his own book. He was writing a history of the Crusade, and like most of his contemporaries he had very little interest in autobiography. He never mentions his own name. Nevertheless it is possible to discover certain facts about him.

From his description of the setting-out of the Crusade, and from the position in which he fought in all the battles up to the end of June 1098, it is clear that he was a vassal of Bohemond, and that he came from southern Italy, almost certainly from Apulia, which he mentions as Karbuqa's[3] ultimate objective. He knew the names of a number of undistinguished men in Bohemond's army, while he sometimes confused those of even the

[1] The 'borrowing' of the *Gesta* from Raymond d'Agiles seems rather doubtful. See below, p. 13

[2] For whose work see *R.H.C. Hist. Occ.*, I-v

[3] For an account of Karbuqa and his expedition, see below, pp. xxxii-xxxiv

noblest of the northern leaders, giving to Hugh of Vermandois the title of 'Magnus' by an apparent confusion with 'maisné' —the younger brother. He knew of Godfrey de Bouillon's march across Europe to Constantinople only by report, and although he was eventually driven to join the forces of Count Raymond of Toulouse he shows no knowledge of the count's dangerous and uncomfortable journey along the Dalmatian coast. Throughout the first nine books of the *Gesta* he calls Bohemond 'dominus' in the feudal sense of 'overlord', and usually describes him, after the manner of an epic hero, by some laudatory epithet such as 'sapiens', 'prudens' or 'bellipotens'. He fought in the ranks of Bohemond's knights at the battles of Dorylaeum and the Lake of Antioch (where he was apparently close enough to his lord to hear what was said to Robert FitzGerard), and he was one of the band of picked men whom Bohemond took with him to undertake the desperate hazard of entering Antioch by night. He knew a few words of Greek, yet he displays, from the beginning of the book, a violent prejudice against the Greek Emperor Alexius Comnenus. He occasionally uses a word such as 'tenda' or 'merula' which is rare in Latin north of the Alps.[1] Moreover, in his reference to Pope Urban's journey to Clermont 'across the mountains' he makes it clear that he normally regarded Italy as his home.

All these indications suggest that he was one of those Normans whose family had followed the sons of Tancred de Hauteville into southern Italy in the eleventh century, when there were good pickings for enterprising mercenaries. Bohemond's father, Robert Guiscard, was one of Tancred's sons. He had been confirmed in possession of the duchy of Apulia in 1059, and, growing more ambitious, had attempted to annex Durazzo from the Greeks in 1081. He was constantly recruiting Norman followers, whom he enfeoffed with Italian lands, and, in fact,

---

[1] Hagenmeyer (p. 8) noted this peculiarity but overstressed it. Such words as 'seniores', 'solarium' and 'cavillae' were by no means confined to Italy.

none of his men who is mentioned in the *Gesta* has an identifiably Italian name, though several of them took their titles from Italian fiefs. We may take it, I think, that Bohemond's immediate followers were of Norman stock, at least on the father's side, although many of them were born in the south.

The Author was a layman, and set out on the Crusade as a knight. It has been suggested by Hagenmeyer, and accepted by Miss Lees, that he lost his horse during the siege of Antioch and that after November 1098, when he had joined the Provençal army, he was serving in the capacity of a foot-soldier.[1] This may be true, but in the summer of 1099 he refers to the 'pauperes homines pedites' as if he were not one of them,[2] and his account of the march from Marra to Jerusalem suggests that the crusaders acquired plenty of horses to replace those which they had lost. Knighthood depended upon training and initiation rather than upon wealth, and a man might be a knight and yet hold no fief. The Author had taken the serious step of cutting himself off from Bohemond, his own feudal lord, because he realised that Bohemond was intent upon founding a principality in Antioch and did not much care whether or not he performed the pilgrimage to the Holy Sepulchre. Normans, however, were adaptable and quite well accustomed to serving as mercenaries, so that there would be nothing surprising in a Norman knight's taking service with Count Raymond of Toulouse.

As a layman and a fighter, the Author saw the Crusade from a completely different standpoint from that of his contemporary authors Raymond of Agiles and Fulcher of Chartres, who, as priests, were debarred from taking part in battles. He was not invited to take part in the councils of the leaders, and could therefore report them only by hearsay. However, he was interested in the ordering of battles and the technique of siege-craft. He was not, considering his circumstances, a brutal man; his accounts of battles and massacres are given in a perfectly straightforward way, with no attempt to emphasise horrid de-

[1] See p. xxxv   [2] See p. 89

tails or to gloat over defeated enemies. He took it for granted that the Turks were unjustly holding the Holy Sepulchre, and that it was therefore desirable that as many as possible of them should be killed, but personally he rather liked them ('you could not find better soldiers anywhere')[1] and his anecdotes of Karbuqa's camp sound like the half-affectionate stories made up by soldiers about an enemy who had, at least, the merit of being a 'bonny fighter'. He knew very little about the Muslim religion, assuming that it involved polytheism and idolatry, and calling the Muslims 'pagans'. He also confused Turks with Arabs, and assumed that the Muslim army was organised in the same way as that of the Franks.

We have no means of knowing whether he wrote the history of the Crusade himself or dictated it to a clerk. Educated knights ('milites literati') were rare in the period, but they did exist, particularly in the case of younger sons, trained for the church, who had not progressed beyond minor orders and had been recalled to a military career by the death of an elder brother. Baldwin I, king of Jerusalem, was a 'miles literatus' of this type, and he was a contemporary of the Author. In any case, the *Gesta* was not extensively remodelled by a clerk. This fact may be appreciated by considering the strictures of Baudri of Dol, and by comparing the book with the ecclesiastical histories of Raymond and Fulcher. The *Gesta* is written throughout in an extremely terse, simple and unadorned style. The sentences are rarely complex, except where the Author is attributing remarks to somebody else. Similes, for example that of the starving lion,[2] are rare but exceedingly vivid. The vocabulary is limited, and the biblical quotations are all drawn from those parts of the Scriptures which would be familiar to a devout layman. There is, however, a slight feeling of reminiscence of the Vulgate about the style (as there is of the Authorised Version about the style of Abraham Lincoln) suggesting that the Author was a religious man who remembered, half-consciously, the words which he had heard in church. That he was a devout

[1] See p. 21   [2] See p. 37

man we know from his conduct in leaving Bohemond and going on to the Holy Sepulchre, turning his back on tempting prospects of enfeoffment in the principality of Antioch, and in his straightforward and unshaken conviction that God intervened miraculously to help the crusaders. Unlike Raymond of Agiles he did not spend time in discussing miracles of rather doubtful validity. He reported three, all of which, so far as he knew, were vouched for by trustworthy witnesses. Like a twentieth-century soldier who had seen the Angels of Mons or the calm sea off Dunkirk, he was convinced that these things were the result of the intervention of God.

The whole work has about it something of the quality of a saga. The Author uses a regular set of conventional epithets to describe people ('sapiens' or 'prudens' for the leaders of the Crusade, 'iniquissimus' or 'infelix' (most undeservedly) for the Greek Emperor, 'inimici Dei et sancte christianitatis' for the Turks). He shows a tendency to slip into stylised refrains reminiscent of the Chansons de Geste in his description of the plunder taken after battles, and in the doxology which he introduced at the end of each section of his work. Whether or not he wrote down the original story with his own hand, he seems to have considered it primarily as a tale of heroic deeds and not as a scholar's chronicle. His creed was that of the Song of Roland: 'Christians are right and pagans are wrong.' In Palestine he found the Holy Sepulchre, which he had braved such dangers to deliver, and there he himself found (so far as we know) a soldier's grave. The account of the tour of the Holy Places, appended to his work in one of the earliest MSS, entitles us to hope that he saw them all (except Nazareth and the Sea of Galilee) before he died.[1]

That the passages describing events in the Muslim camp or in that of the Emperor Alexius are, as Bréhier suggests,[2] the work of a collaborator seems to me extremely doubtful. They are certainly imaginative descriptions of scenes which the Author

[1] Although this 'tour' is no more than an ordinary pilgrims' guide-book.
[2] Bréhier, *Histoire Anonyme*, pp. v-viii

did not see, and he is inclined to make the characters, especially the Turks, speak and write in a high-flown way which contrasts with his own economy of words. Nevertheless, the characteristic terseness of his style keeps on breaking in, as in the conversation between Karbuqa and the amir who was put in charge of the citadel of Antioch, or the description of the retreat of Alexius in the summer of 1098.[1] The imaginative passages do not suggest later interpolations made by a cleric into an unvarnished tale; they are rather, I think, the product of gossip and rumours in the crusaders' camp—the common report of the way in which Muslims or Greeks did actually behave. The Author, who had a sense of humour, probably enjoyed this kind of tale very much and put it into his story with great satisfaction. He would not have expected Karbuqa to speak or behave as Bohemund did, and probably expected him to have a slightly sinister background—hence the curious tale of Karbuqa's second-sighted and rapacious mother. The dramatic outburst of grief attributed to Bohemond's half-brother is quite in keeping with knightly behaviour at the period—a false report of the death of Baldwin I caused his vassal Tancred (who personally disliked him) 'to weep for great sorrow and anguish'.[2]

I do not think that it will ever be possible to determine whether the 'little book' which existed at Jerusalem in 1101 was actually written by the Author or dictated by him to a clerk.[3] In the absence of the original MS we cannot judge, but the style of the whole work seems to reflect faithfully the story told by a devout, observant and intelligent layman with no pretension to learning and no literary background except the Bible.

[1] If the story of Guy's distress and the retreat of Alexius were interpolated after 1105 in order to support Bohemond's claim to Antioch, the writer must have had an unusual capacity for assimilating his style to that of the original Author. See below, p. 63 note 2

[2] Fulcher, in *P.L.*, cLv, 876

[3] The earliest MSS which exist show no signs of the peculiar script written in the Latin kingdom of Jerusalem, and seem to be characteristic of the western book-hand of the middle of the twelfth century.

III

THE TRANSLATION

The translation of the *Gesta* has not been an entirely simple matter, in spite of the fact that the Latin is extremely easy to read, and that the reactions of ordinary soldiers fighting, in countries near the Mediterranean, against an apparently over-whelming force cannot have varied much in the whole period between the battle of Marathon and that of al-Alamein.[1] The Author has a good story to tell, and he tells it with directness. Nevertheless, he lived in a society governed by feudal relation-ships which are not easy to express without using the technical language of historians. His work was to him completely modern —he never, except in a biblical reminiscence, uses an archaic phrase—but he is describing a society which to us would be archaic, in which many things have no exact modern parallel.

I have tried to compromise in a way which I hope will be comprehensible to modern readers. For example, when one of the crusading leaders addresses his fellows in council he usually starts with the phrase 'Seniores et prudentissimi (*or* fortissimi) milites'. The words mean, quite literally, 'Feudal lords and very skilful (*or* valiant) knights', and would indicate exactly the rank of the audience, but they are also the equivalent of a mod-ern commander's 'Gentlemen, you are all experienced officers'. I have generally translated them as 'Gentlemen and very valiant knights', since the word 'senior' (as in modern Italian and Spanish) was a courteous form of address, and the word 'miles' implied not only what we should call an officer but had the precise meaning of a man who had undergone a particular form of training and initiation and who usually held land in return for military service of a particular kind (fighting on horseback in the main line of battle). I have used the word 'soldier'

---

[1] My brother, who had no historical training and had never read the *Gesta*, came extremely close to the style of the book in the letters which he wrote from North Africa in 1942-3.

sparingly except when it applied to a foot-soldier or ranker, because 'solidarius' literally means a man who fights for pay ('solidi' or shillings) as distinct from fighting in return for a grant of land, which a knight, unless hired as a mercenary or enfeoffed on special terms, did not generally do. I have translated 'dominus Boamundus' as 'my lord Bohemond', because the Author generally uses 'dominus' in two senses only, meaning 'the Lord God' and 'my overlord', as distinct from other feudal lords to whom he owed no personal allegiance. The word 'castrum', which I have translated 'castle', can also mean 'a little walled town'. Remembering that this was the eleventh century and that such castles as Caernarvon were yet unbuilt, I have assumed that the small fortified towns of the East would have looked to the Author rather like the 'motte and bailey' castles with which he was familiar.

Adjectives such as 'prudens', 'sapiens' and 'doctus' do not bear their classical meaning, but have the general sense of 'good in dealing with the particular situation which the person had to face'. Therefore in battle or in matters of strategy they seem to convey 'valiant' or 'gallant' or occasionally 'skilful'. (The modern parliamentary custom of addressing a member of military rank as 'the honourable and gallant member for X' appears to convey the same assumption that the man is a good soldier.)

The description of the Emperor Alexius by adjectives such as 'iniquus' or 'infelix' suggests the mixture of dislike and scorn felt by a Catholic for a schismatic, and by a Norman for a man who did not order his life according to Western conventions and was prepared to deal with the Muslims by diplomacy instead of by force. It has a strong suggestion of Kipling's 'lesser breeds without the law', and I have generally translated it as 'wretched' or 'miserable', for this seems to give a genuine impression of the attitude of a Norman to the far more intelligent and sophisticated Greek, who incidentally was far from being 'unfortunate' in his affairs.[1]

---

[1] Compare Liudprand of Cremona, 'The Embassy to Constantinople', trans. F. A. Wright, *The Works of Liudprand of Cremona*, pp. 240-1.

In the scriptural passages, the visions and the prayers I have tried to keep as closely as possible to the text of the Authorised Version of the Bible and to the Book of Common Prayer. It may quite reasonably be argued that the language of English divines of the sixteenth and seventeenth centuries has nothing to do with that of a man born in Apulia in the eleventh century, but I can think of no more adequate way of conveying the Author's meaning.

In the fantastic passages set in the Muslim camp I have tried to convey the peculiar blend of bombast and common-sense which the Author assumed to be the style in which Muslims spoke and wrote. He had been brought up in the South and probably knew a little about the Arabic inhabitants of the Norman lands in Italy and Sicily. It would be natural for him to impute outrageous boastfulness to his enemies, especially when they were defeated, but he does not seem to have wished to hold them up to unmitigated ridicule. They were, after all, brave men.

The names of places and persons have presented some difficulty. A direct translation of the name of a famous place into its modern equivalent (e.g. Istambul for Constantinople) seems to be entirely out of keeping in a crusader's chronicle. On the other hand some small places which lay on the route of the crusaders seem to have retained no tradition of their medieval name. I have tried to make the geography as intelligible as possible, without doing violence to the text, by keeping the ancient traditional name for large cities such as Constantinople and Antioch, the crusader's nick-name for places where the modern form is entirely different (e.g. La Chamelle for Homs) and the modern form for some small places where the medieval name has entirely disappeared, or where a piece of the landscape is described as 'a devilish mountain' or 'a certain river'. I cannot plead consistency, but I have done my best with cross-references. Personal names have generally been given in the modern form which may most easily be found in books of reference. Raymond, Count of Toulouse, was generally known as

the Count of St Gilles from one of his favourite estates. In the
case of Arabic or Turkish names, where the Author makes a
gallant attempt to reproduce a phonetic form, I have restored
the spelling generally used by Professor Sir Hamilton Gibb,
although in my ignorance of the languages involved I have not
ventured to include the diacritical marks.

IV

THE CRUSADE

The history of the First Crusade has been written by many
learned men whose works should be accessible in any good
library, and it is possible, through the works of English,
French and American scholars, to realise something of the
way in which the Crusade was regarded, not only by the
Franks, but also by the Greeks and the Muslims.[1] These brief
notes on the subject are meant to provide nothing more than a
framework into which the text of the *Gesta* can be fitted, in the
hope that they may encourage readers to turn to the works of
those historians, both medieval and modern, who are deeply
versed in the period and write with authority.

It is clearly shown by the *Gesta* that the Crusade was an
extremely complicated affair. Any attempt to explain it in
terms of one motive, such as religious zeal, desire for economic
advantage by Western traders, land-hunger on the part of the
crusading leaders or rivalry between the Franks and the Greeks,
is bound to fail, although every one of these motives was apparent in it. We cannot draw a clear distinction between the
aims of the leading men and those of the crowd of 'poor pilgrims' in whom Raymond of Agiles was so much interested,
for both groups displayed genuine piety and genuine greed.
The password[2] used at the battle of Dorylaeum shows that there

[1] See Bibliography, p. xliii

[2] 'Stand fast all together, trusting in Christ and in the victory of the
Holy Cross. Today, please God, you will all gain much booty.'

was nothing incongruous in begging for God's protection while keeping a hopeful eye open for plunder, and the Author of the *Gesta* came straight out from adoration at the Holy Sepulchre to join in the massacre of a large number of Muslim civilians who were unarmed. No two crusaders can have reacted in the same way, and no-one acted with perfect consistency. Godfrey de Bouillon, who is depicted in most of the twelfth-century texts as a man of devout faith and heroic simplicity, broke a solemn oath to the Emperor Alexius, while Bohemond, whom many people detested and who alienated even the Author of the *Gesta* by his determination to grasp Antioch at any cost, was among those who spent the whole night of Christmas Eve in prayer at Bethlehem with Fulcher of Chartres. The more intimately one comes to know the crusaders the more impossible it becomes to fit them into any preconceived idea, romantic or cynical, of what the crusade was like. We can begin only with the undisputed historical fact that it was the first large-scale attempt by the Franks of the West to drive the Muslims out of Jerusalem.

The city had fallen into the hands of the Muslim Arabs as a result of their great victory over the Greek Emperor Heraclius in 636. On the whole, the Arabs were tolerant towards Christians, whom they regarded as misguided but not absolutely profane in matters of religion. With rare interruptions they allowed Christian pilgrims to visit the Holy Places, at a price, and protected such institutions as the abbey of St Mary of the Latins in Jerusalem. But although Jerusalem was a holy place to the Muslims as well as to the Christians and Jews, it was never the seat of the Muslim Khalifate except for a brief moment at the beginning of the Umayyad dynasty (661-750) which almost immediately adopted Damascus as its capital. In 762 the Abbasids who succeeded to the Umayyads moved even further away, to Baghdad, which was the headquarters of the Khalif at the time of the Crusade. Asia Minor, Syria and Palestine were therefore regarded by the Abbasids as rather remote western provinces, although they contained a holy city and a number

of very important key-fortresses (such as Antioch and Aleppo) as well as valuable trading routes.

During the tenth century the schism between the orthodox (Sunnite) Muslims and the heretical (Shi'ite) sect grew deeper, until at last the Shi'ites, who had already established their own Khalif in Africa, took control of Egypt and set up at Cairo (the 'Babylon' of the Frankish writers) a dynasty which could challenge the powers of the Abbasids. This happened in 972, and from that time onwards the Egyptians were prepared to ally with anyone, even the Christians, against their orthodox rivals. This fact puzzled the Franks. William of Tyre explained it by saying that 'Those who are under the law of Egypt are called Siha, and they are not so far from the true Christian faith as are the others'. The Shi'ites profited by the crusaders' attack on Antioch in 1097 to organise an expedition against Jerusalem, which they captured in 1098. The *Gesta* indicates that they had ambassadors in the Frankish camp at the time, but the crusaders do not seem to have paid much attention to them beyond presenting them with the heads of some decapitated Sunnites.

The Byzantine Empire with its capital at Constantinople had, since the sixth century, grown steadily away from the western half of Christendom, where a rival emperor was set up in the person of Charlemagne in 800. By the time of Liudprand of Cremona's embassy to Constantinople in 971 relations between the two empires were clearly very strained in spite of a projected marriage alliance. Liudprand calls the Emperor Nicephorus Phocas (a distinguished man and a great soldier) a 'miserable burnt-out coal', and remarked that not one of his courtiers had a ceremonial dress which his grandfather had owned when it was new. The schism which occurred between the churches of East and West in 1054 did not make the situation easier. The Greek emperors, with perfect justification, regarded the lands lying west of the Euphrates as lost provinces which they had every right to regain. In the latter half of the tenth century they did temporarily extend their power over the whole of Asia Minor and Syria, but they never recovered Pales-

tine. In the course of prolonged frontier wars the Greeks had grown to regard the Muslims as a foreign power, of different religion but of a high degree of civilisation, with whom they were prepared to treat on equal terms. The Franks, at the time of the Crusade, did not understand this attitude and thought it rather treacherous. For this reason, as well as for their religious, political and economic rivalry, they were never able to take a fair view of Alexius and his subjects.

The trading routes which brought desirable and valuable goods from the East led either to Constantinople or to ports under Muslim control. For this reason the merchants of the great trading cities of Italy were prepared to support the Crusade with fleets, so that they could break the monopoly of Constantinople. Genoese fleets, as the *Gesta* indicates, provided invaluable support during the course of the Crusade, and a little later ships from Venice and Pisa helped in the conquest of other ports in the Levant. A few free-lance sea-captains helped in the Crusade. Such were Guynemer of Boulogne, who supported Baldwin in his raid on the Cilician coast in 1097, and Edgar Atheling, who commanded the fleet which arrived at St Simeon's Port in March 1098. These fleets were invaluable in bringing provisions and military equipment to the hard-pressed army of the Franks, but those of the Italian cities were determined to strike a good bargain, and later obtained substantial concessions in the seaport towns.

During the second half of the eleventh century the lands of the Sunnite Khalifate, including the western provinces, were overrun by Turks migrating from central Asia, who in 1076 captured Jerusalem itself. These Turks were generally known in the West as the Seljuks, from the name of one of their most famous clans, the Saljuqids, but they included also other groups such as the Ortuqids. In Baghdad they set up their own military leader, the Sultan, beside the Muslim religious leader, the Khalif, and the two families generally intermarried. Animists at first, the Turks were converted to Islam, and embraced the Muslim faith with all the fervour of new converts, but in spite

of this they had not, by the time of the Crusade, succeeded in establishing themselves comfortably with the Arabs, who rather despised them, and looked upon them, much as a Roman provincial of the sixth century might have regarded the Gothic army of Theodoric, as a necessary evil, to be placated and if possible brought to a reasonable degree of civilisation.

These Turkish immigrants, who thought little of the sophisticated tolerance with which the Arabs usually regarded the Christians, proceeded to make the pilgrimage to Jerusalem both difficult and dangerous, and the enthusiasm of Peter the Hermit owed a good deal to the fact that he had been ill-treated by the Turks while visiting Jerusalem as a pilgrim. They also dislocated trade, making it harder for the Italian merchants to obtain a plentiful supply of such desirable oriental goods as silk, jewels and spices. At the end of the eleventh century, therefore, two main forces in Western Christendom contributed to the stirring up of the 'valida motio' described by the *Gesta*—the sense of outraged piety and the sense of frustrated trade. In addition to this there were, in France, the Empire and southern Italy, plenty of feudal lords dissatisfied with their own territories—Robert of Normandy, passed over in the succession to the English throne, Hugh of Vermandois, younger brother of the French king, Raymond of Toulouse, ready to mortgage his European possessions in order to seek a new principality in the East, Baldwin, third son of a family with extensive possessions which lay along the western marches of the Empire, and Bohemond the neglected heir of Robert Guiscard. To judge by the speech of Urban II at Clermont, as Fulcher of Chartres reports it, Satan found plenty of mischief for such idle hands to do, and the pope—a Cluniac with a strong feeling of responsibility for the Crusade—was anxious to direct the activities of such men into the safe channel of war against the infidel. That no earlier pope had done so need not surprise us when we remember that the year of the fall of Jerusalem, 1076, had coincided with the excommunication of the Emperor Henry IV by Gregory VII and that the 'investiture contest' was not even formally settled

until 1122, twenty-three years after the crusaders took Jerusalem from the Egyptians.

The part played by Bohemond and his followers in the Crusade demands some explanation. Norman mercenaries had begun to gain a foothold in southern Italy about 1019. The country was inhabited by a mixed population, some of it Greek-speaking and owing allegiance to the emperor and the patriarch at Constantinople, while others were of Italian or Lombardic descent, accepting, without much interest, the primacy of the Western emperor and, more thoroughly, the authority of the pope at Rome. The island of Sicily was controlled by the Arabs but had a large subject Christian population. The Normans established themselves and succeeded, by the Treaty of Melfi in 1059, in obtaining papal sanction for their overlordship of southern Italy and of Sicily when they could conquer it. Bohemond and his followers thus had a reasonable familiarity with both Greeks and Arabs. They had also a strong ambition to extend their lands at the expense of the Eastern Empire. The Byzantine armies had suffered a terrible defeat at the hands of the Turks at Manzikert in 1071, and during the next ten years the position of their empire was highly insecure, and made worse by the intrigues of Bohemond's father Robert Guiscard. In 1081 two things happened. Guiscard crossed the Adriatic and began to besiege Durazzo (the fortress protecting the old Roman road, the Via Egnatia, which led straight to Constantinople), and Alexius Comnenus was proclaimed emperor of the East. Alexius, an extremely capable man, succeeded after four years in beating off the Norman attack led first by Guiscard and then by his son Bohemond, and he used 'Turcopuli', or professional Turkish mercenaries, in order to accomplish his end. In general he treated the Turks diplomatically, and after the death of their Sultan Malikshah in 1092 he was prepared to wait and let dissension do its worst in the Turkish ranks before making a great expedition to recover the lost Asiatic provinces of the empire. He probably sent an appeal to the western Council of Piacenza (1095) for professional soldiers ready to

take his pay and fight under his banner, but he never envisaged anything like the Crusade, which his daughter and biographer Anna Comnena regarded as a new and disastrous barbarian invasion—a view to which the behaviour of the crusaders lent a good deal of colour. He did his best for Peter the Hermit's rabble, and when faced by the official leaders of the Crusade he decided, sensibly enough, to enrol them as mercenaries and pay them good wages, provided that they would hand over to him any lands which they should conquer.

The death of the Sultan Malikshah in 1092 was followed by a disputed succession. The dead man's son Barkyaruq succeeded him in Baghdad, but the western provinces were left in the hands of his brother Tutush, who had strong forces in Syria and Palestine, and had defeated and killed the ruler of Anatolia or Rum (the 'old Suleiman' of the *Gesta*) in 1086. Under the general overlordship of Tutush were many small principalities, some, such as Jerusalem, under Turkish rule, others, such as Shaizar or Tripoli, ruled by Arabic dynasties, and yet others, such as Iconium and Edessa, under the rule of Armenian Christians. The general population was exceedingly mixed in race, language and religion, and this confusion was increased by the Turkish custom of drafting large numbers of foreign slaves into the armies which every Turkish ruler was expected to maintain. Many of the subject Christians were in communion neither with the Latin Catholic nor with the Greek Orthodox church. It is therefore not surprising that the crusaders rarely knew in advance what kind of reception they would get at a city, and the rather ambiguous part played by 'Armenians and Syrians' in the *Gesta* is fully explained by the circumstances in which they lived.

Barkyaruq and Tutush met in battle at Rayy (Teheran) in 1095 and Tutush was defeated and killed. It was this battle, as Professor Gibb has said, 'which decided the fate of the First Crusade'. The western provinces never took kindly to the rule of Barkyaruq and showed great hostility to any army which he might send to them, even on the pretext of bringing help against

the Franks. This fact helps to explain the real weakness which underlay the apparent strength of Karbuqa's expedition in 1098. But the western provinces themselves remained, after 1095, in a state of disunity. Qilij-Arslan, ruler of Rum, refused to ally with the sons of the man who had caused his father's death, and was therefore defeated independently at Dorylaeum in 1097. The two sons of Tutush, Duqaq of Damascus and Rudwan of Aleppo, fell out with one another, and Yaghi Siyan of Antioch had transferred his support from Rudwan to Duqaq shortly before the siege of Antioch began, so that he had no really reliable allies. Duqaq and Rudwan, instead of combining forces, made separate attempts to raise the siege and were in turn defeated, Duqaq's forces at al-Bara and those of Rudwan at the battle of the Lake of Antioch. The Ortuqid family which ruled in Jerusalem was drawn into the strife of the house of Tutush, with the result that Jerusalem was captured fairly easily by the Egyptians in 1098. The small Arabic principalities, on the whole, adopted the policy of 'lying low and saying nothing'. Their rulers, except at Tripoli, came easily to terms with the crusaders during the spring of 1099, and they probably regarded the Franks as simply one more tiresome and rapacious army in a land which had already suffered too much.

The actual history of the Crusade is set forth so clearly in the *Gesta* that a very brief commentary upon it will suffice. The 'popular crusade' stirred up by Peter the Hermit consisted of a few rather disreputable knights and a large, miscellaneous rabble of followers, most of them entirely unsuited to fight against the Turks. (Albert of Aix tells the story of a nun who accompanied this band, was captured in Asia Minor, and later showed a disconcerting unwillingness to be separated from her Muslim husband.) These people arrived in Constantinople in 1096, after committing various atrocities on their way across Europe. They were under no military discipline and made themselves highly obnoxious, so that Alexius, who had begun by warning them to stay in Europe, eventually sent them across the Bosphorus, and most of them were killed or taken prisoner.

Peter the Hermit himself escaped and later joined the forces of Godfrey de Bouillon. The 'princes' crusade', initiated by the Council of Clermont, consisted of large numbers of trained knights under experienced leaders, but they were still hampered

The Route from Durazzo to Constantinople

by the presence of far too many non-combatants. (Since both Raymond of Toulouse and Baldwin took their wives with them, and the *Gesta* mentions the presence of women at the battle of Dorylaeum and the siege of Antioch, it appears that there were a number of women, and probably of babies, with the army. There were also many clergy—technically debarred from bearing arms—of whom Adhémar, bishop of Le Puy, the papal

legate, was the senior representative.) Constantinople was cho-
sen as the meeting-place (apparently without the consent of
Alexius) and the crusaders travelled by three separate routes.
The contingent from Lorraine and the Rhineland went across
Europe by way of the Danube and Maritza valleys and entered
Constantinople from the north. Raymond of Toulouse and
Bishop Adhémar, with the army from southern France and
Provence, came by way of the land route along the Dalmatian
coast (where they suffered a good deal from the attacks of the
local hill tribes) and joined the Via Egnatia at Durazzo. The
French, Flemish and Norman contingents, including Hugh of
Vermandois, Stephen of Blois and Chartres, Robert of Flanders,
Robert of Normandy, Bohemond and Tancred, all used the sea-
route from ports in southern Italy (Bari, Brindisi or Otranto)
to Durazzo, and thence followed the Via Egnatia to Constantinople, although they travelled in various companies. The
whole of the forces arrived at Constantinople between the beginning of December 1096 and the end of April 1097.

The Emperor Alexius tried to induce all the crusading leaders to take an oath to act as his mercenaries. He was successful
with all of them except Raymond of Toulouse (who, although
he impressed the Princess Anna as being the least uncivilised of
the Franks, quarrelled with the emperor and took the oath only
in a modified form) and Tancred (who avoided it by crossing
the Bosphorus in secret). Bohemond, who impressed the princess by his good looks and his skilful diplomacy, although she
regarded him with a kind of fascinated horror, was at great pains
to behave with extreme correctness. He took the oath, and tried
to negotiate a secret treaty with Alexius, although it is doubtful
whether he was successful in gaining the promise of the principality in Syria which the Author of the *Gesta* believed him to
have received. Thereafter the whole army reunited on the
Asiatic side of the Bosphorus and took the city of Nicea, with
substantial help from the imperial troops. Qilij-Arslan failed
to relieve the city, but on 1 July 1097 he lay in ambush and
trapped one part of the crusading army at Dorylaeum. The

Franks were saved by the timely arrival of the rest of their army, which had been separated from the Norman contingent for two days, and Qilij-Arslan suffered such a crushing defeat that he put up no further resistance while the crusaders were crossing

The Route from Constantinople to Antioch

Asia Minor. They followed a route which appears at first sight circuitous, but which was determined by their need to keep, as far as possible, in territory where most of the population was Armenian and Christian, and where it would be possible for them to get enough food and water to supply them in their marches through deserted country. Even so, conditions were bad. Many pack-horses died, and Fulcher of Chartres mentions with

pity the sufferings of unsuitable creatures such as dogs and sheep which were pressed into service as beasts of burden. The crossing of the high passes of the Anti-Taurus range, just before the arrival of the crusaders at Antioch on 20 October, seems to have been almost the last straw for heavily armed knights and a mixed collection of followers encumbered with a good deal of baggage.

During the second week of September Baldwin and Tancred broke away from the main force and marched southwards towards the Cilician coast. Baldwin already had some connections with the Armenians through an Armenian named Bagrat who had become a member of his household, but Tancred's activities seem to have been caused by the Norman love of snatching an opportunity. He nearly succeeded in annexing Tarsus, but Baldwin's larger army drove him off to smaller ports and wrecked his chance of founding a principality in Cilicia. Baldwin afterwards went eastwards, through lands which were mainly Armenian, across the Euphrates to the city of Edessa. Here he succeeded in obtaining the good graces of the Armenian ruler Thoros and was formally adopted as his heir. Thoros was killed soon afterwards in a local revolt (probably with Baldwin's consent), and Baldwin became the independent ruler of Edessa in March 1098, being the first of the crusaders to found a principality. He was successful in holding the city against Karbuqa, whose march to the west he delayed for about three weeks, thereby saving the Frankish forces at Antioch.

Meanwhile the main army had reached Antioch and blockaded it in a somewhat incomplete fashion, since it was far too strong for them to take by direct assault. They were afraid to leave it unconquered in their rear, and moreover Bohemond, always the dominating man among their leaders, was determined to capture it and to establish himself as its ruler, although he does not seem to have spoken openly about his plans until the following spring. Antioch had been taken by the Turks from the Byzantine empire as recently as 1085, and must have contained a large number of people sympathetic towards the crusaders, more especially if they believed them to be fighting as

mercenaries for the emperor. The Turkish ruler, Yaghi Siyan, was in theory the vassal of Rudwan of Aleppo, but he had recently deserted to the side of Rudwan's brother and rival Duqaq of Damascus, to whom he sent his son begging for aid.

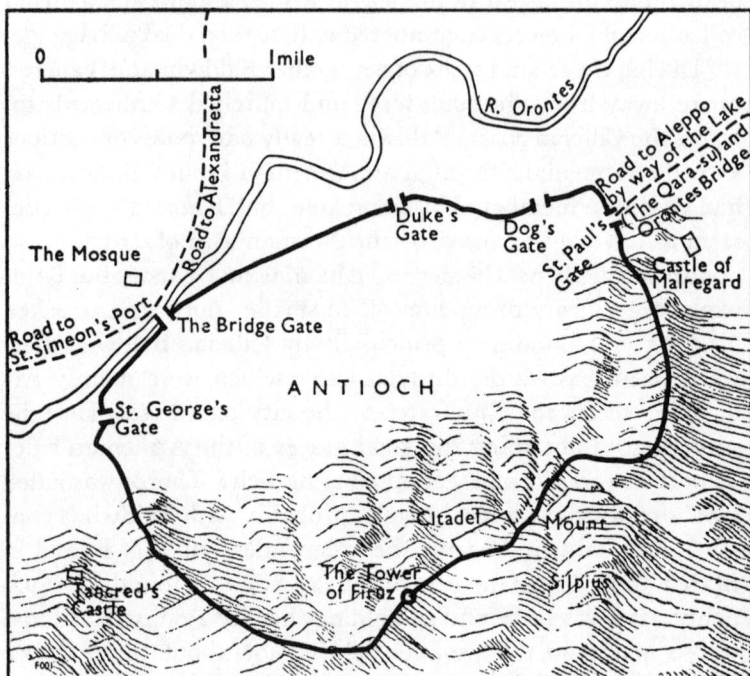

The City of Antioch in 1098

He sent also a message to Karbuqa, amir of Mosul (a town in which the Sultan always took care to establish a man whom he could trust, since it commanded the main route from Baghdad to the western provinces). However, none of Yaghi Siyan's possible supporters trusted him sufficiently to make an immediate effort to relieve him. Duqaq, backed by his formidable atabek[1] Tughtagin, moved first, and was beaten off at the end

[1] An atabek was a kind of military tutor to whom an amir bequeathed the task of bringing up his son. He was usually a distinguished soldier, even if of low birth, and he frequently married into the amir's family. H. A. R. Gibb, *The Damascus Chronicle*, pp. 23-24.

of December by Bohemond's men who had gone out to al-Bara in the hope of picking up supplies. Rudwan's army was defeated in February at the battle of the Lake of Antioch. Yaghi Siyan had on each occasion tried to help the relieving armies by making a sortie, and in March, hearing that his most terrible adversary Bohemond had gone down to the coast to bring up supplies from the crusading fleet there, he decided to risk attacking the Frankish camp without allies. In the battle of the Bridge he nearly succeeded in breaking the siege.

In May reports of Karbuqa's advance were known in the Frankish camp, and it became clear that there would be no time to starve the city into submission. As the situation grew more desperate, Bohemond managed to persuade the other leaders (with the exception of Raymond of Toulouse) to agree to his keeping the city for himself if he could take it, provided that the emperor did not arrive to claim it in person. Bohemond succeeded, by means of treachery within the walls and the exceptional courage of himself and his men, in capturing the whole of Antioch except the citadel. The Author of the *Gesta* was one of the storming-party, and his account of the attack by night is one of the most vivid anecdotes of his story. Karbuqa's army arrived two days too late to save the town.

The Franks were now trapped between a Turkish army outside the walls and a Turkish garrison in the citadel, and eight months of hard fighting and lack of food had left them in poor condition. They were soon starving, and it is not surprising that some of them broke down under the strain. Men took to letting themselves down from the walls under cover of darkness, or skulking in houses until Bohemond drove them out to fight by burning the roofs over their heads. The imperial army, which was in Asia Minor, turned back from its attempt to relieve the city, because Alexius dared not take the risk of lengthening his lines of communication through unfriendly territory in order to save allies who, as Stephen of Chartres suggested, might be dead before he reached them.

At this point the crusading army was given fresh hope by

the report of visions which suggested that God was protecting them, and indicated the presence in Antioch of a precious relic, the Holy Lance of the Crucifixion. The *Gesta* mentions only two sets of visions, one to a Provençal layman named Peter and the other to 'a certain priest'. Raymond of Agiles gives the story in much greater detail and indicates that Peter's visions had begun in the previous January. He also gives the priest's name as Stephen. The Lance was found by a party of Provençals who dug under the floor of St Peter's cathedral, and Raymond records the fact that he kissed the point while the haft was still embedded in the ground. Bishop Adhémar seems never to have believed in the authenticity of this relic, and Fulcher of Chartres (who was not present) treats it as spurious. Peter did, in fact, in the following year undergo an ordeal for the purpose of proving it to be genuine, and died as the result. But whatever the origin of the Lance, its finding had a tremendous psychological effect upon the disconsolate army. Inspired by fresh confidence, the crusaders sent an insulting message to Karbuqa telling him to go away, and followed it up by marching out of the city and utterly defeating the Muslim forces at the Great Battle of Antioch on 28 June. The *Gesta* attributes this victory to the intervention of three warrior saints, much in the way that, according to tradition, the Great Twin Brethren turned the fortunes of the day at Lake Regillus or the Angels stemmed the retreat from Mons. The Author fought in the battle, and I personally see no reason to doubt his explanation, but it is also true that the Muslim camp was rent by quarrels between Karbuqa and the men from the western provinces, and between the forces of Rudwan and those of Duqaq. The citadel surrendered immediately the results of the battle were known, and Bohemond took control of it.

The Great Battle of Antioch may be regarded as the climax of the story of the crusade as set forth by the *Gesta*, although the Author himself clearly felt unsatisfied until he had fulfilled his vow to deliver the Holy Sepulchre. During the heat of the summer the crusaders rested at Antioch, apart from a few minor

The Route from Antioch to Jerusalem

raids, and sent messengers to Alexius asking him to come and take over his lost fief. Since he did not arrive the ownership of the city was left in dispute between Bohemond (who had brought about its capture) and Raymond of Toulouse (who had been the first to hoist his flag over the citadel). On 1 November the crusade was resumed and the army went on to Ma'arat, which was taken by storm. According to Raymond of Agiles, a popular revolt broke out in the ranks against the dilatory behaviour of the leaders, and Count Raymond, seeing that he had not much chance of establishing his claim against Bohemond, put himself at the head of this movement and continued the Crusade. It must have been about this time that he took the Author of the *Gesta* into his service. The crusaders went on, through territory which was predominantly Arab rather than Turkish, by way of Shaizar, Homs, Tripoli, Beyrut, Acre and Ramleh. They were detained for some time besieging Arqa near Tripoli, as a result of Count Raymond's determination to establish a principality at Tripoli if he could not have one at Antioch, but the siege was finally abandoned. In May an embassy from Cairo offering the crusaders 'personally conducted tours' of the Holy Places was rejected, and the army was finally committed to war with the Egyptians, who had profited by the siege of Antioch to capture Jerusalem from the Ortuqids. The army arrived before the walls of Jerusalem in June 1099 and besieged the city for a month, suffering badly from shortage of water but greatly reinforced by a Genoese fleet which had put into the harbour of Jaffa. On 15 July the city fell, and its Muslim inhabitants (with the exception of a few saved by Count Raymond) were slaughtered with the utmost ferocity. The churchmen in the Frankish army succeeded in obtaining the recognition of Jerusalem as an ecclesiastical principality, defended by a lay-advocate in the person of Godfrey de Bouillon. (This arrangement was unsatisfactory in a country where Frankish survival depended in a great measure on the existence of a highly feudalised military society with a fighting ruler whose word could not be disputed, and Godfrey's brother Baldwin succeeded in having

the decision reversed when he was crowned king of Jerusalem in 1100.) An Egyptian relieving force under the command of the wazir of Egypt, al-Afdal, reached Ascalon in August 1099 but was completely defeated. At this point the narrative of the *Gesta* ends, but an appended 'Guide to the Holy Places' which follows the work in all the complete MSS suggests that the Author had the satisfaction of completing his pilgrimage.

The Latin kingdom of Jerusalem, thus precariously founded, survived—mainly because of the disunity of its enemies—until Saladin's capture of the city in 1187, and a few Christian outposts were maintained until the fall of Acre in 1291. The leaders of the Crusade dispersed after the battle of Ascalon, and a brief record of their subsequent activities may be of interest. Godfrey de Bouillon remained as Advocate of the Holy Sepulchre until July 1100, when he died and was succeeded by his brother Baldwin of Edessa, who reigned—on the whole very successfully —until 1118. Bohemond performed a pilgrimage to Jerusalem and then went back to settle himself, with Tancred's help, into the principality of Antioch. He remained on bad terms with Alexius, and in 1105 returned to Italy to plan a new attack on Durazzo.[1] This was unsuccessful, but on Bohemond's death in the autumn of 1108 Tancred succeeded him in Antioch and ruled there until his death in 1112. He left no son, but the Norman dynasty of Hauteville was by this time well established in Syria and resisted all the Greek attempts to turn it out. Raymond of Toulouse, on the strength of his opposition to Bohemond over the fate of Antioch, managed to reconcile himself to the Emperor Alexius and led out a fresh force, supported by a Genoese fleet, to besiege the city of Tripoli. He died in 1105 in his castle of Mount Pilgrim outside the walls, but his successors took Tripoli in 1109 and ruled there as counts under the overlordship of the kings of Jerusalem. Robert of Flanders and Robert of Normandy returned home, accompanied by such

---

[1] It is possible that he took with him a copy of the *Gesta* and used it for the purpose of propaganda. This would explain the presence of the book in Western Europe as early as 1106, when Robert the Monk of Rheims saw it. See above, pp. ix-x and note 3.

of the crusaders as felt that they had discharged their vow by
the recovery of the Holy Sepulchre.

R. M. T. H.

V

MANUSCRIPTS AND EDITIONS

The text of this edition is taken from the earliest and most
authentic of the seven manuscripts known to survive, *Vatican
Reginensis lat. 572* (cited as E), which is very accurately written
and punctuated in a bold round hand of the early twelfth
century. It contains the *Gesta Francorum*, followed by (f. 64ᵛ)
an Itinerary of the Holy Places, (f. 66ᵛ) a Mass in veneration
of the Holy Sepulchre, and (f. 67) the Dimensions of the Sepulchre, all of which are printed here after the text of the *Gesta*,
since they were probably associated with it from its first publication in this form.[1] This ends the original contents of the
volume, but on f. 68 are scribbled some verses on Bohemond
(*Nunc reboat mundus, quia fecit tot Boamundus . . .*), which reinforce
the feeling, inspired by the text itself, that we are not very far
from the circle in which it first saw the light; ff. 69-76 have been
added, and carry in a thirteenth-century hand the letter from
Oliver, *scholasticus* of Cologne (afterwards bishop of Paderborn
and cardinal), about the siege of Damietta in 1219, afterwards
incorporated in his *Historia Damiatina*.[2] There is no ornament
except red capitals; space was left for a heading to each book of
the *Gesta*, but the rubricator got no further with these than the
beginning of book IV, and we have supplied the rest. The
original owner of this precious volume is unfortunately un-

---

[1] The Itinerary is the work printed as 'Innominatus I' by T. Tobler,
Theodorici libellus de locis sanctis (St Gallen 1865), pp. 113-18, and translated
in the publications of the *Palestine Pilgrims' Text Society*, vi (1894), 1-5.
R. Röhricht, *Bibliotheca geographica Palestinae* (Berlin 1890), 28-29, lists 49
manuscripts, in some of which it follows the works of later Crusading
chroniclers such as Robert the Monk or Tudebod, who drew on our *Gesta*.

[2] See his works in the edition of H. Hoogeweg (*Bibliothek des litterarischen
Vereins in Stuttgart*, ccii, Tübingen 1894), p. lix

known; what might have been a name is erased from the top of the last page. In modern times it belonged to the famous French collector Paul Petau (1568-1614), whose name is on f. 69, and passed with many other books from his library to Queen Christina of Sweden.[1]

Close to this is *Madrid, Biblioteca Nacional E.e.103 (9783)*, written in a small hand perhaps of the early fourteenth century, without ornament, which contains also the Itinerary but not the Mass. Of unknown provenance, it was in the eighteenth century at Avignon, in the hands of Joseph-Louis-Dominique de Cambis, Marquis de Valleron, who died in 1772.[2] The book-headings extend, as in E, to book IV and no further; and if we could be sure that this is, as it appears to be, an idiosyncrasy of E and not derived from its exemplar, we should be certain that the Madrid MS is derived from E. In any case, they are very closely related, and the few independent readings in the Madrid text can all be due to error or deliberate alteration; they are therefore not recorded here.

It is otherwise with *Vatican Reginensis lat. 641* (cited as D), which contains *Gesta*, Itinerary and Mass in a neat twelfth-century hand, but had already lost in medieval times its fifth quire (c. xxiii *in mare. Deinde* to c. xxix *Hoc uexillum non est Boa-*). The book divisions are marked by red capitals, without head-ings. It bears at the end an interesting ownership-mark of the fifteenth century: *Iste liber est Reverendissimi D. Alani Cardinalis Auinionensis*, for this is Cardinal Alain de Coëtivy, bishop of Avignon, who was charged by Pope Nicholas V in 1456 with the preaching of his new Crusade in France. When compared with the two copies already mentioned, it shows few additions but many small deliberate alterations: ninety changes of word-order, about a hundred omissions (some of these are accidental), and another hundred substitutions of one word for another of similar meaning. And certain changes (for instance, on pp. 81, 87, 95) betray a desire to exalt Duke Robert of Normandy.

---

[1] The history is told in K. A. de Meyier's *Paul en Alexandre Petau* (Leiden 1947)   [2] Bréhier, *Histoire Anonyme*, p. xxiii

This process of improving the author's syntax and style was carried much further by an unknown editor (cited as X), who shows the same interest in Duke Robert. He worked on a copy of the revision represented by D, which included the Itinerary, the Mass and the Dimensions (all of which survive in the Caius MS), and of his work, which was perhaps entitled *Itinerarium Hierosolimitanum* (or *-tanorum*), we possess three copies, all of English origin:

> *Escorial d.III.11*, part of a volume of Saints' lives formerly at the Premonstratensian abbey of Barlings in Lincolnshire: it is said to be of the late twelfth century, and contains the Itinerary.
>
> *Berlin lat.qu.503*, of the thirteenth century, from Kenilworth, an Austin priory in Warwickshire; when sold in London in 1895 it had been the property of an English collector, A. C. Ranyard. One leaf (cc. xxvii-xxix) is badly mutilated, and several have been lost (including part of c. xxxiv, the end of the *Gesta*, and whatever may have followed it), and the rest of the volume is occupied by an incomplete text of Eutropius, the Roman historian.
>
> *Cambridge, Gonville and Caius College 162/83*, of unknown provenance, in a thirteenth or fourteenth century English hand, includes the *Gesta* and its three appendices in a corpus of works on Oriental history and religion.[1]

From a copy of this revision was derived, with minor alterations, a somewhat abbreviated text preserved in *Cambridge, Corpus Christi College 281*, which shows its devotion to the duke of Normandy still more by moving his name to stand first in any list of Crusading captains, and by calling him *dux* instead of *comes*.

---

[1] It was perhaps from a volume akin to this that the Dimensions of the Sepulchre passed (with the length of line exactly copied) into Cambridge University Library Dd. 1.17, an immense corpus of historical works from Glastonbury Abbey, which includes most of the contents of the Caius MS, but not the *Gesta* nor the Itinerary. Another Cambridge MS, Dd. 1.2, has the longer line drawn on f. 180v, but casually and of the wrong length. It would be interesting to know how far the later circulation of the *Linea Christi* is indebted to our *Gesta* manuscripts of the English family, and whether the length of the lines is accurately maintained.

The commonest changes made by the unknown reviser X are again in word-order (150, on top of 50 changes already found in D) and in vocabulary (about 260)—all these designed to raise the level of the Latinity, e.g. *nuntius* becomes *legatus*, and *capti erant* becomes *in uinculis tenebantur*, and *non diu morans furtim recessit* becomes *non diu moratus latenter aufugit*. There are 55 changes of tense, 60 corrections of syntax, 70 cases of re-arrangement of phrases, 75 of words omitted and 80 of words added. One point in particular receives special care: the re-viser held strong views on the correct articulation of an his-torical narrative, and in 170 places he alters the connecting particle at the beginning of a sentence, ringing the changes on *igitur* and *enim* and *autem* and *ergo* and the rest as his nice ear dictated. Of all his labours we had in mind to give an accurate account based on collation of all the MSS, until it became clear that this would burden the brief text of the *Gesta* with nearly a thousand notes, not one of which would contribute (as it seems) to our knowledge of the original.[1] The reader who cares for such things is therefore invited to gain an idea of the nature of the revision from Bréhier's textual notes or Miss Lees's report of the Caius MS, and we have recorded only those readings where the combined testimony of D and X differs from E, and it is thus at least theoretically possible that E is in error.

The first edition of the *Gesta Francorum* was published by J. Bongars in volume I of his *Gesta Dei per Francos* (Hanau, 1611), 1-29. He used our manuscript E, which was lent to him by Paul Petau, and another copy belonging to William Camden, the great English antiquary (1551-1623), which has never been identified. It concluded, he tells us, with the colophon *Explicit uia bona*: and to judge by the additions which he made from it to the text of the original *Gesta*, must have been a copy not of

[1] For this edition the two Reginenses have been collated partly in the original and also completely in microfilm. Of the others, the Madrid and Berlin MSS have been collated in microfilm, those at Cambridge in the original, and the readings of the Escorial MS have been taken from Hagen-meyer. In this connection we wish to express our gratitude to Dr H. Boese (Berlin), Dr Gebhardt (Marburg), Mr P. Grierson and Dr R. Vaughan (Cambridge).

the *Gesta* proper, but of another Crusading chronicle based upon it. Misled by the defective rubrication of E, he divided the text into four books only, of which the fourth was inordinately long; and he also offered a division into 39 chapters, which is not found in any of our manuscripts.

Two and a half centuries later, this was followed by the majestic edition of Ph. Le Bas in the *Recueil des Historiens des Croisades, Historiens occidentaux*, iii (Paris 1866), 121-63. Le Bas purports to base his text on E and Bongars, with some help from the Corpus Christi copy; but it is clear, from the account that he gives of his principal manuscript, that what he had was a collation not of E but D. A new standard was set by H. Hagenmeyer in his edition, published at Heidelberg in 1890. His valuable introduction and commentary were accompanied by a text based on all the manuscripts—mainly known to him from the collations of Comte Paul Riant; but unfortunately he confused the two Vatican copies, misunderstood the stages of the transmission of the text, and drew principally on the Madrid MS and on Bongars. An edition for students, published by Miss B. A. Lees at Oxford in 1924, modestly aims to do no more for the text than reprint Bongars (with all the interpolations of three hundred years before), accompanied by a new collation of the Caius MS. In the same year appeared the attractive edition of Louis Bréhier, with French translation and short notes, as fascicule 4 of the *Classiques de l'Histoire de France au Moyen Age*. Even here one observes with regret that the readings of MS D are often attributed to MS E also, which leads the learned and accomplished editor into a false view of the relationships of the principal MSS.

An English version is incorporated into the composite narrative of A. C. Krey's *The First Crusade* (Princeton, N.J. 1921), but the first separate translation is that published in England by the Golden Cockerel Press in 1945, and made by Mr Somerset de Chair. It is the modest claim of this edition to be the first to give the text of the oldest and best manuscript with no admixture of alien material.

R. A. B. M.

SELECT BIBLIOGRAPHY

(including full titles of all works referred to in the notes
in abbreviated form)

I

EARLIER EDITIONS OF THE 'GESTA FRANCORUM'
(IN ORDER OF PUBLICATION)

BONGARS, J.: *Gesta Dei per Francos*, I, 1-29 (Hanoviae 1611).
LE BAS, P.: in *Recueil des Historiens des Croisades, Historiens occidentaux*,
III, 121-63 (Paris 1866).
HAGENMEYER, H.: *Anonymi Gesta Francorum* (Heidelberg 1890).
LEES, B. A.: *Anonymi Gesta Francorum* (Oxford 1924).
BRÉHIER, L.: *Histoire Anonyme de la première Croisade* (with French
translation, Classiques de l'Histoire de France, IV, Paris
1924).
DE CHAIR, SOMERSET: *The Deeds of the Franks and other Jerusalemites*
(English translation, Golden Cockerel Press, 1945).

II

OTHER ORIGINAL SOURCES

The contemporary Latin sources may be most conveniently
studied in

P.L.—J.-P. Migne, *Patrologiae Cursus Completus, series Latina*, and
R.H.C. Hist. Occ.—*Recueil des Historiens des Croisades* (16 volumes,
Paris 1841-1906), *Historiens occidentaux*.

The most important of these are three eye-witness accounts of
the crusade:

Tudebodi sacerdotis Sivracensis Historia de Hierosolymitano itinere, R.H.C.
Hist. Occ., III, 1-117; *P.L.*, CLV, 763-820.
Raimundi de Agiles Historia Francorum, R.H.C. Hist. Occ., III, 139-83;
P.L., CLV, 591-666.
Fulcherii Carnotensis Gesta Francorum Iherusalem peregrinantium, *P.L.*, CLV,
821-940.

xliii

The following are of particular interest in their relationship to the text of the *Gesta*, although none was written by an eye-witness of the crusade:

Ekkehardi Uraugiensis Hierosolymita, R.H.C. Hist. Occ., v, 1 ff.

Roberti Remensis Monachi Historia Hierosolymitana, R.H.C. Hist. Occ., III, 717-882; P.L., CLV, 667-758.

Baldrici Dolensis Episcopi Historia Hierosolymitana, R.H.C. Hist. Occ., IV, 1-111; P.L., CLXVI, 1057 ff.

Guiberti Historia quae dicitur Gesta per Francos, R.H.C. Hist. Occ., IV, 115 ff.; P.L., CLVI, 675 ff.

The following are available in English translations:

DAWES, E. A. S.: *The Alexiad of Anna Comnena* (London 1928).

GIBB, H. A. R.: *The Damascus Chronicle* (London 1932).

JOHNSON, C.: *Constitutio Domus Regis* (in *Dialogus de Scaccario*, Nelson's Medieval Texts, 1950).

KREY, A. C.: *The First Crusade, accounts of eye-witnesses* (Princeton 1921).

POTTER, G. R.: *The Autobiography of Ousama* (London 1929).

WRIGHT, F. A.: *The Embassy to Constantinople* (in *The Works of Liudprand of Cremona*, London 1930).

III

A FEW MODERN WORKS OF REFERENCE

BALDWIN, M. W. (ed.): *A History of the Crusades*, I, *The First Hundred Years* (Philadelphia 1958).

BRÉHIER, L.: *L'Église et l'Orient: Les Croisades* (Paris 1912).

CAHEN, C.: *La Syrie du nord à l'époque des Croisades* (Paris 1940).

CHALANDON, F.: *Essai sur le règne d'Alexis Comnene* (Paris 1900).

GROUSSET, R.: *Histoire des Croisades*, I (Paris 1934).

HEYD, W. (tr. and ed. Furcy-Raynaud): *Histoire du commerce du Levant au moyen âge* (2 vols., Leipzig 1885-6).

PAETOW, L. J. (ed.): *The Crusades and other historical essays presented to Dana C. Munro* (New York 1928).

PRESCOTT, H. F. M.: *Jerusalem Journey* (London 1954).

RUNCIMAN, S.: *A history of the Crusades* (3 vols., Cambridge 1951-5).

RUNCIMAN, S.: *The Medieval Manichee* (Cambridge 1955).

SMAIL, R. C.: *Crusading Warfare, 1097-1193* (Cambridge 1956).

IV

Manuscripts Referred to in the Apparatus Criticus
(see above, pp. xxxviii-xlii)

D   Vatican MS Reginensis lat. 641.
E   Vatican MS Reginensis lat. 572.
X   Text of unknown editor from which were derived MSS Escorial
      d.III.11, Berlin lat.qu.503, and Cambridge, Gonville and
      Caius College, 162/83.

LATIN TEXT
and
ENGLISH TRANSLATION

GESTA FRANCORVM ET
ALIORVM HIEROSOLIMITANORVM

I

[i] Cum iam appropinquasset ille terminus quem dominus Iesus cotidie suis demonstrat fidelibus, specialiter in euangelio dicens: 'Si quis uult post me uenire, abneget semetipsum et tollat crucem suam et sequatur me',[1] facta est igitur motio ualida per uniuersas Galliarum regiones, ut si aliquis Deum studiose puroque corde et mente sequi desideraret, atque post ipsum crucem fideliter baiulare uellet, non pigritaretur Sancti Sepulchri uiam celerius arripere. Apostolicus namque Romanae sedis[a][2] ultra montanas partes quantocius profectus est cum suis archiepiscopis, episcopis, abbatibus, et presbiteris, coepitque subtiliter sermocinari et predicare, dicens, ut si quis animam suam saluam facere uellet, non dubitaret humiliter uiam incipere Domini, ac si denariorum ei deesset copia, diuina ei satis daret misericordia. Ait namque domnus apostolicus 'Fratres, uos[b] oportet multa pati pro nomine Christi, uidelicet miserias, paupertates, nuditates, persecutiones, egestates, infirmitates, fames, sites et alia huiusmodi, sicuti Dominus ait

[a] DX *add* Vrbanus secundus
[b] *corrected in* E *to* nos

[1] Matthew 16:24
[2] Urban II, 1088-99. Fulcher of Chartres makes it clear that in preaching the crusade he was also trying to divert the Frankish lords from breaking the Truce of God by indiscriminate attacks upon one another. The sermon to which the Anonymous alludes was preached at the Council of Clermont in 1095 (*P.L.*, CLV, 825-9).

THE DEEDS OF THE FRANKS AND THE OTHER PILGRIMS TO JERUSALEM

I

[i] When that time had already come, of which the Lord Jesus warns his faithful people every day, especially in the Gospel where he says, 'If any man will come after me, let him deny himself, and take up his cross, and follow me'[1], there was a great stirring of heart throughout all the Frankish lands, so that if any man, with all his heart and all his mind, really wanted to follow God and faithfully to bear the cross after him, he could make no delay in taking the road to the Holy Sepulchre as quickly as possible. For even the pope[2] set out across the Alps as soon as he could, with his archbishops, bishops, abbots and priests, and he began to deliver eloquent sermons and to preach, saying, 'If any man wants to save his soul, let him have no hesitation in taking the way of the Lord in humility, and if he lacks money, the divine mercy will give him enough.' The lord pope said also, 'Brothers, you must suffer for the name of Christ many things, wretchedness, poverty, nakedness, persecution, need, sickness, hunger, thirst and other such troubles, for the Lord says to his dis-

suis discipulis: "Oportet uos pati multa pro nomine
meo",[1] et: "Nolite erubescere loqui ante facies hominum; ego uero dabo uobis os et eloquium",[2] ac deinceps:
"Persequetur uos larga retributio".'[3] Cumque iam hic
sermo paulatim per uniuersas regiones ac Galliarum
patrias coepisset crebrescere, Franci audientes talia
protinus in dextra crucem[a] suere scapula, dicentes sese
Christi unanimiter sequi uestigia, quibus de manu erant
redempti tartarea. Iamiamque Galliae suis remotae
sunt domibus.

[ii] Fecerunt denique Galli tres partes. Vna pars
Francorum in Hungariae intrauit regionem, scilicet
Petrus Heremita,[4] et dux Godefridus,[5] et Balduinus frater
eius,[6] et Balduinus comes de Monte.[7] Isti potentissimi
milites et alii plures quos ignoro uenerunt per uiam
quam iamdudum Karolus Magnus mirificus rex Franciae aptari fecit usque Constantinopolim.[8]

Petrus uero supradictus primus uenit Constantinopolim in kalendis Augusti et cum eo maxima gens Ala-
mannorum. Illic inuenit Lombardos et Longobardos
et alios plures congregatos, quibus imperator[9] iusserat

---

[a] crucem X; E *and* D *omit it; the Madrid MS adds* cruces inceperunt
after scapula

[1] Acts 9:16. The Anonymous here, and on many subsequent occasions,
gives a scriptural quotation in a slightly inaccurate form. Being a devout
layman, he probably remembered it by ear and did not collate it with the
Vulgate.

[2] 2 Timothy 1:8, and Luke 21:15

[3] Matthew 5:12

[4] Leader of the popular crusade of unorganised enthusiasts

[5] Godfrey de Bouillon, duke of Lower Lorraine, who became in 1099
Advocate of the Holy Sepulchre. He was a man of great physical prowess
and deep devotion, but he seems to have had no outstanding qualities as a
statesman.

[6] Baldwin, Godfrey's younger brother, had been educated as a clerk
since there seemed to be no prospect of his acquiring a suitable estate in the
West. His exploits during the Crusade gained him first the position of count
of Edessa and afterwards that of king of Jerusalem. He was far more intelligent and less scrupulous than his brother.

ciples,"You must suffer many things for my name",[1] and "Be not ashamed to speak before men, for I will give you what you shall say"[2] and afterwards "Great will be your reward.""[3] And when these words had begun to be rumoured abroad through all the duchies and counties of the Frankish lands, the Franks, hearing them, straightway began to sew the cross on the right shoulders of their garments, saying that they would all with one accord follow in the footsteps of Christ, by whom they had been redeemed from the power of hell. So they set out at once from their homes in the lands of the Franks.

[ii] The Franks ordered themselves in three armies. One, which entered into Hungary, was led by Peter the Hermit[4] and Duke Godfrey,[5] Baldwin his brother[6] and Baldwin, count of Hainault.[7] These most valiant knights and many others (whose names I do not know) travelled by the road which Charlemagne, the heroic king of the Franks, had formerly caused to be built to Constantinople.[8]

The aforesaid Peter was the first to reach Constantinople on 1 August, and many Germans came with him. There they found men from northern and southern Italy and many others gathered together. The emperor[9] ordered such provisions as there were in the city

---

[7] Baldwin, count of Mons in Hainault

[8] This was the traditional route by way of the valleys of the Danube, the Morava and the Maritza. The ascription to Charlemagne is legendary.

[9] Alexius Comnenus. He was the most dangerous enemy of Bohemond and of the Normans of the Two Sicilies, and the anonymous Author of the Gesta, being a follower of Bohemond, is understandably unfair to him. Later MSS of the Gesta, written after 1204, describe him in even more unflattering terms. He was, however, a great emperor, and his own point of view is given in the Alexiad written by his daughter, Anna Comnena, and by the modern historians Chalandon and Runciman.

dari mercatum, sicuti erat in ciuitate, dixitque illis
'Nolite transmeare Brachium, donec ueniat maxima
Christianorum uirtus, quoniam uos tanti non estis, ut
cum Turcis preliari ualeatis.' Ipsique Christiani ne-
quiter deducebant se, quia palatia urbis sternebant et
ardebant, et auferebant plumbum quo ecclesiae erant
coopertae et uendebant Grecis. Vnde imperator iratus
est iussitque eos transmeare Brachium. Postquam transfretauerunt, non cessabant agere omnia mala, combu-
rentes et deuastantes domos et ecclesias. Tandem peruenerunt Nicomediam, ubi diuisi sunt Lombardi et
Longobardi, et Alamanni a Francis,[1] quia Franci tume-
bant superbia. Elegerunt Lombardi et Longobardi
seniorem super se, cui nomen Rainoldus, Alamanni
similiter. Et intrauerunt in Romaniam[2] et per quatuor
dies ierunt ultra Nicenam urbem inueneruntque quoddam castrum cui nomen Exerogorgo, quod erat uacuum
gente. Et apprehenderunt illud, in qua inuenerunt satis
frumenti et uini et carnis, et omnium bonorum abundantiam. Audientes itaque Turci quod Christiani essent
in castro, uenerunt obsidere illud. Ante portam castri
erat puteus, et ad pedem castri fons uiuus, iuxta quem
exiit Rainaldus[3] insidiari Turcos. Venientes uero Turci
in festo sancti Michahelis, inuenerunt Rainaldum et qui
cum eo erant, occideruntque Turci multos ex eis. Alii
fugerunt in castrum. Quod confestim Turci obsederunt,
eisque aquam abstulerunt. Fueruntque nostri in tanta
afflictione sitis, ut flebotomarent suos equos et asinos,
quorum sanguinem bibebant.[a] Alii mittebant zonas
atque panniculos in piscinam, et inde exprimebant

---

[a] et sanguinem biberent DX

[1] Here used in the specialised sense of the subjects of Philip I Capet.
[2] Romania, the modern Asia Minor
[3] The variants in the spelling of this name are given in the MS.

to be given to them, and he said, 'Do not cross the Hellespont until the great army of the Christians arrives, for there are not enough of you to fight against the Turks.' But those Christians behaved abominably, sacking and burning the palaces of the city, and stealing the lead from the roofs of the churches and selling it to the Greeks, so that the emperor was angry, and ordered them to cross the Hellespont. After they had crossed they did not cease from their misdeeds, and they burned and laid waste both houses and churches. At last they reached Nicomedia, where the Italians and Germans broke away from the Franks,[1] because the Franks were intolerably proud. The Italians chose a leader called Rainald; the Germans also chose a leader, and they all went into Rum[2] and travelled for four days' journey beyond the city of Nicea, where they found a deserted castle named Xerigordo which they took, finding therein plenty of corn and wine and meat and abundance of all good things. But when the Turks heard that the Christians were in the castle, they came and besieged it. Before its gate was a well, and beneath its walls a spring, where Rainald[3] went out to lay an ambush for the Turks, but when they arrived on Michaelmas Day they caught Rainald and his company, and killed many of them. The survivors fled into the castle, which the Turks at once besieged, cutting off the water-supply. Our men were therefore so terribly afflicted by thirst that they bled their horses and asses and drank the blood; others let down belts and clothes into a sewer and squeezed out the liquid into their mouths; others

aquam in os suum. Alii mingebant in pugillo alterius,
et bibebant. Alii fodiebant humidam terram, et supina-
bant se, terramque sternebant super pectora sua, pro
nimia ariditate sitis. Episcopi uero et presbiteri confortabant nostros et commonebant ne deficerent. Haec
tribulatio fuit per octo dies. Denique dominus Alaman-
norum concordatus est cum Turcis, ut traderet socios
illis, et fingens se exire ad bellum, fugit ad illos et multi
cum eo. Illi autem qui Deum negare noluerunt, capitalem sententiam susceperunt. Alios quos ceperunt uiuos
adinuicem diuiserunt quasi oues. Alios miserunt ad
signum et sagittabant eos; alios uendebant et donabant
quasi animalia. Quidam conducebant suos in domum
suam, alios in Corosanum,[1] alios in Antiochiam, alios in
Aleph, aut ubi ipsi manebant. Isti primo felix acceperunt martirium pro nomine Domini Iesu.

Audientes denique Turci quod Petrus Heremita et
Guualterius Sinehabere[2] fuissent in Cyuito, quae supra
Nicenam urbem est, uenerunt illuc cum magno gaudio
ut occiderent illos et eos qui cum ipsis erant. Cumque
uenissent obuiauerunt Guualterio cum suis, quos Turci
mox occiderunt. Petrus uero Heremita paulo ante ierat
Constantinopolim, eo quod nequibat refrenare illam
diuersam gentem, quae nec illum nec uerba eius audire
uolebat. Irruentes uero Turci super eos occiderunt
multos ex eis; alios inuenerunt dormientes, alios nudos,
quos omnes necauerunt, cum quibus quemdam sacer-
dotem inuenerunt missam celebrantem, quem statim
super altare martirizauerunt. Illi uero qui euadere

---

[1] This name, literally descriptive of the north-eastern part of the modern
Iran, is sometimes used by the author to denote Persia in general.

[2] Walter de Poissi, a knight and a leader of one of the disorderly bands
which had followed Peter the Hermit

passed water into one another's cupped hands and drank; others dug up damp earth and lay down on their backs, piling the earth upon their chests because they were so dry with thirst. The bishops and priests encouraged our men and told them not to despair. This miserable state of affairs went on for eight days. Then the leader of the Germans made an agreement to betray his comrades to the Turks, and pretending that he was going out to fight he fled to them, and many men went with him. Of the remainder, those who would not renounce God were killed; others, whom the Turks captured alive, were divided among their captors like sheep, some were put up as targets and shot with arrows, others sold and given away as if they were brute beasts. Some of the Turks took their prisoners home to Khorasan,[1] Antioch or Aleppo or wherever they happened to live. These men were the first to endure blessed martyrdom for the Name of our Lord Jesus.

Afterwards, when the Turks heard that Peter the Hermit and Walter the Penniless[2] were in Kivotos, which is beyond the city of Nicea, they came thither full of glee intending to kill them and their comrades, and when they had come they found Walter and his men, and killed them at once. Peter the Hermit, however, had gone off to Constantinople a little before this happened, for he could not control such a mixed company of people who would not obey him or listen to what he said. The Turks fell upon his men and killed most of them—some they found asleep, others naked, and all these they slaughtered. Among the rest they found a priest saying mass, and they killed him at once upon the altar. Those who managed to

potuerunt Cyuito fugerunt; alii precipitabant se in mare,
alii latebant in siluis et montanis. Turci uero persequentes illos in castrum adunauerunt ligna, ut eos
comburerent cum castro. Christiani igitur qui in castro
erant miserunt ignem in ligna congregata, et uersus ignis
in Turcos quosdam eorum concremauit, sed ab illo
incendio Deus nostros tunc liberauit. Tandem Turci
apprehenderunt illos uiuos, diuiseruntque illos sicut prius
fecerant alios, et disperserunt illos per uniuersas regiones
has, alios in Corosanum, alios in Persidem. Hoc totum
est factum in mense Octobri.ᵃ Audiens imperator quod
Turci sic dissipassent nostros, gauisus est ualde, et mandauit fecitque eos Brachium transmeare. Postquam
ultra fuerunt, comparauit omnia arma eorum.

[iii] Secunda uero pars intrauit in Sclauiniae partes,¹
scilicet comes de Sancto Egidio Raimundus² et Podiensis
episcopus.³ Tertia autem pars per antiquam Romae
uiam uenit.⁴ In hac parte fuerunt Boamundus,⁵ et
Richardus de Principatu,⁶ Rotbertus comes Flandrensis,
Rotbertus Nortmannus,⁷ Hugo Magnus,⁸ Eurardus de
Puisatio, Achardus de Monte Merloi, Isuardus de
Musone,ᵃ⁹ et alii plures. Deinde uenerunt ad portum
Brandosim aut Barim siue Otrentum. Hugo denique
Magnus et Willelmus Marchisi filius¹⁰ intrauerunt mare

ᵃ DX *omit* Hoc . . . Octobri   ᵇ Musione *or* Niusione DX

¹ The modern Jugoslavia
² Raymond of Saint Gilles, count of Toulouse. He was a man of over
fifty, and by far the eldest of the leaders of the crusade. He seems to have
made arrangements to settle permanently in the East. Raymond d'Agiles,
his chaplain, wrote the history of the crusade from his point of view (*P.L.*,
CLV).
³ Adhémar, bishop of Le Puy, appointed papal legate by Urban II.
⁴ The Via Egnatia, running from Durazzo to Constantinople
⁵ Son of Robert Guiscard by his first wife Aubrée, disinherited in favour
of the children of a second wife. He was a man of great courage and ability
and of no scruples. Anna Comnena, who disliked him, described him as an
intelligent man, extremely plausible in speech (*Alexiad*, x, 11).

escape fled to Kivotos. Some leapt into the sea, and others hid in the woods and mountains. The Turks chased some of our men into the castle, and piled up wood so that they could burn them and the castle together, but the Christians in the castle set fire to the pile of wood, and the flames were blown back against the Turks and burned some of them, but God delivered our men from that fire. At last the Turks took them alive and apportioned them as they had done with the others, sending them away through all the neighbouring lands, some to Khorasan and some to Persia. All this happened in October. When the emperor heard that the Turks had inflicted such a defeat on our men he rejoiced greatly, and gave orders for the survivors to be brought back over the Hellespont. When they had crossed over he had them completely disarmed.

[iii] Our second army came through the Dalmatian lands,[1] and it was led by Raymond, count of Saint Gilles,[2] and the bishop of Le Puy.[3] The third came by way of the old Roman road.[4] In this band were Bohemond[5] and Richard of the Principality,[6] Robert count of Flanders, Robert the Norman,[7] Hugh the Great,[8] Everard of Puiset, Achard of Montmerle, Isard of Mouzon[9] and many others. Some of them came to the port of Brindisi, others to Bari or Otranto. Hugh the Great and William son of the Marquis[10] embarked

---

[6] Bohemond's cousin, the count of Salerno
[7] Eldest son of William the Conqueror
[8] Hugh of Vermandois, younger son of Philip I of France. 'Magnus' is described by Bréhier as a corruption of 'maisné', i.e. the younger (Bréhier, *Histoire Anonyme*, p. 14).
[9] French barons
[10] Bohemond's nephew, son of his sister Emma

ad portum Bari, et transfretantes uenerunt Durachium. Audiens uero dux illius loci hos prudentissimos uiros[a] illic esse applicatos, mox mala cogitatio cor eius tetigit, illosque apprehendit, ac iussit Constantinopolim imperatori caute duci, quo ei fidelitatem facerent.

Dux denique Godefridus primus omnium seniorum Constantinopolim uenit cum magno exercitu, duobus diebus ante Domini nostri Natale, et hospitatus est extra urbem, donec iniquus imperator iussit eum hospitari in burgo urbis. Cumque fuisset hospitatus dux, secure mittebat armigeros suos per singulos dies, ut paleas et alia equis necessaria asportarent.[b] Et cum putarent exire fiducialiter quo uellent, iniquus imperator Alexius imperauit Turcopolis[1] et Pinzinacis[2] inuadere illos et occidere. Balduinus itaque frater ducis haec audiens misit se in insidiis, tandemque inuenit eos[c] occidentes gentem suam, eosque inuasit forti animo, ac Deo iuuante superauit eos. Et apprehendens sexaginta ex eis, partem occidit, partem duci fratri suo presentauit. Quod cum audisset imperator, ualde iratus est. Videns uero dux inde iratum imperatorem, exiit cum suis de burgo et hospitatus est extra urbem. Sero autem facto, infelix imperator iussit suis exercitibus inuadere ducem cum Christi gente. Quos dux persequens inuictus cum Christi militibus septem ex illis occidit, persequendo alios usque ad portam ciuitatis. Reuersusque dux[d] ad sua tentoria mansit inibi per quinque dies, donec pactum iniit cum

---

[a] DX *omit* uiros	[b] DX *correct to* apportarent
[c] illos DX	[d] DX *omit* dux

[1] Turkish mercenaries recruited by the Emperor Alexius
[2] Mercenaries recruited from the Mongolian tribes settled between the Dnieper and the Don.

at Bari and sailed to Durazzo, but the governor of that place, hearing that warriors of such experience were arriving, immediately devised a treacherous plan, and he arrested them and sent them under guard to the emperor at Constantinople, so that they might swear fealty to him.

After this Duke Godfrey was the first of all our leaders to reach Constantinople with a great army, and he arrived two days before Christmas, and encamped outside the city until that wretch of an emperor gave orders that quarters were to be assigned to him in the suburbs. When the duke had settled in, he sent his squires out each day, quite confidently, to get straw and other things necessary for the horses; but, when they thought that they could go out freely wherever they liked, the wretched Emperor Alexius ordered his Turcopuli[1] and Patzinaks[2] to attack and kill them. So Baldwin, the duke's brother, hearing of this, lay in ambush, and when he found the enemy killing his men he attacked them bravely and by God's help defeated them. He took sixty prisoners, some of whom he killed and others he presented to the duke his brother. When the emperor heard of this he was very angry, and the duke, realising this, led his men out of the city and encamped outside the walls. Late that evening the miserable emperor ordered his men to attack the duke and the Christian army, but our unconquered leader with his Christian knights drove back the imperial troops, killing seven men and driving the rest to the gates of the city. Afterwards he came back to his camp and stayed there for five days, until he came to an

imperatore, dixitque illi imperator ut transfretaret Brachium sancti Georgii, permisitque eum habere omnem mercatum ibi sicut est Constantinopoli; et pauperibus elemosinam erogare, unde potuissent uiuere.

[iiii] At bellipotens Boamundus qui erat in obsidione Malfi, Scafardi Pontis, audiens uenisse innumerabilem gentem Christianorum de Francis, ituram ad Domini Sepulchrum, et paratam ad prelium contra gentem paganorum, coepit diligenter inquirere quae arma pugnandi haec gens deferat, et quam ostensionem Christi in uia*a* portet, uel quod signum in certamine sonet. Cui per ordinem haec dicta sunt: 'Deferunt arma ad bellum congrua, in dextra uel inter utrasque scapulas crucem Christi baiulant; sonum uero "Deus uult, Deus uult, Deus uult!" una uoce conclamant.' Mox Sancto commotus Spiritu, iussit preciosissimum pallium quod apud se habebat incidi, totumque statim in cruces expendit. Coepit tunc ad eum uehementer concurrere maxima pars militum qui erant in obsidione illa, adeo ut Rogerius comes[1] pene solus remanserit, reuersusque Siciliam dolebat et merebat quandoque gentem amittere suam. Denique reuersus iterum in terram suam[2] dominus Boamundus diligenter honestauit sese ad incipiendum Sancti Sepulchri iter. Tandem transfretauit mare cum suo exercitu, et cum eo Tancredus Marchisi filius,[3] et Richardus princeps, ac Rainulfus frater eius, et Rotbertus de Ansa, et Hermannus de Canni, et Rotbertus de Surda Valle, et Robertus filius Tostani, et Hunfredus filius

---

a in uia Christi DX

[1] Younger brother of Robert Guiscard, and therefore Bohemond's uncle
[2] Taranto
[3] Bohemond's nephew, brother of William (see p. 5 above). He was the youngest of the crusading leaders, not yet twenty at the time of the events described by the *Gesta*. His subsequent career as Prince of Antioch showed him to be extremely intelligent and adaptable, courageous and quite unscrupulous (Fulcher of Chartres, in *P.L.*, CLV).

agreement with the emperor, who told him to cross the Hellespont and promised that he would have as good provision there as he had in Constantinople; moreover the emperor promised to give alms to the poor so that they could live.

[iiii] As for Bohemond, that great warrior, he was besieging Amalfi when he heard that an immense army of Frankish crusaders had arrived, going to the Holy Sepulchre and ready to fight the pagans. So he began to make careful inquiries as to the arms they carried, the badge which they wore in Christ's pilgrimage and the war-cry which they shouted in battle. He was told, 'They are well-armed, they wear the badge of Christ's cross on their right arm or between their shoulders, and as a war-cry they shout all together "God's will, God's will, God's will!"' Then Bohemond, inspired by the Holy Ghost, ordered the most valuable cloak which he had to be cut up forthwith and made into crosses, and most of the knights who were at the siege began to join him at once, for they were full of enthusiasm, so that Count Roger[1] was left almost alone, and when he had gone back to Sicily he grieved and lamented because he had lost his army. My lord Bohemond went home to his own land[2] and made careful preparations for setting out on the way to the Holy Sepulchre. Thereafter he crossed the sea with his army, and with him went Tancred son of the Marquis,[3] Richard of the Principality and Ranulf his brother, Robert of Anse, Herman of Cannes, Robert of Sourdeval, Robert Fitz-Toustan, Humphrey Fitz-

Radulfi, et Ricardus filius comitis Rainulfi, et comes de
Russignolo cum fratribus suis, et Boello Carnotensis,
et Alberedus de Cagnano, et Hunfredus de Monte
Scabioso.[1] Hi omnes transfretauerunt ad Boamundi
famulatum, et applicuerunt Bulgariae partibus; ubi inuenerunt nimiam abundantiam frumenti et uini et ali-
mentorum corporis. Deinde descendentes in uallem
de Andronopoli[2]; expectauerunt gentem suam, donec
omnes pariter transfretassent. Tunc Boamundus ordi-
nauit concilium cum gente sua, confortans et monens
omnes ut boni et humiles essent; et ne depredarentur
terram istam quia Christianorum erat, et nemo acciperet
nisi quod ei sufficeret ad edendum.[3]

Tunc exeuntes inde, uenerunt per nimiam plenitu-
dinem de uilla in uillam, de ciuitate in ciuitatem, de
castello in castellum, quousque peruenimus Castoriam[4];
ibique Natiuitatem Domini solemniter celebrauimus;
fuimusque ibi per plures dies, et quesiuimus mercatum,
sed ipsi noluerunt nobis assentire, eo quod ualde timebant nos, non putantes nos esse peregrinos, sed uelle
populari terram et occidere illos. Quapropter appre-
hendebamus boues, equos et asinos, et omnia quae
inueniebamus. Egressi de Castoria, intrauimus Pala-
goniam,[5] in qua erat quoddam hereticorum[6] castrum.
Quod undique aggressi sumus, moxque nostro succubuit
imperio. Accenso itaque igne, combussimus castrum
cum habitatoribus suis. Postea peruenimus ad flumen
Bardarum. Denique perrexit dominus Boamundus ultra

---

[1] Norman or Frankish knights and barons who had acquired fiefs in
southern Italy.
[2] Probably the river Drino or Drim
[3] Bohemond had already fought against the Emperor Alexius 1084-5.
He seems now to have been anxious to create a good impression, since he
hoped to gain a principality in the imperial lands.
[4] Kastoria
[5] Monastir

Ralph, Richard son of Count Ranulf, the count of Russignolo and his brothers, Boel of Chartres, Aubré of Cagnano and Humphrey of Monte Scaglioso.[1] All these crossed at Bohemond's expense, and reached western Macedonia, where they found plenty of corn and wine and other things to eat, and going down into the valley of Andronopolis[2] they waited for their men, until all had crossed over. Then Bohemond called a council to encourage his men, and to warn them all to be courteous and refrain from plundering that land, which belonged to Christians, and he said that no-one was to take more than sufficed for his food.[3]

Then we set out and travelled through very rich country from one village to another, and from one city to another and from one castle to another, until we came to Castoria,[4] where we held the feast of Christmas and stayed for some days trying to buy provisions, but the inhabitants would sell us none, because they were much afraid of us, taking us to be no pilgrims but plunderers come to lay waste the land and to kill them. So we seized oxen, horses and asses, and anything else we could find, and leaving Castoria we went into Palagonia,[5] where there was a castle of heretics.[6] We attacked this place from all sides and it soon fell into our hands, so we set fire to it and burnt the castle and its inhabitants together. After this we reached the river Vardar, and my lord Bohemond crossed over

---

[6] Probably Manichaeans, of whom there were a great number in the Balkans. See S. Runciman, *The Medieval Manichee*. The Author of the *Gesta*, as an orthodox Catholic, clearly thought heretics fair game, and was outraged when the Byzantine troops avenged their murder by an attack at the Vardar river.

cum sua gente, sed non tota. Remansit enim ibi comes
de Russignolo, cum fratribus suis. Venit exercitus imperatoris, et inuasit comitem cum fratribus suis, et omnes
qui erant cum eis. Quod audiens Tancredus rediit retro,
et proiectus in flumen natando peruenit ad alios, et duo
milia miserunt se in flumen sequendo Tancredum. Tandem inuenerunt Turcopulos et Pinzinacos dimicantes
cum nostris. Quos repente fortiter inuaserunt, et prudenter eos superauerunt. Et apprehenderunt plures ex
illis, et duxerunt illos ligatos ante domini Boamundi
presentiam. Quibus ait ipse, 'Quare miseri occiditis
gentem Christi et meam? Ego cum uestro imperatore
nullam altercationem habeo.' Qui responderunt: 'Nos
nequimus aliud agere. In roga imperatoris locati sumus,
et quicquid nobis imperat nos oportet implere.' Quos
Boamundus impunitos permisit abire. Hoc bellum factum est in quarta feria, quae est caput ieiunii.[1] Per
omnia benedictus Deus. Amen.

Explicit liber I. Incipit liber secundus.

[1] 18 February 1097

with some of his men, but not all, for the count of Russignolo and his brothers stayed behind. The emperor's army came up and attacked the count and his brothers and all their men, so when Tancred heard of this he went back and, diving into the river, he swam across to the others, with two thousand men following him. They found Turcopuli and Patzinaks fighting with our men, so they made a sudden and gallant attack and, since they were men of experience, they defeated the enemy and took many prisoners whom they bound and led before my lord Bohemond. He said to them, 'You scoundrels, why do you kill Christ's people and mine? I have no quarrel with your emperor!' They answered, 'We cannot do anything else. We are at the emperor's command, and whatever he orders, that we must do.' Bohemond let them go scot-free. This battle was fought on the fourth day of the week, which was Ash Wednesday.[1] Blessed be God in all his works! Amen.

Here ends the first book, and the second book begins.

II

[v] Mandauit infelix imperator simul cum nostris
nuntiis uni ex suis, quem ualde diligebat, quem et cor-
palatium[1] uocant, ut nos secure deduceret per terram
suam, donec ueniremus Constantinopolim. Cumque
transiremus ante illorum ciuitates, iubebat habitatoribus
terrae ut nobis asportarent mercatum, sicut faciebant et
illi quos diximus. Certe tantum timebant fortissimam
gentem domni Boamundi, ut nullum nostrorum sinerent
intrare muros ciuitatum. Volueruntque nostri quoddam
castrum aggredi et apprehendere, eo quod erat plenum
omnibus bonis. Sed uir prudens Boamundus noluit con-
sentire, tantum pro iustitia terrae quantum pro fiducia
imperatoris. Vnde ualde iratus est cum Tancredo et
aliis omnibus. Hoc factum est uespere. Mane uero
facto, exierunt habitatores castri, et cum processione
deferentes in manibus cruces, uenerunt in presentiam
Boamundi. Ipse uero gaudens recepit eos, et cum letitia
abire permisit illos. Deinde uenimus ad quamdam
urbem quae dicitur Serra,[2] ubi nostra fiximus tentoria,
et sat habuimus mercatum, illis diebus conueniens. Ibi
Boamundus concordatus est cum duobus corpalatiis, et
pro amicitia eorum ac pro iustitia terrae iussit reddi
omnia animalia quae nostri depredata tenebant. Deinde
peruenimus ad Rusam ciuitatem.[3] Grecorum autem

---

[1] 'Lord of the Palace', a high official of the imperial household. Later
the Author speaks of two Kyriopalatioi.

[2] In eastern Macedonia

[3] This place has never been satisfactorily identified. It seems to have
lain west of the Maritza ('vallem plenam omnibus bonis') and may have
been Xanthi or Komotini. The name seems to mean 'Russian'.

II

[v] The wretched emperor commanded one of his own men, who was very dear to him and whom they call the *kyriopalatios*,[1] to accompany our messengers so that he might guide us safely through his country until we came to Constantinople. Whenever we passed by any of their cities this man used to tell the people of the land to bring us provisions, as those whom we have mentioned before used to do. It was clear that they were so much afraid of my lord Bohemond's strong army that they would not allow any of our men to go inside the walls of the cities. Our men wanted to attack one of the castles and take it, because it was full of goods of all kinds, but the valiant Bohemond would not allow this, for he wished to treat the country justly and to keep faith with the emperor, so he was furious with Tancred and all the others. This happened one evening, and next morning the inhabitants of the castle emerged in procession, carrying crosses in their hands, and came into the presence of Bohemond, who received them with joy and let them also go away rejoicing. After this we reached a town called Serres,[2] where we encamped and had provisions good enough for Lent. While we were there Bohemond made an agreement with two of the *kyriopalatioi*, and because of his friendship with them and his desire to treat the country justly he ordered all the animals which our men had stolen and kept to be given back. Thereafter we reached the city of Rusa.[3] The Greek inhabitants came out and ap-

gens exibat et ueniebat gaudens in occursum domini
Boamundi, nobis deferens maximum mercatum, ibique
nostros tetendimus papiliones in quarta feria ante Cenam
Domini[1]; ibi etiam Boamundus totam gentem suam
dimisit, perrexitque loqui cum imperatore Constantinopolim, ducens tamen secum paucos milites. Tancredus
remansit caput militiae Christi, uidensque peregrinos
cibos emere, ait intra se quod exiret extra uiam, et hunc
populum conduceret ubi feliciter uiueret. Denique intrauit in uallem quamdam plenam omnibus bonis quae
corporalibus nutrimentis sunt congrua; in qua Pascha
Domini deuotissime celebrauimus.[2]

[vi] Cum imperator audisset honestissimum uirum
Boamundum ad se uenisse, iussit eum honorabiliter
recipi, et caute hospitari extra urbem. Quo hospitato,
imperator misit pro eo, ut ueniret loqui simul secreto
secum. Tunc illuc uenit dux Godefridus cum fratre
suo; ac deinde comes Sancti Egidii appropinquauit
ciuitati. Tunc imperator anxians et bulliens ira, cogi-
tabat quemadmodum callide fraudulenterque compre-
henderet hos Christi milites. Sed diuina gratia reuelante,
neque locus neque nocendi spatium ab eo uel a suis
inuenta sunt. Nouissime uero congregati omnes maiores
natu qui Constantinopoli erant, timentes ne sua priua-
rentur patria, reppererunt in suis consiliis atque ingeni-
osis scematibus quod nostrorum duces, comites, seu
omnes maiores imperatori sacramentum fideliter facere
deberent.[3] Qui[a] omnino prohibuerunt, dixeruntque:

---

[a] quod DX

[1] 1 April 1097
[2] This was the first of Tancred's independent enterprises. His later
attacks on Tarsus and Bethlehem showed that he had his own ideas of how
a crusade should be conducted.
[3] Alexius, whose predecessors had lawfully held the whole of Palestine,

proached my lord Bohemond rejoicing, bringing us plenty of provisions, so we pitched our tents there on the Wednesday in Holy Week.[1] While we were there Bohemond left his army, and went ahead to Constantinople with a few knights to take counsel with the emperor. Tancred stayed behind with the army of Christ, and when he saw that the pilgrims were buying food he had the idea of turning aside from the road and bringing the people where they could live in plenty; so that he went into a certain valley full of all kinds of things which are good to eat, and there we kept the festival of Easter with great devotion.[2]

[vi] When the emperor had heard that Bohemond, that most distinguished man, had come, he ordered him to be received with proper ceremony, but took care to lodge him outside the city. After Bohemond had settled in, the emperor sent to invite him to a secret conference. Duke Godfrey and his brother were also present, and the count of St Gilles was near the city. Then the emperor, who was troubled in mind and fairly seething with rage, was planning how to entrap these Christian knights by fraud and cunning, but by God's grace neither he nor his men found place or time to harm them. At last all the elders of Constantinople, who were afraid of losing their country, took counsel together and devised a crafty plan of making the dukes, counts and all the leaders of our army swear an oath of fealty to the emperor.[3] This our leaders flatly refused to do, for they said, 'Truly, this is unworthy of us, and

---

Syria and Romania, wished, reasonably enough, to compel the crusading leaders to admit that they were re-conquering these lands in his name (*Alexiad*, x, 9).

'Certe indigni sumus, atque iustum nobis uidetur nullatenus ei sacramentum iurare.'[1]

Forsitan adhuc a nostris maioribus sepe delusi erimus.
Ad ultimum quid facturi erunt? Dicent quoniam necessitate compulsi nolentes uolentesque[a] humiliauerunt se
ad nequissimi imperatoris uoluntatem.

Fortissimo autem uiro Boamundo quem ualde timebat, quia olim eum sepe cum suo exercitu eiecerat de
campo dixit, quoniam si libenter ei iuraret, quindecim
dies eundi terrae in extensione ab Antiochia retro daret,
et octo in latitudine. Eique tali modo iurauit, ut si ille
fideliter teneret illud sacramentum, iste suum nunquam
preteriret.[2] Tam fortes et tam duri milites, cur hoc
fecerunt? Propterea igitur, quia multa coacti erant
necessitate.[3]

Imperator quoque omnibus nostris fidem et securi-
tatem dedit, iurauit etiam quia ueniret nobiscum pariter
cum suo exercitu per terram et per mare; et nobis mercatum terra marique fideliter daret, ac omnia nostra
perdita diligenter restauraret, insuper et neminem nostrorum peregrinorum conturbari uel contristari in uia
Sancti Sepulchri uellet aut permitteret.

---

^a uolentes nolentesque DX

[1] Frankish (i.e. Western European) feeling against the Greek emperor
had been hardening ever since the production of the forged Donation of
Constantine c. 750. Since 1054 the western Catholic church had regarded
the Greek Orthodox church as schismatic. Robert Guiscard's attack on
Durazzo, beaten off in 1085, seems to have been designed as a first step in
the conquest of the Eastern Empire.
[2] Anna Comnena confirms the fact that Bohemond demanded a special
position in the imperial court, but says that Alexius gave him an incon-
clusive answer (*Alexiad*, x, 11). The story as told by the Anonymous was
probably circulated to explain Bohemond's later claim to Antioch, and may
have been inserted into the original text for the purpose of propaganda (see
Introduction, p. x). It is worthy of note that in the summer of 1098
Bohemond never cited this treaty in order to support his claim to Antioch,
and this suggests to Professor Krey that no such treaty existed. He may
very well be right, but it is also true that the crusading leaders in the summer
of 1098 had, in general, an unjustifiably low opinion of Alexius, and that a

it seems unjust that we should swear to him any oath at all.'[1]

Perhaps, however, we were fated to be misled often by our leaders, for what did they do in the end? They may say that they were constrained by need, and had to humble themselves willy-nilly to do what that abominable emperor wanted.

Now the emperor was much afraid of the gallant Bohemond, who had often chased him and his army from the battlefield, so he told Bohemond that he would give him lands beyond Antioch, fifteen days' journey in length and eight in width, provided that he would swear fealty with free consent, and he added this promise, that if Bohemond kept his oath faithfully he would never break his own.[2] But why did such brave and determined knights do a thing like this? It must have been because they were driven by desperate need.[3]

The emperor for his part guaranteed good faith and security to all our men, and swore also to come with us, bringing an army and a navy, and faithfully to supply us with provisions both by land and sea, and to take care to restore all those things which we had lost. Moreover he promised that he would not cause or permit anyone to trouble or vex our pilgrims on the way to the Holy Sepulchre.

---

suggestion of a secret treaty with him would have been extremely unpopular.
[3] The Author was not present at the council, and shows a natural reluctance to believe his own lord capable of deliberate duplicity. He seems to have been disillusioned in the autumn of 1098, but even then he utters no explicit condemnation of Bohemond. This was a right and proper attitude for a vassal to take to his lord. If, however, Bohemond used the *Gesta* as a justification of his claim to Antioch, it is odd that he did not omit from this passage the mention of his own oath, the breach of which left him with no justifiable pretext for continuing to hold the city (see Krey in *The Crusades and other historical essays presented to D. C. Munro*, ed. L. J. Paetow, pp. 57-79, and C. Cahen, *La Syrie du Nord*, pp. 8-9).

Comes autem Sancti Egidii erat hospitatus extra
ciuitatem in burgo, gensque sua remanserat retro. Mandauit itaque imperator comiti, ut faceret ei hominium
et fiduciam sicut alii fecerant. Et dum imperator haec
mandabat, comes meditabatur qualiter uindictam de
imperatoris exercitu habere posset.[a] Sed dux Godefridus
et Rotbertus comes Flandrensis aliique principes dixerunt ei, iniustum fore, contra Christianos pugnare. Vir
quoque sapiens Boamundus dixit, quia si aliquid iniustum imperatori faceret, et fiduciam ei facere pro-
hiberet, ipse ex imperatoris parte fieret. Igitur comes
accepto consilio a suis, Alexio uitam et honorem iurauit,
quod nec per se nec per alium ei auferre consentiat,
cumque de hominio appellaretur, non se pro capitis
periculo id facturum.[b][1] Tunc gens domni Boamundi
appropinquauit Constantinopoli.[c]

[vii] Tancredus uero et Richardus de Principatu
propter iusiurandum imperatoris latenter transfretauerunt Brachium, et fere omnis gens Boamundi iuxta illos.
Et mox exercitus comitis Sancti Egidii appropinquauit
Constantinopoli.[c] Comes uero remansit ibi cum ipsa
sua gente. Boamundus itaque remansit cum imperatore,
ut cum eo consilium acciperet, quomodo mandarent
mercatum gentibus quae erant ultra Nicenam ciuitatem.
Dux itaque Godefridus iuit prius Nicomediam simul cum

---

[a] potuisset DX
[b] DX *add* respondit
[c] Constantinopolim DX

[1] Count Raymond's passage through the imperial lands had been a
particularly stormy one, and his chronicler Raymond d'Agiles describes a
good deal of fighting on the way. Nevertheless, he was the only one of the
crusading leaders to take his oath seriously. The wording of the passage
'Mandat . . . facturum' is close to, although not identical with, the similar

The count of St Gilles was encamped outside the city in the suburbs, and his army had stayed behind, so the emperor ordered him to do homage and swear fealty as the others had done; but when the emperor sent him this message the count was planning how to revenge himself on the imperial army. Duke Godfrey and Robert, count of Flanders, and the other leaders, however, told him that it would be improper to fight against fellow Christians, and the valiant Bohemond said that if Count Raymond did any injustice to the emperor, or refused to swear fealty to him, he himself would take the emperor's part. Therefore the count took the advice of his friends and swore that he would respect the life and honour of Alexius, and neither destroy them nor permit anyone else to do so; but when he was asked to do homage he said that he would not, even at the peril of his life.[1] After this my lord Bohemond's army came up to Constantinople.

[vii] Tancred and Richard of the Principality crossed the Hellespont secretly, because they did not want to take the oath to the emperor, and nearly all Bohemond's forces went with them. Soon afterwards the count of St Gilles approached Constantinople, and he stayed on there with his forces. Bohemond stayed with the emperor in order to consult him about the supply of provisions to the people who had gone on beyond Nicea, so Duke Godfrey was the first to go to

---

passage in Raymond d'Agiles (*P.L.*, CLV, 395). Raymond omits the description of Bohemond as 'vir sapiens', which the Author of the *Gesta* uses frequently throughout the first nine books, and I think that he was here using, and emending, the MS of the *Gesta*, unless we may assume the not impossible hypothesis that two historians may describe the same event in very similar words.

Tancredo, et aliis omnibus, fueruntque ibi per tres dies.
Videns uero dux quod nulla uia pateret per quam posset
conducere has gentes usque Nicenam ciuitatem, quoniam
per illam uiam per quam prius alii transierant non posset
modo tanta gens transire, misit ante se tria milia hominum cum securibus et gladiis, qui incidissent et aperuis-
sent hanc viam, quae patefacta fieret nostris peregrinis
usque Nicenam*a* urbem. Quae uia fuit aperta per
angustam et nimis immensam montanam,[1] et faciebant
retro per uiam cruces ferreas ac ligneas, quas ponebant
super stipites ut eas nostri peregrini cognoscerent.
Interea peruenimus ad Niceam, quae est caput totius
Romaniae, in quarto die, II nonas Maii, ibique castrametati sumus. Priusquam autem Boamundus uenisset
ad nos, tanta inopia panis fuit inter nos, ut unus panis
uenderetur uiginti aut triginta denariis. Postquam uenit
uir prudens Boamundus, iussit maximum mercatum conduci per mare, et pariter utrinque ueniebant, ille per
terram et ille per mare, et fuit maxima ubertas in tota
Christi militia.

[viii] In die autem Ascensionis Domini[2] coepimus
urbem circumquaque inuadere, et aedificare instrumenta
lignorum atque turres ligneas, quo possemus murales
turres sternere. Tam fortiter et tam acriter aggredimur
urbem per duos dies, ut etiam foderemus murum urbis.
Turci quippe qui erant in urbe, miserunt nuntios aliis
qui uenerant adiutorium ciuitati dare, in hunc modum,
quo audacter secureque approximent, et per meridianam
introeant portam, quoniam ex illa*b* nemo eis erit obuiam
nec contristabit. Quae porta ipsa die a comite sancti

a Niceam DX
b illa parte DX

[1] The mountains here rise to more than four thousand feet.
[2] 14 May 1097

Nicomedia, taking with him Tancred and all the others. They stayed there for three days, and when the duke saw that there was no road by which he could lead these people to Nicea (for there were so many of them that they could not go by the route which the other crusaders had followed) he sent ahead three thousand men with axes and swords so that they could go on and hack open a route for our pilgrims as far as the city of Nicea. This route led over a mountain,[1] steep and very high, so the pathfinders made crosses of metal and wood, and put them upon stakes where our pilgrims could see them. Eventually we came to Nicea, which is the capital of Rum, on Wednesday the sixth of May, and there we encamped. Before my lord the valiant Bohemond came to us we were so short of food that a loaf cost twenty or thirty pence, but after he came he ordered plenty of provisions to be brought to us by sea, so goods poured in both by land and sea, and all Christ's army enjoyed great abundance.

[viii] On Ascension Day[2] we began to lay siege to the town, and to build siege-engines and wooden towers by means of which we could knock down the towers on the wall. We pressed the siege so bravely and fiercely for two days that we managed to undermine the wall of the city, but the Turks who were inside sent messengers to the others who had come to their help, telling them that they might come and enter, fearlessly and safely, by way of the south gate, for there was no-one there to stand in their way or attack them. This gate, however, was blocked on that very day (the Saturday after Ascension Day) by the count of

Egidii in die sabbati post Ascensionem Domini et episcopo Podiensi hospitata fuit. Qui comes, ueniens ex
alia parte, protectus diuina uirtute ac terrenis fulgebat
armis cum suo fortissimo exercitu. Hic itaque inuenit
contra nos uenientes Turcos. Qui undique signo crucis
armatus, uehementer irruit super illos atque superauit.
Dederuntque fugam, et fuit mortua maxima pars illorum.
Qui rursus uenerunt auxilio aliorum gaudentes et exultantes ad certum bellum, trahentes secum funes, quibus
nos ligatos ducerent Corosanum. Venientes autem
letantes, coeperunt ex cacumine montis paulatim descendere. Quotquot descenderunt, illic cesis capitibus
a manibus nostrorum remanserunt. Proiiciebant autem
nostri capita occisorum funda in urbem, ut inde Turci
magis terrerentur.

Denique comes sancti Egidii et episcopus Podiensis
consiliati sunt in unum qualiter facerent subfodi quamdam turrim, quae erat ante tentoria eorum. Ordinati
sunt homines qui hanc suffodiant, et arbalistae et sagit-
tarii qui eos undique defendant. Foderunt namque
illam usque ad radices muri, summiseruntque postes et
ligna, ac deinde miserunt ignem. Sero autem facto,
cecidit turris iam in nocte, sed quia nox erat, non potuerunt preliari cum illis. Nocte uero illa surrexerunt
festinanter Turci, et restaurauerunt murum tam fortiter,
ut ueniente die nemo posset eos laedere ex illa parte.

Modo uenit comes de Nortmannia,[a] et comes Stephanus,[1] et alii plures, ac deinceps Rogerius de Barna-

---

[a] Rotbertus comes Normanniae DX

[1] Count of Blois and Chartres. He had married Adela, daughter of
William the Conqueror, and was therefore brother-in-law to Robert of
Normandy.

St Gilles and the bishop of Le Puy. The count, who came from the other side of the city with a very strong army, trusting in God's protection and glorious in his earthly weapons, found the Turks coming towards the gate against our men. Protected on all sides by the sign of the Cross, he made a fierce attack upon the enemy and defeated them so that they took to flight and many of them were killed. The survivors rallied with the help of other Turks and came in high spirits, exulting in their certainty of victory, bringing with them ropes with which to lead us bound into Khorasan. They came along gleefully and began to descend a little way from the top of the mountain, but as many as came down had their heads cut off by our men, who threw the heads of the slain into the city by means of a sling, in order to cause more terror among the Turkish garrison.

After this the count of St Gilles and the bishop of Le Puy took counsel together how they could undermine a tower which stood over against their camp, so they set men to sap it, with arbalists and archers to protect them. The sappers dug down to the foundations of the wall and inserted beams and pieces of wood, to which they set fire, but because all this was done in the evening it was already night when the tower fell, and since it was dark our men could not fight with the defenders. That night the Turks arose in haste and rebuilt the wall so strongly that at daybreak there was no chance of defeating them at that point.

Soon afterwards Robert count of Normandy and Count Stephen[1] arrived with many others, and Roger

uilla.[1] Boamundus denique obsedit urbem in prima
fronte, et iuxta eum Tancredus, et postea dux Godefridus, ac deinde comes Flandrensis, iuxta quem Rotbertus Nortmannus,[a] et iuxta eum comes Sancti Egidii,
iuxta quem Podiensis episcopus. Ita uero per terram
fuit obsessa, ut nemo auderet exire neque intrare.[b]
Fueruntque ibi omnes congregati in unum. Et quis
poterat numerare tantam Christi militiam? Nullus ut
puto tot prudentissimos milites nec antea uidit nec ultra
uidere poterit.

Erat autem ex una parte urbis immensus lacus, in
quo Turci suas mittebant naues, et exibant et intrabant,
et afferebant herbam, ligna et alia plura. Tunc nostri
maiores, consiliati in unum, miserunt nuntios Constantinopolim dicturos imperatori, ut faceret naues conduci
ad Ciuito, ubi portus est, atque iuberet congregari boues
qui eas traherent per montanas et siluas, usque approximent lacui. Quod continuo factum fuit, suosque Turcopulos mandauit cum eis. Die uero quo naues fuerant
conductae, noluerunt eas statim mittere in lacum; sed
nocte superueniente miserunt eas in ipsum lacum, plenas
Turcopolis, bene ornatis armis. Summo autem diluculo
stabant naues optime ordinatae, per lacum properantes
contra urbem. Videntes eas[c] Turci mirabantur, igno-
rantes an esset eorum gens an imperatoris. Postquam
autem cognouerunt esse gentem imperatoris, timuerunt
usque ad mortem, plorantes et lamentantes; Francique
gaudebant, et dabant gloriam Deo. Videntes autem

---

[a] comes Rotbertus (Rotb. comes X) Normanniae DX, *and so in other
places*
[b] intrare neque (aut D) exire DX
[c] DX *add* autem

[1] Barneville-sur-mer (Manche)

of Barneville[1] followed them. Then Bohemond took up his station in front of the city, with Tancred next to him, then Duke Godfrey and the count of Flanders, next to whom was Robert of Normandy, and then the count of St Gilles and the bishop of Le Puy. The city was therefore so closely besieged by land that no-one dared go out or in. Our men were all, for the first time, collected together in this place, and who could count such a great army of Christians? I do not think that anyone has ever seen, or will ever again see, so many valiant knights.

On one side of the city was a great lake, on which the Turks launched boats, and they went in and out bringing fodder and wood and many other things, so our leaders took counsel together and sent messengers to Constantinople to ask the emperor to have boats brought to Kivotos, where there is a harbour, and to have oxen collected to drag these boats over the mountains and through the woods until they reached the lake. The emperor had this done immediately, and sent his Turcopuli with them. His men would not launch the boats at once on the day on which they arrived, but they put out on the lake at nightfall, with the boats full of Turcopuli who were well armed. At daybreak there were the boats, all in very good order, sailing across the lake towards the city. The Turks, seeing them, were surprised and did not know whether it was their own fleet or that of the emperor, but when they realised that it was the emperor's they were afraid almost to death, and began to wail and lament, while the Franks rejoiced and gave glory to God. Then the

Turci quod nullatenus ex suis exercitibus adiutorium habere possent, legationem mandauerunt imperatori, quia ciuitatem sponte redderent, si eos omnimodo abire permitteret cum mulieribus et filiis et omnibus substantiis suis. Tunc imperator, plenus uana et iniqua cogitatione, iussit illos impunitos abire sine ullo timore, ac sibi eos Constantinopolim cum magna fiducia adduci. Quos studiose seruabat, ut illos ad Francorum nocumenta et obstacula paratos haberet.

Fuimusque in obsidione illa per septem ebdomadas et tres dies, et multi ex nostris illic receperunt martyrium, et letantes gaudentesque reddiderunt felices animas Deo; et ex pauperrima gente multi mortui sunt fame pro Christi nomine. Qui in caelum triumphantes portarunt stolam recepti martyrii, una uoce dicentes: 'Vindica Domine sanguinem nostrum, qui pro te effusus est; qui es benedictus et laudabilis in secula seculorum Amen.'

Explicit liber II. Incipit liber III.

Turks, realising that their armies could do no more to help them, sent a message to the emperor saying that they would surrender the city to him if he would let them go free with their wives and children and all their goods. The emperor, who was a fool as well as a knave, told them to go away unhurt and without fear; he had them brought to him at Constantinople under safe-conduct, and kept them carefully so that he could have them ready to injure the Franks and obstruct their crusade.

We besieged this city for seven weeks and three days, and many of our men suffered martyrdom there and gave up their blessed souls to God with joy and gladness, and many of the poor starved to death for the Name of Christ. All these entered Heaven in triumph, wearing the robe of martyrdom which they have received, saying with one voice, 'Avenge, O Lord, our blood which was shed for thee, for thou art blessed and worthy of praise for ever and ever. Amen.'

Here ends the second book, and the third book begins.

III

[ix] Interea reddita ciuitate et Turcis deductis Constantinopolim, unde imperator magis magisque gauisus quod ciuitas reddita sit eius potestati, iussit maximas elemosinas erogari nostris pauperibus. Denique prima die qua recessimus a ciuitate, uenimus ad quemdam pontem, ibique mansimus per duos dies. Tertia autem die, priusquam lux coepisset oriri, surrexerunt nostri; et quia nox erat non uiderunt tenere unam uiam, sed sunt diuisi per duo agmina, et uenerunt diuisi per duos dies. In uno agmine fuit uir Boamundus, et Rotbertus Normannus, et prudens Tancredus, et alii plures. In alio fuit comes Sancti Egidii, et dux Godefridus, et Podiensis episcopus, et Hugo Magnus, comesque Flandrensis, et alii plures.

Tertia uero die irruerunt Turci uehementer super Boamundum, et eos qui cum ipso erant.[1] Continuo Turci coeperunt stridere et garrire ac clamare, excelsa uoce dicentes diabolicum sonum nescio quomodo in sua lingua.[2] Sapiens uir Boamundus uidens innumerabiles Turcos procul, stridentes et clamantes demoniaca uoce, protinus iussit omnes milites descendere, et tentoria celeriter extendere. Priusquam tentoria fuissent extensa, rursus dixit omnibus militibus: 'Seniores[3] et fortissimi milites Christi, ecce modo bellum angustum est undique

---

[1] Anna Comnena gives the site of this battle as 'in the plains of Dorylaeum', i.e. near the modern Eski-Cheir (*Alexiad*, xi, 3). See also Smail, *Crusading Warfare*, pp. 168-70.

[2] Ralph of Caen describes the Turkish war-cry on another occasion as 'Allachibar' (*P.L.*, CLV, 521). It was probably 'Allah akbar' ('God is great').

[3] There is no adequate modern English translation for this word (see Introduction, p. xvii) so I have used the formal method of address which a

III

[ix] When the city had surrendered, and the Turks had been taken to Constantinople, the emperor was exceedingly glad because the city was put under his authority, and he ordered alms to be distributed bountifully to our poor pilgrims. On the first day after we left the city we came to a bridge, and there we stayed for two days. On the third day, before dawn, our men arose, and because it was dark they could not see to keep together, but divided into two bands, and thus they travelled for two days. In one band were the brave Bohemond, Robert the Norman and the gallant Tancred, with many others; in the other were the count of St Gilles and Duke Godfrey, the bishop of Le Puy, Hugh the Great and the count of Flanders, with many others.

On the third day the Turks made a fierce and sudden attack upon Bohemond and his comrades.[1] These Turks began, all at once, to howl and gabble and shout, saying with loud voices in their own language some devilish word which I do not understand.[2] The valiant Bohemond saw that there were innumerable Turks some distance off, howling and shouting like demons, so he ordered all the knights to dismount at once and to pitch camp quickly. Before the camp was pitched he said to all the knights, 'Gentlemen,[3] most valiant soldiers of Christ, you can see that we are encircled and that the battle will be hard, so let the knights go out

---

modern commander would use in speaking to his officers. Although not absolutely correct in a feudal army it seems to convey Bohemond's meaning.

circa nos. Igitur omnes milites eant uiriliter obuiam illis, et pedites prudenter et citius extendant tentoria.'[1]

Postquam uero hoc totum factum est, Turci undique iam erant circumcingentes nos, dimicando et iaculando, ac spiculando,[a] et mirabiliter longe lateque sagittando. Nos itaque quamquam[b] nequiuimus resistere illis, neque sufferre pondus tantorum hostium, tamen pertulimus illuc unanimiter gradum. Feminae quoque nostrae in[c] illa die fuerunt nobis in maximo refugio, quae afferebant ad bibendum aquam nostris preliatoribus, et fortiter semper confortabant illos, pugnantes et defendentes. Vir itaque sapiens Boamundus protinus mandauit aliis, scilicet comiti de Sancto Egidio, et duci Godefrido, et Hugoni Magno, atque Podiensi episcopo, aliisque omnibus Christi militibus, quo festinent, et ad bellum citius approximent, dicens: 'Et si hodie luctari uolunt, uiriliter ueniant.' Dux itaque Godefridus audax et fortis, ac Hugo Magnus simul uenerunt prius cum suis exercitibus; episcopus quoque Podiensis prosequutus est illos, una cum suo exercitu, et comes de Sancto Egidio iuxta illos cum magna gente.

Mirabantur ergo nostri ualde unde esset exorta tanta multitudo Turcorum, et Arabum et Saracenorum, et aliorum quos enumerare ignoro; quia pene omnes montes et colles et ualles et omnia plana loca intus et extra undique erant cooperta de illa excommunicata generatione. Factus est itaque sermo secretus inter nos laudantes et consulentes atque dicentes: 'Estote omnimodo

[a] DX *omit* ac spiculando
[b] DX *omit* quamquam
[c] DX *omit* in

[1] The crusaders seem to have defended a 'laager' or hollow square in which they had placed their non-combatants.

to fight bravely, while the foot-soldiers are careful and quick in pitching the camp.'[1]

After we had set ourselves in order the Turks came upon us from all sides, skirmishing, throwing darts and javelins and shooting arrows from an astonishing range. Although we had no chance of withstanding them or of taking the weight of the charge of so many foes we went forward as one man. The women in our camp were a great help to us that day, for they brought up water for the fighting men to drink, and gallantly encouraged those who were fighting and defending them. The valiant Bohemond made haste to send a message to the others (the count of St Gilles and Duke Godfrey, Hugh the Great and the bishop of Le Puy, with all the rest of the Christian knights) telling them to hurry and come to the battlefield with all speed, and saying, 'If any of you wants to fight today, let him come and play the man.' So Duke Godfrey, who was reckless and brave, with Hugh the Great, came first and arrived together, with their forces, and the bishop of Le Puy followed them with his, and the count of St Gilles came next with a great force.

Our men could not understand whence could have come such a great multitude of Turks, Arabs, Saracens and other peoples whose names I do not know, for nearly all the mountains and hills and valleys, and all the flat country within and without the hills, were covered with this accursed folk. For our part we passed a secret message along our line, praising God and saying, 'Stand fast all together, trusting in Christ

unanimes in fide Christi et Sanctae Crucis uictoria, quia hodie omnes diuites si Deo placet effecti eritis.'[1]

Continuo fuerunt ordinatae nostrorum acies. In sinistra parte fuit uir sapiens Boamundus, et Rotbertus Nortmannus, et prudens Tancredus, ac Robertus de Ansa et Richardus de Principatu.[2] Episcopus uero Podiensis uenit per alteram montanam, undique circumcingens[a] incredulos Turcos. In sinistra quoque parte equitauit fortissimus miles Raimundus comes de Sancto Egidio. In dextera uero parte fuit dux Godefridus, et acerrimus miles Flandrensis comes, et Hugo Magnus, et alii plures, quorum nomina ignoro.

Statim autem uenientibus militibus nostris, Turci et Arabes, et Saraceni et Agulani[b][3] omnesque barbarae nationes dederunt uelociter fugam, per compendia montium et per plana loca. Erat autem numerus Turcorum, Persarum, Publicanorum,[4] Saracenorum, Agulanorum, aliorumque paganorum trecenta sexaginta milia extra Arabes, quorum numerum nemo scit nisi solus Deus.[5] Fugerunt uero nimis uelociter[c] ad sua tentoria, ibique eos diu morari non licuit. Iterum uero arripuerunt fugam, nosque illos persecuti sumus occidentes[d] tota una die. Et accepimus spolia multa, aurum, argentum, equos et[e] asinos, camelos, oues, et boues et plurima alia quae ignoramus. Et nisi Dominus fuisset nobiscum in bello, et aliam cito nobis misisset aciem, nullus nostrorum

---

[a] circumcingentes DX   [b] Angulani DX, *as always*
[c] DX *omit* uelociter   [d] occidendo DX
[e] DX *omit* et

---

[1] This is an interesting example of the way in which the crusaders combined genuine devotion with an eye to mundane advantage.
[2] The Author himself fought on the left wing.
[3] Unexplained, but possibly the Caucasian Albanians (Aghovanians), for whom see Runciman, *The Medieval Manichee*, pp. 59-60.

and in the victory of the Holy Cross. Today, please
God, you will all gain much booty.'[1]

Our line of battle formed up at once. On the left
wing were the valiant Bohemond, Robert the Norman,
the gallant Tancred, Robert of Anse and Richard of
the Principality.[2] The bishop of Le Puy came round
by the other mountain, so that he could take those
misbelieving Turks in the rear, and Raymond, count
of St Gilles and a very gallant knight, rode also on the
left wing. On the right wing were Duke Godfrey and
the count of Flanders, who was very eager to fight,
and Hugh the Great with many others whose names I
do not know.

As soon as our knights charged, the Turks, Arabs,
Saracens, Agulani[3] and all the rest of the barbarians
took to their heels and fled through the mountain
passes and across the plains. There were three hundred
and sixty thousand Turks, Persians, Paulicians,[4] Saracens and Agulani, with other pagans, not counting the
Arabs, for God alone knows how many there were of
them.[5] They fled very fast to their camp, but they
were not allowed to stay there long, so they continued
their flight and we pursued them, killing them, for a
whole day, and we took much booty, gold, silver,
horses, asses, camels, oxen, sheep and many other
things about which we do not know. If God had not
been with us in this battle and sent us the other army
quickly, none of us would have escaped, because the

---

[4] This should properly mean followers of the heresiarch Paul of Samosata, for whom see Runciman, op. cit. pp. 26-62. The Author of the *Gesta*
had no specialised knowledge of heresies, and used the word to denote
heretics in general.
[5] The numbers given in chronicles of the First Crusade are unreliable.

euasisset, quia ab hora tertia usque in horam nonam perdurauit haec pugna. Sed omnipotens Deus pius et misericors qui non permisit suos milites perire, nec in manibus inimicorum incidere, festine nobis adiutorium misit. Sed fuerunt illic mortui duo ex nostris milites honorabiles, scilicet Gosfredus de Monte Scabioso,[1] et Willelmus Marchisi filius frater Tancredi, aliique milites et pedites quorum nomina ignoro.

Quis unquam tam sapiens aut doctus audebit describere prudentiam militiamque[a] et fortitudinem Turcorum? Qui putabant terrere gentem Francorum minis suarum sagittarum, sicut terruerunt Arabes, Saracenos, et Hermenios, Suranios et Grecos. Sed si Deo placet nunquam tantum ualebunt, quantum nostri. Verumtamen dicunt se esse de Francorum generatione, et quia nullus homo naturaliter debet esse miles nisi Franci et illi. Veritatem dicam quam nemo audebit prohibere. Certe si in fide Christi et Christianitate sancta semper firmi fuissent, et unum Deum in trinitate confiteri uoluissent Deique Filium natum de Virgine matre, passum, et resurrexisse a mortuis et in caelum ascendisse suis cernentibus discipulis, consolationemque Sancti Spiritus perfecte misisse; et eum in caelo et in terra regnantem recta mente et fide credidissent, ipsis potentiores uel[b] fortiores uel bellorum ingeniosissimos nullus inuenire potuisset. Et tamen gratia Dei uicti sunt a nostris.[2] Hoc bellum est factum, primo die Iulii.

Explicit liber III. Incipit IIII.

---

fighting went on from the third hour until the ninth, but Almighty God, who is gracious and merciful, delivered his knights from death and from falling into the hands of the enemy and sent us help speedily. Yet two distinguished knights were killed, Godfrey of Monte Scaglioso[1] and William son of the Marquis, Tancred's brother, together with other knights and foot-soldiers whose names I do not know.

What man, however experienced and learned, would dare to write of the skill and prowess and courage of the Turks, who thought that they would strike terror into the Franks, as they had done into the Arabs and Saracens, Armenians, Syrians and Greeks, by the menace of their arrows? Yet, please God, their men will never be as good as ours. They have a saying that they are of common stock with the Franks, and that no men, except the Franks and themselves, are naturally born to be knights. This is true, and nobody can deny it, that if only they had stood firm in the faith of Christ and holy Christendom, and had been willing to accept One God in Three Persons, and had believed rightly and faithfully that the Son of God was born of a virgin mother, that he suffered, and rose from the dead and ascended in the sight of his disciples into Heaven, and sent them in full measure the comfort of the Holy Ghost, and that he reigns in Heaven and earth, you could not find stronger or braver or more skilful soldiers; and yet by God's grace they were beaten by our men.[2] This battle was fought on 1 July.

Here ends the third book, and the fourth begins.

[1] Possibly 'Humphrey of Monte Scaglioso'. See p. 8.
[2] See Introduction, p. xiv.

IV

[x] Postquam uero Turci inimici Dei et sanctae Christianitatis omnino fuerunt deuicti, per quatuor dies et noctes fugientes huc et illuc, contigit ut Solimanus dux illorum, filius Solimani ueteris,[1] fugeret de Nicea. Qui inuenit decem milia Arabum, qui dixerunt ei: 'O infelix et infelicior omnibus gentilibus, cur tremefactus fugis?' Quibus Solimanus lacrimabiliter respondit: 'Quoniam olim cum habuissem omnes Francos deuictos, eosque putarem iam in captiuitate ligatos, dum paulatim uoluissem ligare adinuicem,[2] tunc respiciens retro, uidi tam innumerabilem gentem eorum, ut si uos aut aliquis illic adesset, putaret quod omnes montes et colles uallesque et omnia plana loca plena essent illorum multitudine. Nos igitur illos cernentes, statim coepimus capere subitaneum iter, timentes tam mirabiliter, ut uix euaserimus de illorum manibus, unde adhuc in nimio terrore sumus. Et si michi et uerbis meis uelletis credere, auferretis uos hinc, quia si et ipsi potuerint uos solummodo scire, unus ex uobis uix amplius euadet uiuens.'[a] At illi audientes talia, retrorsum uerterunt dorsa, et se expanderunt per uniuersam Romaniam. Tunc ueniebamus nos persequentes iniquissimos Turcos, cotidie fugientes ante nos. At illi uenientes ad cuncta castra siue urbes, fingentes et deludentes habitatores terrarum illarum dicebant: 'Nos deuicimus Christianos omnes, et super-

---

[a] uiuus DX

[1] Qilij-Arslan II, amir of Rum, son of Qilij-Arslan I who had killed himself after his defeat at the hands of Malikshah's brother Tutush in 1086.
[2] This passage is obscure, but the Author deliberately makes all his

IV

[x] After the Turks, who are enemies of God and holy Christendom, were altogether defeated, they fled wildly for four days and nights. It happened that Suleiman their leader, son of old Suleiman,[1] was fleeing from Nicea when he met ten thousand Arabs who thus accosted him, 'O unhappy man, more miserable than all our people, why are you fleeing in terror?' Suleiman answered them weeping, 'Because when I had just (as I thought) defeated all the Franks and bound them as captives—in fact I wanted to have them bound together in pairs[2]—I happened to look back, and saw such an innumerable army of their men that if you or anyone else had been there you would have thought that all the mountains and hills and valleys and all the plains were full of them. So when we saw them we were terribly afraid and took to flight at once, barely escaping from their hands, and that is why we are still terror-stricken. If you will believe me and trust my words, be off, because if they but know that you are here, hardly one of you will escape with his life.' The Arabs, having heard such a tale, turned back and went in scattered bands throughout Rum. Meanwhile we were coming in pursuit of those abominable Turks, who were fleeing before us every day, and when they came to castles or cities they used to deceive and mislead the inhabitants, saying, 'We have defeated and

Muslim characters speak in a slightly bizarre fashion. See Introduction, pp. xv-xvi.

auimus illos, ita ut nullus eorum iam unquam audeat
erigere se ante[a] nos; tantum permittite nos intus intrare.'
Qui intrantes spoliabant ecclesias et domos et alia omnia,
et ducebant equos[b] secum et asinos et mulos, aurum et
argentum et ea quae reperire poterant. Adhuc quoque
filios Christianorum secum tollebant,[1] et ardebant ac
deuastabant omnia conuenientia siue utilia, fugientes et
pauentes ualde ante faciem nostram. Nos itaque per-
sequebamur eos per deserta[c] et inaquosam et inhabita-
bilem terram,[2] ex qua uix uiui euasimus uel exiuimus.
Fames uero et sitis undique coartabant nos, nihilque
penitus nobis erat ad edendum, nisi forte uellentes et
fricantes spicas manibus nostris, tali cibo quam miserrime
uiuebamus. Illic fuit mortua maxima pars nostrorum
equorum, eo quod multi ex nostris militibus remanserunt
pedites; et pro penuria equorum, erant nobis boues loco
caballorum, et pro nimia necessitate succedebant nobis
capri et multones ac canes ad portandum.

Interea coepimus intrare in terram optimam, plenam
corporalibus alimentis et deliciis[d] omnibusque bonis; ac
deinceps appropinquauimus Yconio.[3] Habitatores uero
terrae illius suadebant et ammonebant nos, nobiscum
ferre utres plenos aqua, quia illic in itinere diei unius est
maxima penuria aquae. Nos uero ita fecimus, donec
peruenimus ad quoddam flumen, ibique hospitati sumus
per duos dies. Coeperunt autem cursores nostri ante ire,
donec peruenerunt ad Erachiam,[4] in qua erat Turcorum
nimia congregatio, exspectans et insidians, quomodo
posset Christi milites[e] nocere. Quos Turcos Dei omni-

---

[a] contra DX   [b] DX *omit* equos
[c] desertam DX   [d] diuitiis DX
[e] militibus DX

conquered all the Christians so that none of them will ever dare to oppose us again, so let us come in.' Once inside, they used to loot the churches and houses and other places, and carry off horses, asses, mules, gold and silver and anything else they could find. They also kidnapped Christian children,[1] and burned or destroyed everything that might be helpful or useful to us, as they fled in great terror at our approach. We therefore pursued them through a land which was deserted, waterless and uninhabitable,[2] from which we barely emerged or escaped alive, for we suffered greatly from hunger and thirst, and found nothing at all to eat except prickly plants which we gathered and rubbed between our hands. On such food we survived wretchedly enough, but we lost most of our horses, so that many of our knights had to go on as foot-soldiers, and for lack of horses we had to use oxen as mounts, and our great need compelled us to use goats, sheep and dogs as beasts of burden.

At last we began to reach fertile country, full of good and delicious things to eat and all sorts of provisions, and finally we reached Iconium,[3] where the inhabitants of that country gave us advice, warning us to carry skins full of water, for it is very scarce for a day's journey from that city. So we did this, and came at last to a river where we encamped for two days, and then our scouts took the road before us until they came to Heraclea,[4] in which a large Turkish garrison was waiting in ambush to attack the Christian knights. Our knights, trusting in Almighty God, found these

[1] A common Turkish habit. Compare the later Janissaries.
[2] The Anatolian desert
[3] Konieh
[4] Eregli

potentis milites inuenientes audacter inuaserunt. Superati itaque sunt inimici nostri in illa die, tamque celeriter
fugiebant quam sagitta fugit emissa ictu ualido cordae
et arcus.ᵃ Nostri igitur intrauerunt statim in ciuitatem,
ibique mansimus per quatuor dies.

Illic diuisit se ab aliis Tancredus Marchisi filius, et
Balduinus comes frater ducis Godefridi, simulque intrauerunt uallem de Botrenthrot.¹ Diuisit quoque se Tancredus, et uenit Tharsum ² cum suis militibus. Exierunt
denique Turci de urbe, et uenerunt obuiam eis, atque in
unum congregati properauerunt ad bellum contra Christianos. Appropinquantibus itaque nostris et pugnanti-
bus, dederunt inimici nostri fugam, reuertentes in urbem
celeri gressu. Tancredus uero miles Christi peruenit
laxatis loris, et castrametatus est ante portam urbis. Ex
alia igitur parte uenit uir inclitus comes Balduinus cum
suo exercitu, postulans Tancredum, quatinus eum amicissime in societatem ciuitatis dignaretur suscipere. Cui
ait Tancredus: 'Te omnimodo in hac societate denego.'
Nocte itaque superueniente, omnes Turci tremefacti
fugam una arripuerunt. Exierunt denique habitatores
ciuitatis sub illa noctis obscuritate, clamantes excelsa
uoce: 'Currite inuictissimi Franci currite, quia Turci
expergefacti uestro timore omnes pariter recedunt.'

Orta autem die, uenerunt maiores ciuitatis, et reddiderunt sponte ciuitatem, dicentes illis qui super hoc
litigabant adinuicem: 'Sinite modo seniores sinite, quia
uolumus et petimus dominari et regnare super nos illum
qui heri tam uiriliter pugnauit cum Turcis.' Balduinus
itaque mirificus comes altercabatur et litigabat cum Tan-

ᵃ corda et arcu DX

¹ Going directly south towards the Cilician coast
² Tarsus in Cilicia, birthplace of St Paul. Its population in 1097 was
composed mainly of Greek and Armenian Christians.

Turks and attacked them boldly, so on that day our enemies were defeated and fled as quickly as an arrow, shot by a strong hand, flies from the bowstring. Our men entered the city at once, and we stayed there for four days.

While we were there Tancred son of the Marquis and Count Baldwin, Duke Godfrey's brother, went off together and entered the valley of Botrenthrot.[1] Tancred and his knights struck out by themselves and came to Tarsus,[2] where the Turks sallied from the city and came against them in one band, ready to fight with the Christians, so our men attacked them and fought with them and put them to flight, and they rushed back to the city as fast as they could. Tancred the knight of Christ galloped up and encamped before the city gate. The noble Count Baldwin came up with his army from the other direction and asked Tancred to make a friendly agreement about sharing the city, but Tancred said, 'I flatly refuse to make this pact with you.' When night fell, all the Turks fled away together, for they were terrified, and thereupon the inhabitants of the city came out in the dark, shouting at the tops of their voices, 'Come on, unconquered Franks, come on! The Turks have all gone because they are so much afraid of you!'

At dawn the chief men of the city came and surrendered it, saying to Tancred and Baldwin, who were quarrelling over it, 'Sirs, let be. We desire and seek to have for our ruler and lord the man who yesterday fought so gallantly against the Turks.' Count Baldwin, a man with great achievements to his credit, went on arguing and quarrelling with Tancred, saying, 'Let us

credo dicens: 'Intremus simul et spoliemus ciuitatem, et qui plus potuerit habere, habeat, et qui poterit capere, capiat.' Cui Tancredus fortissimus dixit: 'Absit hoc a me. Ego namque Christianos nolo expoliare. Homines huius ciuitatis elegerunt me dominum super se, meque habere desiderant.' Tandem nequiuit uir fortis Tancredus diu luctari cum Balduino comite, quia illi magnus erat exercitus; tamen uolens nolensque dimisit eam, et uiriliter recessit cum suo exercitu; fueruntque ei statim traditae duae optimae ciuitates, uidelicet Athena[1] et Manustra,[2] et plurima castra.

[xi] Maior uero exercitus scilicet Raimundus comes de Sancto Egidio, et doctissimus Boamundus, duxque Godefridus, et alii plures, in Hermeniorum intrauerunt terram,[3] sitientes atque aesfuantes Turcorum sanguinem. Tandem peruenerunt ad quoddam castrum, quod tam forte erat, ut nichil ei possent facere. Erat autem ibi homo quidam nomine Symeon, qui in illa ortus fuit[a] regione, quique hanc petiit terram, quo eam de manibus defenderet inimicorum Turcorum, cui sponte illi dederunt terram, quique remansit ibi cum sua gente. Nos denique exeuntes inde peruenimus feliciter, usque[b] Cesaream[4] Cappadociae. A Cappadocia autem egressi, uenimus ad quamdam ciuitatem pulcherrimam et nimis uberrimam,[5] quam paululum ante nostrum aduentum obsederant Turci per tres ebdomadas, sed non superauerant. Mox illuc aduenientibus nobis, continuo tradidit se in manu nostra cum magna laetitia. Hanc igitur petiit quidam miles cui nomen Petrus de Alpibus,[6] ab

---

[a] fuerat DX
[b] usque ad DX

[1] Adana
[2] Missis, the classical Mopsuestia
[3] Between 1069 and 1085 an Armenian principality under the rule of Philaretos had existed in the south-eastern parts of Asia Minor and had

go in together and sack this city, and whoever can get most, let him keep it, and whoever can take most, let him take it.' The most valiant Tancred replied, 'Far be this from me. I have no wish to plunder Christians. The men of this city have chosen me, and they want me to be their lord.' At last, however, brave as he was, he could not stand up to Count Baldwin because of the strength of his forces. And so, willy-nilly, he left the city and boldly led his men away. Two fine cities, Athena[1] and Manustra[2] together with many castles, surrendered to him directly.

[xi] The main army, led by Raymond count of St Gilles and the most excellent Bohemond, Duke Godfrey and many others, entered the land of the Armenians,[3] thirsting and craving for the blood of the Turks. They came at last to a castle which was so strong that they could not prevail against it. They had with them a man called Simeon, who was born in that country, and he asked for this place, so that he could defend it from the hands of the Turkish enemies. Our leaders granted it to him, and he stayed there with his people. We, however, went on and had a good journey to Caesarea[4] in Cappadocia, and when we left Cappadocia we came to a city of great splendour and wealth[5] which the Turks had been besieging for three weeks a little before our arrival, but they could not take it. When we came the city surrendered to us at once with great rejoicing. A knight called Peter d'Aups[6] asked our leaders to let

---

extended as far south as Antioch. The local population was still, in 1097, predominantly Christian.
    [4] Kaisarieh   [5] Probably Plastencia
    [6] A Provençal knight who had served first under Robert Guiscard and then under Alexius Comnenus

omnibus senioribus, quatinus eam defenderet in fidelitate
Dei et Sancti Sepulchri, et seniorum atque imperatoris.
Cui cum nimio amore gratis concesserunt eam. Sequenti
nocte audiuit Boamundus quod Turci qui fuerant in
obsessione ciuitatis, frequenter precederent nos. Mox
preparauit se solummodo cum militibus, quatinus illos
undique expugnaret, sed eos inuenire non potuit.

Deinde uenimus ad quamdam urbem nomine Coxon,[1]
in qua erat maxima ubertas omnium bonorum quae
nobis erant necessaria. Christiani igitur uidelicet alumni
urbis illius reddiderunt se statim, nosque fuimus ibi
optime per tres dies, et illic maxime sunt recuperati
nostri. Audiens itaque Raimundus comes quod Turci
qui erant in custodia Antiochiae discessissent, in suo
inuenit consilio, quod mitteret illuc aliquos ex suis militibus, qui eam diligenter custodirent. Tandem elegit
illos quos legare uolebat, uidelicet Petrum de Castellione
vicecomitem, Willelmum de Monte Pislerio, Petrum de
Roasa, Petrum Raimundum de Pul, cum quingentis
militibus. Venerunt itaque in uallem prope Antiochiam
ad quoddam castrum Publicanorum, illicque audierunt
Turcos esse in ciuitatem[a] eamque fortiter defendere pre-
parabant. Petrus de Roasa diuisit se ibi ab aliis, et
proxima nocte transiuit prope Antiochiam, intrauitque
uallem de Rugia; et inuenit Turcos et Saracenos, et
preliatus est cum eis, et occidit multos ex eis, et alios
persecutus est ualde. Videntes hoc Hermenii habitatores
terrae illius, illum[b] fortiter superasse paganos, continuo

[a] ciuitate DX   [b] illum scilicet DX

[1] Gueuk-su

him hold it in fealty to God and the Holy Sepulchre, and to our leaders and the emperor, and this they freely granted to him with a very good will. During the next night Bohemond heard that great numbers of the Turks who had been besieging the city were just ahead of us, so he and his own knights got ready to attack them wherever they were, but he could not find them.

After this we came to a city called Coxon,[1] in which there were plentiful supplies of provisions of which we were badly in need. The Christians who lived in that city surrendered it at once, and we stayed there, very comfortably, for three days, and our men were much recovered. Count Raymond, hearing that the Turkish garrison of Antioch had made off, held a council and decided to send thither some of his knights, so that they could take charge of it. Those whom he appointed for this mission were Peter the seneschal of Castillon, William of Montpellier, Peter of Roaix, Peter Raymond of Hautpoul and five hundred knights. These men came into a valley near Antioch and reached a castle held by the Paulicians, where they heard that the Turks were in the city and were preparing to defend it in strength. Peter of Roaix left the others and approached Antioch on the following night, entering the valley of Rugia where he found Turks and Saracens whom he attacked, killing many of them and driving the others into headlong flight. When the Armenians who lived in this country saw that he had been so brave in defeating the pagans they surrendered to him at once,

reddiderunt se. Ipse uero statim cepit Rusam*a* ciuitatem, et plurima castra.[1]

Nos autem qui remansimus, exeuntes inde intrauimus
in diabolicam montanam,[2] quae tam erat alta et angusta,
ut nullus nostrorum auderet per semitam, quae in monte
patebat, ante alium preire. Illic precipitabant se equi,
et unus saumarius precipitabat alium. Milites ergo stabant undique tristes, feriebant se manibus pre nimia
tristitia et dolore, dubitantes quid facerent de semetipsis
et de suis armis uendentes*b* suos clipeos et loricas optimas
cum galeis, solummodo propter tres aut quinque dena-
rios, uel prout quisque poterat habere.[3] Qui autem uen-
dere nequibant, gratis a se iactabant et ibant. Exeuntes
igitur de exsecrata montana, peruenimus ad ciuitatem
quae uocatur Marasim. Cultores uero illius ciuitatis
exierunt obuiam nobis letantes, et deferentes maximum
mercatum, illicque habuimus omnem copiam, expec-
tando*c* donec ueniret domnus Boamundus. Venerunt
itaque nostri milites in uallem, in qua regalis ciuitas
Antiochia sita est,[4] quae est caput totius Syriae, quam-
que dominus Iesus Christus*d* tradidit beato Petro apostolorum principi, quatinus eam ad cultum sanctae fidei
reuocaret; qui uiuit et regnat cum Deo Patre in unitate
Spiritus Sancti Deus, per omnia secula seculorum.
Amen.[5]

[*Explicit liber IIII. Incipit liber V.*]

a Rursam E
b uendebant ergo (autem X) DX
c expectantes DX
d DX *omit* Christus

[1] The valley of Riha lies to the east of Antioch on the road to Aleppo.
Rusa may be Ruweha, a village to the south-east of the road, but the
identification is uncertain.
[2] The Anti-Taurus range
[3] Because coats of mail were heavy as well as hot, and most people

and he immediately occupied the city of Rusa and many castles.[1]

We, who stayed at Coxon, set out and began to cross a damnable mountain,[2] which was so high and steep that none of our men dared to overtake another on the mountain path. Horses fell over the precipice, and one beast of burden dragged another down. As for the knights, they stood about in a great state of gloom, wringing their hands because they were so frightened and miserable, not knowing what to do with themselves and their armour, and offering to sell their shields, valuable breastplates and helmets for three-pence or fivepence or any price they could get.[3] Those who could not find a buyer threw their arms away and went on. When we had crossed that accursed mountain we came to a city called Marash. The peasants came out of that city to meet us, rejoicing and bringing plenty of merchandise, and there we had all kinds of provisions, and waited for the arrival of my lord Bohemond. So at last our knights came into the valley where stands the royal city of Antioch,[4] capital of Syria, which was granted to blessed Peter, prince of the Apostles, to restore it to the holy faith, by Our Lord Jesus who liveth and reigneth with God the Father in the unity of the Holy Ghost, One God, world without end. Amen.[5]

Here ends the fourth book, and the fifth book begins.

---

regarded mountains as places to be avoided. The epithet 'mountaineer' was considered an insult as late as the time of Shakespeare (*Cymbeline*, iv, 2).

[4] This city was built on the true left (i.e. south-east) bank of the Orontes, the valley of which it controlled. It was extremely strongly fortified. The Saljuqid Turks had captured it in 1085, but it still had a large number of Christians among its population.

[5] The MSS make it clear that Book IV ends at this point.

V

[xii] Cum coepissemus appropinquare ad Pontem Farreum,[a1] cursores nostri, qui semper solebant nos precédere, inuenerunt Turcos innumerabiles congregatos obuiam eis, qui dare adiutorium Antiochiae festinabant. Irruentes igitur nostri uno corde et mente super illos, superauerunt Turcos. Consternati sunt barbari dederuntque fugam, et multi mortui sunt ex eis in ipso certamine. Nostri igitur superantes illos Dei gratia, acceperunt spolia multa, equos, camelos, mulos, asinos, honustos frumento et uino. Venientes denique nostri, castrametati sunt super ripam fluminis. Protinus uir sapiens Boamundus cum quatuor milibus militum uenit ante portam ciuitatis, uigilare si forte aliquis nocte latenter exiret aut intraret ciuitatem. Crastina uero die peruenerunt usque ad Antiochiam media die, in quarta feria quae est XII kalendas Novembris, et obsedimus mirabiliter tres portas ciuitatis, quoniam in alia parte deerat nobis locus obsidendi, quia alta et nimis angusta montana nos coartabat.[2] Tantum autem timebant nos undique inimici nostri Turci, qui erant intus in urbe, ut nemo eorum auderet offendere aliquem ex nostris, fere per spatium dierum quindecim. Mox hospitantes nos circa Antiochiam, repperimus illic omnem abundantiam, uidelicet uineas undique plenas, foueas plenas frumento, arbores refertas pomis, et alia multa bona corporibus utilia.

---

[a] ferreum D, *as always*

[1] The Orontes was called the Far. The name 'Pons Ferreus' or 'the

V

[xii] When we drew near to the bridge over the Orontes[1] our scouts, who used always to go ahead of us, found barring their way a great number of Turks who were hurrying to reinforce Antioch, so they attacked the Turks with one heart and mind and defeated them. The barbarians were thrown into confusion and took to flight, leaving many dead in that battle, and our men who by God's grace overcame them took much booty, horses, camels, mules and asses laden with corn and wine. Afterwards, when our main forces came up, they encamped on the bank of the river, and the gallant Bohemond came at once with four thousand knights to guard the city gate, so that no-one could go out or come in secretly by night. Next day, Wednesday 21 October, the main army reached Antioch about noon, and we established a strict blockade on three gates of the city, for we could not besiege it from the other side because a mountain, high and very steep, stood in our way.[2] Our enemies the Turks, who were inside the city, were so much afraid of us that none of them tried to attack our men for nearly a fortnight. Meanwhile we grew familiar with the surroundings of Antioch, and found there plenty of provisions, fruitful vineyards and pits full of stored corn, apple-trees laden with fruit and all sorts of other good things to eat.

Iron Bridge', found in MS Vat. Reginensis 641 seems to be a soldiers' corruption of a local name, like 'Wipers' for 'Ypres' in the First World War.
    [2] Mount Silpius

Hermenii et Suriani qui erant intus in urbe exeuntes et ostendentes se fugere, cotidie erant nobiscum, sed eorum uxores in ciuitate. Illi uero ingeniose inuestigabant nostrum esse nostramque qualitatem, referebantque omnia his qui erant in urbe inclusi. Postquam uero Turci fuerunt edocti de nostra essentia, coeperunt paulatim de urbe exire, nostros[a] peregrinos undique coangustare, non solum ex una parte, sed undique erant latentes obuiam nobis ad mare et ad montanam.

Erat autem non longe castrum cui nomen Aregh,[1] ubi erant congregati multi Turci fortissimi, qui frequenter conturbabant nostros. Audientes itaque nostri seniores talia, nimis doluerunt, miseruntque ex militibus suis qui diligenter explorarent locum ubi erant Turci. Reperto igitur loco ubi latebant, nostri milites qui quaerebant illos obuiant eis. At nostris paulatim retrogredientibus ubi sciebant Boamundum esse cum suo exercitu, statim fuerunt illic mortui duo ex nostris. Hoc audiens Boamundus surrexit cum suis ut fortissimus Christi athleta, et barbari irruerunt contra illos, eo quod nostri erant pauci; tamen simul iuncti inierunt bellum. Mortui sunt uero multi ex nostris inimicis, et capti alii ducti sunt ante portam urbis, ibique decollabantur, ut magis tristes fierent qui erant in urbe.

Exibant quidem alii de ciuitate, et ascendebant in quamdam portam, et sagittabant nos, ita ut sagittae eorum caderent in domini Boamundi plateam; et una mulier occubuit ictu sagittae.

---

[a] nostrosque DX

[1] East of Antioch. It guarded the Orontes bridge.

The Armenians and Syrians who lived in the city came out and pretended to flee to us, and they were daily in our camp, but their wives were in the city. These men spied on us and on our power, and reported everything we said to those who were besieged in the city. After the Turks had found out about us, they began gradually to emerge and to attack our pilgrims wherever they could, not on one flank only but wherever they could lay ambush for us, either towards the sea or towards the mountain.

Not far off there stood a castle called Aregh,[1] manned by many of the bravest of the Turks, who often used to make attacks on our men. When our leaders heard that such things were happening, they were very troubled and sent some of our knights to reconnoitre the place where the Turks had established themselves. When our knights, who were looking for the Turks, found the place where they used to hide, they attacked the enemy, but had to retreat a little way to where they knew Bohemond to be stationed with his army. Two of our men were killed there in the first attack. When Bohemond heard of this he went out, like a most valiant champion of Christ, and his men followed him. The barbarians fell upon our men because they were few, yet they joined battle in good order and many of our enemies were killed. Others, whom we captured, were led before the city gate and there beheaded, to grieve the Turks who were in the city.

There were others who used to come out of the city and climb upon a gate, whence they shot arrows at us, so that the arrows fell into my lord Bohemond's camp, and a woman was killed by a wound from one of them.

[xiii] Congregati sunt itaque omnes maiores nostri, et ordinauerunt concilium dicentes: 'Faciamus castrum in uertice montis Maregart,[1] quo securi atque tuti possimus esse a Turcorum formidine.' Facto itaque castro atque munito, omnes maiores illud inuicem custodiebant.

Iamiam coeperant frumentum et omnia nutrimenta corporum nimis esse cara ante Natale Domini. Foras penitus non audebamus exire, nichilque penitus in terra Christianorum inuenire poteramus ad edendum. In Saracenorum namque terram nemo intrare audebat nisi cum magna gente. Ad ultimum statuerunt nostri seniores concilium, ordinando qualiter regerent tantas gentes. Inuenerunt in consilio, ut una pars nostri iret diligenter attrahere stipendium, et ubique custodire exercitum; alia quoque pars fiducialiter remaneret custodire hostem.[a][2] Boamundus denique dixit: 'Seniores et prudentissimi milites, si uultis et bonum uobis uidetur, ego ero cum Flandrensi comite, iturus cum eo.' Celebratis itaque gloriosissimae solempnitatibus Natiuitatis in die lunae secunda scilicet feria[3] egressi sunt illi et alii plus quam uiginti milia militum et peditum, ac sani et incolumes intrauerunt terram Saracenorum. Congregati quippe erant multi Turci et Arabes et Saraceni, ab Hierusalem et Damasco et Aleph, et ab aliis regionibus,[4] qui ueniebant fortitudinem Antiochiae dare. Audientes itaque isti Christianorum gentem conductam esse in illorum terram, illico preparauerunt se ad bellum contra Chris-

---

[a] hostes DX

[1] This fort was established to the north-east of the city, opposite St Paul's Gate. Its name, 'Mal regard' is a nickname given by the crusaders, in the same category as 'Longstop Hill' in the Second World War. It means, in terms of modern slang, 'dirty look'.

[2] The Author stayed in the camp before Antioch.

[3] 28 December 1097

[xiii] Thereafter all our leaders met together and summoned a council. They said, 'Let us build a castle on top of Mount Malregard,[1] so that we can stay here safe and sound, without fear of the Turks.' The castle was built and fortified, and all our leaders took turns in guarding it.

By and by, before Christmas, corn and all foodstuffs began to be very dear, for we dared not go far from the camp and we could find nothing to eat in the land of the Christians. (No-one dared to go into the land of the Saracens except with a strong force.) Finally our leaders held a council to decide how they should provide for so many people, and in this council they determined that one part of our army should go and do its best to get supplies and to protect the flanks of our forces, while the other part should stay behind, faithfully to guard the non-combatants.[2] Then Bohemond said, 'Gentlemen and most gallant knights, if you wish, and if it seems to you a good plan, I will go on this expedition, with the count of Flanders.' So when we had celebrated Christmas with great splendour these two set out on Monday the second day of the week,[3] and with them went others, more than twenty thousand knights and foot-soldiers in all, and they entered, safe and sound, into the land of the Saracens. Now it happened that many Turks, Arabs and Saracens had come together from Jerusalem and Damascus and Aleppo and other places[4] and were approaching to relieve Antioch, so when they heard that a Christian force had been led into their country they prepared at

---

[4] Led by Duqaq, amir of Damascus, Tughtagin his atabek, and Janah al-Dawla amir of Homs.

tianos; atque summo diluculo uenerunt in locum[1] ubi gens nostra erat in unum. Diuiseruntque se barbari et fecerunt duas acies, unam ante et aliam retro, cupientes ex omni parte circumcingere nos. Egregius itaque comes Flandrensis undique regimine fidei signoque crucis quam fideliter cotidie baiulabat armatus, occurrit illis una cum Boamundo. Irrueruntque nostri unanimiter super illos. Qui statim arripuerunt fugam, et festinanter uerterunt retro scapulas, ac mortui sunt ex illis plurimi, nostrique coeperunt equos eorum et alia spolia. Alii uero, qui uiui remanserant uelociter fugerunt, et in iram perditionis[2] abierunt. Nos autem reuertentes cum magno tripudio, laudauimus et magnificauimus trinum et unum Deum, qui uiuit et regnat nunc et in aeuum. Amen.[3]

Explicit liber V. Incipit liber VI.

[1] al-Bara
[2] Romans 9:22
[3] The MSS make it clear that Book V ends at this point.

once for battle, and at daybreak they came to the place[1] where our men were assembled. The barbarians split up their forces into two bands, one before and one behind, for they wanted to surround us on all sides, but the noble count of Flanders, armed at all points with faith and with the sign of the Cross (which he bore loyally every day) made straight for the enemy with Bohemond at his side, and our men charged them in one line. The enemy straightway took to flight, turning tail in a hurry; many of them were killed and our men took their horses and other plunder. Others, who remained alive, fled quickly and went into 'the wrath fitted for destruction',[2] but we came back in great triumph, and praised the glorified God the Three in One, who liveth and reigneth now and eternally. Amen.[3]

Here ends the fifth book, and the sixth book begins.

VI

[xiiii] Turci denique, inimici Dei et sanctae christianitatis, qui erant intus in custodia ciuitatis Antiochiae,
audientes dominum Boamundum et Flandrensem comitem in obsessione*a* non esse, exierunt de ciuitate, et
audacter ueniebant preliari nobiscum, insidiantes undique in qua parte obsidio esset languidior, scientes prudentissimos milites foris esse; inueneruntque quod in una
martis die[1] possent obsistere nobis et ledere. Venerunt
uero iniquissimi barbari caute,*b* et irruerunt uehementer
super nos, et incautos occiderunt multos ex nostris militibus et peditibus. Episcopus quoque Podiensis in illa
amara die perdidit suum senescalcum, conducentem et
regentem eius*c* uexillum. Et nisi esset flumen quod erat
inter nos et illos, sepius inuasissent nos, atque maximam
lesionem fecissent in nostram gentem.

Egrediebatur tunc uir prudens Boamundus cum suo
exercitu de terra Saracenorum, uenitque in Tancredi
montanam,[2] cogitans an forte ibi ualeret inuenire aliquid
quod potuisset deferri. Nam totam terram in expendio
miserant; alii quippe inuenerant, alii uero uacui redi-
erant. Tunc uir sapiens Boamundus increpauit eos
dicens: 'O infelix et miserrima gens, O uilissima omnium
Christianorum, cur tam celeriter uultis abire? Sinite
modo sinite, usquequo erimus congregati in unum, et

a obsidione DX
b nocte DX
c suum DX

[1] Tuesday, 29 December 1097
[2] The mountain south-west of the city, where Tancred in the following
April volunteered to guard a fort. See below, p. 43.

VI

[xiiii] While this was going on the Turks (enemies of God and holy Christendom) who were acting as garrison to the city of Antioch, heard that my lord Bohemond and the count of Flanders were not with the besieging army, so they sallied from the city and came boldly to fight with our men, seeking out the places where the besiegers were weakest, for they knew that some very valiant knights were away, and they found that on the Tuesday[1] they could withstand us and do us harm. Those wretched barbarians came up craftily and made a sudden attack upon us, killing many knights and foot-soldiers who were off their guard. On that grievous day the bishop of Le Puy lost his seneschal, who was carrying his banner and guarding it, and if there had not been a river between us and them they would have attacked us more often and done very great harm to our people.

Just then the valiant Bohemond arrived with his army from the land of the Saracens, and he came over Tancred's mountain[2] thinking that he might find some-thing which could be carried off, for our men had pillaged all the land. Some of his followers had found plunder, but others were coming back empty-handed. Then the gallant Bohemond shouted at the fugitives from our camp, 'You wretched and miserable creatures! You scum of all Christendom! Why do you want to run away so fast? Stop now, stop until we all join

nolite errare sicut oues non habentes pastorem. Si autem inimici nostri inuenerint uos errantes, occident uos, quia die noctuque uigilant, ut uos sine ductore segregatos siue solos inueniant, uosque cotidie occidere et in captiuitatem ducere laborant.' Cumque finis esset dictis, rediit ad suam hostem, cum suis plus uacuis quam honustis.

Videntes autem Hermenii et Surani quod nostri penitus uacui rediissent, consiliati in unum abibant per montaneas et prescita loca, subtiliter inquirentes et ementes frumentum et corporea alimenta, quae ad hostem deferebant in qua erat fames immensa; et uendebant onus unius asini octo purpuratis, qui appreciabantur centum uiginti solidis denariorum. Ibi quidem sunt mortui multi ex nostris, non habentes pretium unde tam carum emere potuissent.

[xv] Willelmus igitur Carpentarius[1] et Petrus Heremita, pro immensa infelicitate ac miseria ipsa, latenter recesserunt. Quos Tancredus persequens apprehendit, secumque reduxit cum dedecore; qui dextram et fidem illi dederunt, quia libenter ad hostem redirent et satisfactionem senioribus facerent. Tota denique nocte Willelmus uti mala res in tentorio domini Boamundi iacuit. Crastina uero die summo diluculo, ueniens erubescendo ante Boamundi presentiam stetit. Quem alloquens Boamundus dixit: 'O infelix et infamia totius Franciae, dedecus et scelus Galliarum, O nequissime omnium quos terra suffert, cur tam turpiter fugisti? Forsitan ob hoc quod uoluisti tradere hos milites et hostem Christi, sicut

---

[1] Lord of Melun

forces, and do not rush about like sheep without a shepherd. If our enemies find you rushing all over the place they will kill you, for they are on the watch day and night to catch you without a leader or alone, and they are always trying to kill you or to lead you into captivity.' When he had said this he returned to his camp together with his men, but more of them were empty-handed than carrying plunder.

The Armenians and Syrians, seeing that our men had come back with scarcely any supplies, took counsel together and went over the mountains by paths which they knew, making careful inquiries and buying up corn and provisions which they brought to our camp, in which there was a terrible famine, and they used to sell an ass's load for eight hyperperoi, which is a hundred and twenty shillings in our money. Many of our people died there, not having the means to buy at so dear a rate.

[xv] Because of this great wretchedness and misery William the Carpenter[1] and Peter the Hermit fled away secretly. Tancred went after them and caught them and brought them back in disgrace. (They gave him a pledge and an oath that they were willing to return to the camp and give satisfaction to the leaders.) William spent the whole of the night in my lord Bohemond's tent, lying on the ground like a piece of rubbish. The following morning, at daybreak, he came and stood before Bohemond, blushing for shame. Bohemond said to him, 'You wretched disgrace to the whole Frankish army—you dishonourable blot on all the people of Gaul! You most loathsome of all men whom the earth has to bear, why did you run off in such a shameful way? I suppose that you wanted to betray

tradidisti alios in Hispania.'[1] Qui omnino tacuit, et
nullus sermo ex eius ore processit.[2] Adunauerunt sese
omnes fere Francigenae,[3] rogaueruntque humiliter ne
deterius ei facere[a] permitteret. Annuit ille sereno uultu,
et ait: 'Hoc pro uestri amore libenter consentiam, si
mihi toto corde et mente iurauerit quod nunquam re-
cedet ab Hierosolimitano itinere siue bono siue malo; et
Tancredus neque per se neque per suos aliquid contrarii
ei consentiet fieri.' Qui auditis his uerbis uoluntarie
concessit. Ipse uero protinus dimisit eum. Postmodum
uero Carpentarius maxima captus turpitudine, non diu
morans furtim recessit.

Hanc paupertatem et miseriam pro nostris delictis
concessit nos habere Deus. In tota namque hoste non
ualebat aliquis inuenire mille milites, qui equos haberent
optimos.

[xvi] Interea inimicus Tetigus[4] audiens quod exercitus Turcorum uenissent super nos, ait se timuisse,
arbitransque nos omnes perisse atque in manibus inimicorum incidisse, fingens omnia falsa, dixit: 'Seniores et
uiri prudentissimi, uidete quia nos sumus hic in maxima
necessitate, et ex nulla parte nobis adiutorium succedit.
Ecce modo sinite me in Romaniae patriam[b] reuerti, et
ego absque ulla dubitatione faciam huc multas naues
uenire per mare, onustas frumento, uino, hordeo, carne,
farina et caseis, omnibusque bonis quae sunt nobis necessaria. Faciam et equos conduci ad uendendum, et

---

[a] fieri X (E *has* uel fieri *in the margin*)
[b] Romaniam DX

[1] He had taken part in an expedition against the Moors in Spain and
had deserted.
[2] A rather archaic phrase, perhaps a reminiscence of St Matthew 4:4
[3] Men from northern France, William's compatriots
[4] The official representative of the Emperor Alexius

these knights and the Christian camp, just as you betrayed those others in Spain?'¹ William kept quiet, and never a word proceeded out of his mouth.² Nearly all the Franks³ assembled and humbly begged my lord Bohemond not to allow him to suffer a worse punishment. He granted their request without being angry, and said, 'I will freely grant this for the love I bear you, provided that the man will swear, with his whole heart and mind, that he will never turn aside from the path to Jerusalem, whether for good or ill, and Tancred shall swear that he will neither do, nor permit his men to do, any harm to him.' When Tancred heard these words he agreed, and Bohemond sent the Carpenter away forthwith; but afterwards he sneaked off without delay, for he was greatly ashamed.

God granted that we should suffer this poverty and wretchedness because of our sins. In the whole camp you could not find a thousand knights who had managed to keep their horses in really good condition.

[xvi] While all this was going on, our enemy Tatikios,⁴ hearing that the Turkish army had attacked us, admitted that he had been afraid that we had all perished and fallen into the hands of the enemy. So he told all sorts of lies, and said, 'Gentlemen and most gallant knights, you see that we are here in great distress and that no reinforcements can reach us from any direction. Let me therefore go back to the country of Rum, and I will guarantee without delay to send by sea many ships, laden with corn, wine, barley, meat, flour, cheese and all sorts of provisions which we need; I will also have horses brought here to sell, and will

mercatum per terram in fidelitate imperatoris huc ad-
uenire faciam. Ecce haec omnia uobis fideliter iurabo,
et attendam. Adhuc quoque et domestici mei et papilio
meus sunt in campo, unde et firmiter credite, quia
quantocius redibo.'

Sic itaque fecit finem dictis. Fuit ille inimicus, omnia
sua dimisit in campo, et in periurio manet et manebit.
Itaque tali modo inerat nobis maxima necessitas, quia
Turci undique prestringebant nos, ita ut nullus nostrorum
auderet iam exire extra tentoria. Nam illi constringe-
bant nos ex una parte, et fames cruciabat ex alia.
Succursus uero et adiutorium nobis deerat; gens minuta
et pauperrima fugiebat Cyprum, Romaniam, et in montaneas. Ad mare utique non audebamus ire propter
timorem pessimorum Turcorum; nusquam erat nobis
uia patefacta.

[xvii] Itaque audiens dominus Boamundus innumerabilem gentem Turcorum[1] uenientem super nos, caute
uenit ad alios, dicens: 'Seniores et prudentissimi milites,
quid facturi erimus? Nos namque tanti non sumus, ut
in duabus partibus pugnare ualeamus. Sed scitis quid
faciemus? Faciamus ex nobis duas partes. Pars peditum remaneat iugiter custodire papiliones, et quibit
nimis obsistere his qui in ciuitate sunt. Alia uero pars
militum nobiscum ueniat obuiam inimicis nostris, qui
hic hospitati sunt prope nos, in castello Areg ultra pontem
Farreum.'

Sero autem facto, exiit e tentoriis uir prudens Boamundus cum aliis prudentissimis militibus, iuitque iacere

---

[1] Led by Rudwan, amir of Aleppo, and Suqman ibn Ortuq

cause goods to be brought hither by land under the emperor's safe-conduct. See, I will swear faithfully to do all this, and I will attend to it myself. Meanwhile my household and my pavilion shall stay in the camp as a firm pledge that I will come back as soon as I can.'

So that enemy of ours made an end of his speech. He left all his possessions in the camp; but he is a liar, and always will be. We were thus left in direst need, for the Turks were harrying us on every side, so that none of our men dared to go outside the encampment. The Turks were menacing us on the one hand, and hunger tormented us on the other, and there was no-one to help us or bring us aid. The rank and file, with those who were very poor, fled to Cyprus or Rum or into the mountains. We dared not go down to the sea for fear of those brutes of Turks, and there was no road open to us anywhere.

[xvii] Now when my lord Bohemond heard rumours that an immense force of Turks[1] was coming to attack us, he thought the matter over and came to the other leaders, saying, 'Gentlemen and most valiant knights, what are we to do? We have not sufficient numbers to fight on two fronts. Do you know what we might do? We could divide our forces into two, the foot-soldiers staying here in a body to guard the tents and to contain, so far as possible, those who are in the city. The knights, in another band, could come out with us against our enemies, who are encamped not far off, at the castle of Aregh beyond the Orontes bridge.'

That evening the valiant Bohemond went out from the camp with other very gallant knights, and took up

inter flumen et lacum.¹ Summo diluculo iussit protinus
exploratores exire, et uidere quot sunt Turcorum turmae,
et ubi sint, aut certe quid agant. Exierunt illi, coeperunt-
que ᵃ subtiliter inquirere, ubi essent acies Turcorum re-
conditae. Viderunt tandem Turcos innumerabiles segregatos uenire ex parte fluminis diuisos per duas acies;
maxima uero uirtus illorum ueniebat retro. Reuersi sunt
namque celeriter speculatores, dicentes: 'Ecce, ecce
ueniunt! Igitur estote omnes parati, quia iam prope
nos sunt.' Dixitque uir sapiens Boamundus aliis: 'Seniores et inuictissimi milites, ordinate adinuicem bellum.'
Responderuntque illi: 'Tu sapiens et prudens, tu magnus
et magnificus, tu fortis et uictor, tu bellorum arbiter et
certaminum iudex, hoc totum fac; hoc totum super te
sit. Omne bonum quod tibi uidetur, nobis et tibi operare
et fac.' Tunc Boamundus iussit, ut unusquisque prin-
cipum per se dirigeret aciem suam ordinatim. Feceruntque ita; et ordinatae sunt sex acies. Quinque uero ex eis
ierunt adunatim inuadere illos. Boamundus itaque paulatim gradiebatur retro cum sua acie. Iunctis igitur
prospere nostris, unus comminus percutiebat alium.
Clamor uero resonabat ad celum. Omnes preliabantur
insimul. Imbres telorum obnubilabant aerem. Postquam uenit maxima uirtus illorum quae erat retro,
acriter inuasit nostros, ita ut nostri paululum ᵇ iam
cederent retro. Quod ut uidit uir doctissimus Boamundus, ingemuit. Tunc precepit suo conostabili scilicet
Rotberto filio Girardi, dicens: 'Vade quam citius potes

ᵃ et coeperunt DX
ᵇ paulatim DX

¹ Bohemond forced his enemies to attack him in a strip of land running
between the river and a marshy lake north-east of Antioch, where the
advantage of their numbers would be lost to them. Smail, *Crusading Warfare*,
p. 171.

his position between the river and the lake.[1] At dawn he ordered his scouts to go out forthwith and to discover the number of Turkish squadrons, and where they were, and to make sure what they were doing. The scouts went out and began to make careful inquiries as to where the army of the Turks was hidden, and they saw great numbers of the enemy coming up from the river in two bands, with the main army following them. So the scouts returned quickly, saying, 'Look, look, they are coming! Be ready, all of you, for they are almost upon us!' The valiant Bohemond said to the other leaders, 'Gentlemen and unconquered knights, draw up your line of battle!' They answered, 'You are brave and skilful in war, a great man of high repute, resolute and fortunate, and you know how to plan a battle and how to dispose your forces, so do you take command and let the responsibility rest with you. Do whatever seems good to you, both for your own sake and for ours.' Then Bohemond gave orders that each commander should arrange his own forces in line of battle. This was done, and they drew up in six lines. Five of them together charged the enemy, while Bohemond held his men a little in reserve. Our army joined battle successfully and fought hand-to-hand; the din arose to heaven, for all were fighting at once and the storm of missiles darkened the sky. After this the main army of the Turks, which was in reserve, attacked our men fiercely, so that they began to give back a little. When Bohemond, who was a man of great experience, saw this, he groaned, and gave orders to his constable, Robert Fitz-Gerard, saying, 'Charge at top

ut uir fortis, et esto acer in adiutorium Dei Sanctique
Sepulchri. Et reuera scias quia hoc bellum carnale non
est sed spirituale. Esto igitur fortissimus athleta Christi.
Vade in pace; Dominus sit tecum ubique.' Fuit itaque
ille, undique signo crucis munitus, qualiter leo perpessus
famem per tres aut quatuor dies, qui exiens a suis
cauernis, rugiens ac sitiens sanguinem pecudum sicut
improuide ruit inter agmina gregum, dilanians oues
fugientes huc et illuc; ita agebat iste inter agmina Turcorum. Tam uehementer instabat illis, ut linguae uexilli
uolitarent super Turcorum capita.

Videntes autem aliae acies quod uexillum Boamundi
tam honeste esset ante alios delatum, ilico redierunt
retrorsum, nostrique unanimiter inuaserunt Turcos; qui
omnes stupefacti arripuerunt fugam. Nostri itaque persecuti sunt illos et detruncauerunt usque ad pontem
Farreum. Reuersi sunt autem Turci festinanter in castrum suum, acceperuntque omnia quae ibi reperire
potuerunt, totumque[a] castrum spoliauerunt, miseruntque ignem et fugerunt. Hermenii et Surani scientes
Turcos omnino perdidisse bellum, exierunt et excuba-
uerunt per arta loca, et occiderunt et apprehenderunt
multos ex eis.

Superati sunt itaque, Deo annuente, in illo die inimici
nostri. Satis uero recuperati sunt nostri de equis et de
aliis multis quae erant illis ualde necessaria. Et centum
capita mortuorum detulerunt ante portam ciuitatis, ubi
legati ammirati[b] Babyloniae[1] castrametati fuerant, qui

---

[a] ac totum DX
[b] admirati D; admiralii X, *which is the normal spelling elsewhere in both*
X *and* D

[1] Cairo (the Author never uses *Babylonia* in any other sense). The
Fatimids of Cairo, who were Arabs and Shi'ites, were bitter opponents of

speed, like a brave man, and fight valiantly for God and the Holy Sepulchre, for you know in truth that this is no war of the flesh, but of the spirit. So be very brave, as becomes a champion of Christ. Go in peace, and may the Lord be your defence!' So Bohémond, protected on all sides by the sign of the Cross, charged the Turkish forces, like a lion which has been starving for three or four days, which comes roaring out of its cave thirsting for the blood of cattle, and falls upon the flocks careless of its own safety, tearing the sheep as they flee hither and thither. His attack was so fierce that the points of his banner were flying right over the heads of the Turks.

The other troops, seeing Bohemond's banner carried ahead so honourably, stopped their retreat at once, and all our men in a body charged the Turks, who were amazed and took to flight. Our men pursued them and massacred them right up to the Orontes bridge. The Turks fled in a hurry back to their castle, picked up everything they could find, and then, having thoroughly looted the castle, they set fire to it and took to flight. The Armenians and Syrians, knowing that the Turks had been completely defeated, came out and laid ambushes in passes, killing or capturing many men.

Thus, by God's will, on that day our enemies were overcome. Our men captured plenty of horses and other things of which they were badly in need, and they brought back a hundred heads of the dead Turks to the city gate, where the ambassadors of the amir of Cairo[1] (for he had sent them to our leaders) were en-

---

the orthodox Sunnite dynasty ruling in Baghdad (which was under the influence of the Saljuqid Turks), and were trying to ally with the Franks against the coalition of orthodox Muslims and Turks.

mittebantur senioribus. Illi qui remanserant in tentoriis, tota die preliati sunt cum illis qui erant in ciuitate,
ante tres portas ciuitatis.[1] Factum est hoc bellum in die
martis ante caput ieiunii, quinto idus Februarii, fauente[a]
domino nostro Iesu Christo, qui cum Patre et Spiritu
Sancto uiuit et regnat Deus, per immortalia secula
seculorum, Amen.[2]

[*Explicit liber VI.   Incipit liber VII.*]

[a] regnante DX

[1] There were five gates into Antioch, the three most important being
the Bridge Gate on the north-west, St Paul's Gate on the north-east, and
St George's Gate on the south-west (Grousset, I, 69).
[2] The MSS make it clear that Book VI ends at this point.

camped. The men who had stayed in the camp had spent the whole day in fighting with the garrison before the three gates[1] of the city. This battle was fought on Shrove Tuesday, 9 February, by the power of Our Lord Jesus Christ, who with the Father and the Holy Ghost liveth and reigneth, One God, world without end. Amen.[2]

Here ends the sixth book, and the seventh book begins.

VII

[xviii] Reuersi sunt nostri agente Deo triumphantes,
et gaudentes de triumpho quem in die illo habuerunt
deuictis inimicis, qui sunt per omnia superati semper,
fugientes huc et illuc; uagantes et errantes, alii in Corrozanam, alii uero*ᵃ* in Saracenorum introierunt terram.
Videntes autem nostri maiores quod male tractarent et
constringerent nos inimici nostri qui erant in ciuitate,
die ac nocte uigilantes et insidiantes qua parte nos ledere
possent, congregati in unum dixerunt: 'Priusquam per-
damus gentem nostram, faciamus castrum ad machumariam quae est ante urbis portam, ubi pons est, ibique
forsitan poterimus nostros constringere inimicos.' Con-
senserunt omnes, et laudauerunt quod bonum esset ad
faciendum.   Comes de Sancto Egidio primus dixit:
'Estote mihi in adiutorium ad faciendum castrum, et ego
muniam ac seruabo.' Respondit Boamundus: 'Si uos
uultis et alii, ibo uobiscum ad portum Sancti Simeonis[1]
diligenter conducere illos qui illic sunt homines, ut per-
agant hoc opus[2]; alii qui sunt remansuri muniant se
undique ad defendendum.'

Comes igitur et Boamundus perrexerunt ad Sancti
Simeonis portum. Nos uero, qui remansimus, congregati in unum, castrum incipiebamus, dum Turci preparauerunt se ilico, et exierunt extra ciuitatem obuiam

---

ᵃ DX *omit* uero

[1] At the mouth of the Orontes, about fourteen miles from Antioch
[2] Genoese and English ships were lying in the harbour, so that men and

VII

[xviii] Our men, by God's will, came back exulting and rejoicing in the triumph which they had that day. Their conquered enemies, who were totally defeated, continued to flee, scurrying and wandering hither and thither, some into Khorasan and some into the land of the Saracens. Then our leaders, seeing that our enemies who were in the city were constantly harrying and vexing us, by day and night, wherever they might do us harm, met in council and said, 'Before we lose all our men, let us build a castle at the mosque which is before the city gate where the bridge stands, and by this means we may be able to contain our enemies.' They all agreed and thought that it was a good plan. The count of St Gilles was the first to speak, and he said, 'Help me to build this castle, and I will fortify and hold it.' 'If you wish it,' replied Bohemond, 'and if the other leaders approve, I will go with you to St Simeon's Port[1] and give safe conduct to the men who are there, so that they can construct this building.[2] The people who are to stay here must keep watch on all sides so as to defend themselves.'

The count and Bohemond therefore set out for St Simeon's Port. We who stayed behind gathered together, and were beginning to build the castle, when the Turks made ready and sallied out of the city to

---

materials to complete the fort could easily be brought up to Antioch (Grousset, i, 88-89).

nobis ad prelium. Sic itaque irruerunt super nos, et
miserunt nostros in fugam, occideruntque plures ex
nostris, unde tristes ualde fuimus.

Crastina autem die[1] uidentes Turci quod maiores
nostri deessent et quod preterita die iuissent ad portum,
preparauerunt se, et ierunt obuiam illis uenientibus e
portu. Tunc uidentes comitem et Boamundum uenientes et conducentes illam gentem, mox coeperunt
stridere et garrire ac clamare uehementissimo clamore,
circumcingendo undique nostros, iaculando, sagittando,
uulnerando, et crudeliter detruncando. Nam tam
acriter inuaserunt nostros ut illi inirent fugam per
proximam montaneam, et ubi uia eundi patebat. Qui
potuit celeri se gressu expedire euasit uiuus, qui uero
fugere nequiuit mortem suscepit. Fueruntque in illa
die martyrizati ex nostris militibus seu peditibus plus
quam mille, qui ut credimus in caelum ascenderunt, et
candidati stolam martyrii receperunt.

Itaque Boamundus uiam quam tenuerant non tenuit,
sed celerius cum paucis militibus ad nos uenit, qui
eramus in unum congregati.[a][2] Tunc nos accensi occisione
nostrorum, Christi nomine inuocato et Sancti Sepulchri
confidentes itinere, iuncti simul peruenimus contra eos
ad bellum, eosque inuasimus uno corde et animo. Stabant uero inimici Dei et nostri undique iam stupefacti et
uehementer perterriti, putantes nostros se deuincere et
occidere, sicut fecerant gentem comitis et Boamundi.
Sed Deus omnipotens hoc illis non permisit. Milites
igitur ueri Dei undique signo crucis armati irruerunt

[a] congregati in unum, annuntians quae illis euenerant X

[1] 6 March 1098
[2] The Anonymous had stayed in the camp, probably because Bohemond had taken only a small force of his men to act as escort to the builders.

attack us. They rushed upon us and put our men to flight, killing many, which was a great grief to us.

Next day[1] the Turks, realising that some of our leaders were away, and that they had gone to the port on the previous day, got ready and sallied out to attack them as they came back from the port. When they saw the count and Bohemond coming back and escorting the builders, they began to gnash their teeth and gabble and howl with very loud cries, wheeling round our men, throwing darts and shooting arrows, wounding and slaughtering them most brutally. Their attack was so fierce that our men began to flee over the nearest mountain, or wherever there was a path. Those who could get away quickly escaped alive, and those who could not were killed. On that day more than a thousand of our knights or foot-soldiers suffered martyrdom, and we believe that they went to Heaven and were clad in white robes and received the martyr's palm.

Bohemond did not follow the same route which they had followed, but came more quickly with a few knights to where we were gathered together,[2] and we, angry at the loss of our comrades, called on the Name of Christ and put our trust in the pilgrimage to the Holy Sepulchre and went all together to fight the Turks, whom we attacked with one heart and mind. God's enemies and ours were standing about, amazed and terrified, for they thought that they could defeat and kill us, as they had done with the followers of the count and Bohemond, but Almighty God did not allow them to do so. The knights of the True God, armed at all points with the sign of the Cross, charged them fiercely and made a

acriter super illos et fortiter inuaserunt. Illi autem celeriter fugerunt, per medium angusti pontis, ad illorum introitum. Illi qui uiui nequiuerunt transire pontem pre nimia multitudine gentium et caballorum, ibi receperunt sempiternum interitum cum diabolo et angelis eius. Nos itaque illos superauimus, impellentes in flumen et deicientes. Vnda uero rapidi fluminis undique uidebatur fluere rubea Turcorum sanguine. Et si forte aliquis eorum uoluisset reptare super pontis columnas, aut natando ad terram moliretur exire, uulneratus est a nostris, undique stantibus super ripam fluminis. Rumor quoque et clamor nostrorum et illorum resonabat ad caelum. Pluuiae telorum et sagittarum tegebant polum, et claritatem diei. Mulieres Christianae urbis ueniebant ad muri fenestras, spectantes misera fata*a* Turcorum, et occulte plaudebant manibus. Hermenii et Surani iussu maiorum Turcorum, inuiti seu spontanei sagittas iaciebant foras ad nos. Mortui sunt etiam in anima et corpore duodecim ammiralii de Turcorum agmine in prelio illo, et alii prudentissimorum et fortiorum*b* militum, qui melius ciuitatem pugnando defendebant; numerus quorum fuit mille et quingenti. Alii qui remanserant uiui, iam amplius non audebant clamitare, uel garrire, die neque nocte*c* sicut ante solebant. Omnes itaque nos uel illos solummodo separauit*d* nox, noxque diuisit utrosque in preliando, iaculando, spiculando, sagittando. Sic superati sunt inimici nostri uirtute Dei et Sancti Sepulchri, et ulterius non ualuerunt talem uirtutem habere, neque in uoce, neque in opere sicuti*e* prius. Nos itaque ualde fuimus refecti in illa die multis rebus quae satis erant nobis necessariae, et de equis.

---

a facta DX   *b* fortium DX   *c* neque die nocte E, die noctuque X
d superauit DX   *e* sicut DX

brave attack upon them, and they fled swiftly across the middle of the narrow bridge to their gate. Those who did not succeed in crossing the bridge alive, because of the great press of men and horses, suffered there everlasting death with the devil and his imps; for we came after them, driving them into the river or throwing them down, so that the waters of that swift stream appeared to be running all red with the blood of Turks, and if by chance any of them tried to climb up the pillars of the bridge, or to reach the bank by swimming, he was stricken by our men who were standing all along the river bank. The din and the shouts of our men and the enemy echoed to heaven, and the shower of missiles and arrows covered the sky and hid the daylight. The Christian women who were in the city came to the windows in the walls, and when they saw the wretched fate of the Turks they clapped their hands secretly. (The Armenians and Syrians who were under the command of Turkish leaders had to shoot arrows at us, whether they liked it or not.) Twelve amirs of the Turkish army suffered death in body and soul in the course of that battle, together with fifteen hundred more of their bravest and most resolute soldiers, who were the best in fighting to defend the city. The survivors no longer had the courage to howl and gabble day and night, as they used to do. Darkness alone separated the two sides, and night put an end to the fighting with darts, spears and arrows. Thus our enemies were defeated by the power of God and the Holy Sepulchre, so that henceforth they had less courage than before, both in words and works. On that day we recouped ourselves very well, with many things of which we were badly in need, as well as horses.

Crastina uero die summo diluculo exierunt alii Turci
de ciuitate, et colligerunt omnia cadauera foetentia Turcorum mortuorum, quae reperire potuerunt super ripam
fluminis, exceptis illis quae in alueo latebant eiusdem
fluminis*a* ; et sepelierunt ad machumariam quae est ultra
pontem ante portam urbis; simulque illis consepelierunt
pallia, bisanteos aureos, arcus, sagittas, et alia plurima
instrumenta, quae nominare nequimus. Audientes itaque nostri quod humassent mortuos suos Turci, omnes
sese preparauerunt, et uenerunt festinantes ad diabolicum
atrium, et iusserunt desepeliri et frangi tumbas eorum,
et trahi eos extra sepulchra. Et eiecerunt omnia cadauera eorum in quandam foueam, et deportauerunt cesa
capita ad tentoria nostra quatinus perfecte sciretur eorum
numerus, excepto quod onerauerant quatuor equos, de
nuntiis ammiralii Babiloniae, et miserant ad mare. Quod
uidentes Turci doluerunt nimis, fueruntque tristes usque
ad necem. Nam cotidie dolentes, nichil aliud agebant
nisi flere et ululare. Tertia uero die coepimus simul
iuncti cum gaudio magno aedificare castrum supra-
dictum, de lapidibus scilicet quos abstraximus de tumulis
Turcorum. Peracto itaque castro, mox coepimus ex omni
parte coangustare inimicos nostros, quorum superbia ad
nichilum iam erat redacta. Nos autem secure ambula-
bamus huc et illuc, ad pórtam*b1* et ad montaneas, laudantes et glorificantes Dominum Deum nostrum, cui est
honor et gloria per omnia seculorum secula. Amen.[2]

[*Explicit liber VII. Incipit liber VIII.*]

a DX *omit* exceptis . . . fluminis   *b* portum DX

[1] Bréhier reads 'portum' (DX, supported by Tudebod), saying that
'portam' does not make sense (*Histoire Anonyme*, p. 96). It does, however,
if one looks at the plan of Antioch, Grousset, 1, 69. The castle at the mosque

Next day, at dawn, other Turks came out from the city and collected all the stinking corpses of the dead Turks which they could find on the river bank, except those that were concealed in the actual river-bed, and buried them at the mosque which is beyond the bridge before the gate of the city, and together with them they buried cloaks, gold bezants, bows and arrows, and other tools the names of which we do not know. When our men heard that the Turks had buried their dead, they made ready and came in haste to that devil's chapel, and ordered the bodies to be dug up and the tombs destroyed, and the dead men dragged out of their graves. They threw all the corpses into a pit, and cut off their heads and brought them to our tents (so that they could count the number exactly), except for those which they loaded on to four horses belonging to the ambassadors of the amir of Cairo and sent to the sea-coast. When the Turks saw this, they were very sad and grieved almost to death, for they lamented every day and did nothing but weep and howl. On the third day we combined together, with great satisfaction, to build the castle already mentioned, with stones we had taken from the tombs of the Turks. When the castle was finished, we began to press hard from every side upon our enemies whose pride was brought low. But we went safely wherever we liked, to the gate[1] and to the mountains, praising and glorifying our Lord God, to whom be honour and glory, world without end. Amen.[2]

Here ends the seventh book, and the eighth book begins.

---

dominated the bridge over the river and the Bridge Gate. It would not have been useful in protecting the road to St Simeon's Port.

[2] The MSS make it clear that Book VII ends at this point.

VIII

[xix] Iamiam omnes semitae pene prohibitae et in-
cisae undique erant Turcis, nisi ex illa parte fluminis ubi
erat castrum et quoddam monasterium.[1] Quod castrum
si fuisset a nobis perfecte munitum, iam nullus eorum
auderet extra ciuitatis portam exire. Conciliauerunt se
denique nostri, et una uoce concorditer dixerunt: 'Eli-
gamus unum ex nobis, qui robuste teneat illud castrum,
et nostris inimicis prohibeat montaneas et plana, et introitum urbis ac[a] exitum.' Tancredus igitur primus
protulit se ante alios dicens: 'Si scirem quid proficui
mihi attigerit, ego sedule cum meis solummodo hominibus corroborarem castrum, et uiam per quam inimici
nostri solent frequentius saeuire, uiriliter deuetabo illis.'
Qui continuo spoponderunt ei quater centum marcas
argenti. Non adquieuit Tancredus; tamen perrexit cum
suis honestissimis militibus ac seruientibus, et extemplo
abstulit undique uias Turcis, ita ut nulli auderent ex eis
iam timore eius perterriti extra urbis portam exire; neque
propter herbam neque propter ligna neque propter ulla
necessaria. Remansit uero ibi Tancredus cum suis,
coepitque uehementer ubique coangustare ciuitatem.
Ipsa quoque die ueniebat maxima pars Hermeniorum et
Suranorum secure de montaneis, qui ferebant alimenta
Turcis in adiutorium ciuitatis. Quibus aduenit obuiam
Tancredus et apprehendit eos, et omnia quae deferebant;
uidelicet frumentum, uinum, hordeum, oleum, et alia

[a] et DX

[1] The monastery of St George, situated south-west of the city on the
hillside above St George's Gate

VIII

[xix] By this time all the paths were shut and blocked against the Turks, except for that by the river, where there was a castle and also a monastery.[1] If we could have succeeded in fortifying this castle in strength, none of the enemy would have dared to go out of the city gate. So our men held a council, and agreed unanimously, saying, 'Let us choose one of our number who can hold that castle strongly, and keep our enemies from the mountains and the plain, and prevent them from going into and out of the city.' Then Tancred was the first to stand forward among the others, and he said, 'If I may know what reward I shall have, I will guard the castle carefully with only my own followers, and I will do all that a man may to cut the path by which our enemies most often launch their cruel attacks.' The council immediately offered him four hundred marks of silver, so he made no delay, but arose at once with his best knights and followers, and forthwith blocked the paths against the Turks, so that none of them dared to go out of the city gate, either for fodder, wood or anything else which they needed, because they were very much afraid of him. Tancred stayed there with his men and began to blockade the city closely. That same day a very large number of Armenians and Syrians came confidently down from the mountains, carrying provisions for the Turks, to help those who were besieged in the city. Tancred met them and captured both them and all their loads—corn, wine, barley, oil and other such things. He was so forceful

huiusmodi. Sic itaque robuste et prospere deducebat se Tancredus, iamque habebat prohibitas et incisas omnes *a* semitas Turcis, donec Antiochia esset capta.

Omnia quae egimus antequam urbs esset capta nequeo enarrare, quia nemo est in his partibus siue clericus siue laicus qui omnino possit scribere uel narrare, sicut res gesta est. Tamen aliquantulum dicam.

[xx] Erat quidam ammiratus de genere Turcorum cui nomen Pirus,[1] qui maximam amicitiam receperat cum Boamundo. Hunc sepe Boamundus pulsabat nuntiis adinuicem missis, quo eum infra ciuitatem amicissime reciperet; eique christianitatem liberius promittebat, et eum se diuitem facturum cum multo honore mandabat. Consensit ille dictis et promissionibus dicens: 'Tres turres custodio, eique libenter ipsas promitto, et quacunque hora uoluerit in eas eum recolligam.' Erat itaque Boamundus iam securus de introitu ciuitatis, et gauisus serenaque mente, placido uultu uenit ad omnes seniores eisque iocunda uerba intulit, dicens: 'Viri prudentissimi milites, uidete quomodo nos omnes in nimia paupertate et miseria sumus, maiores siue minores; et ignoramus penitus qua parte melius succedat nobis. Igitur si uobis bonum et honestum uidetur, eligat se ante alios unus ex nobis, et si aliquo modo uel ingenio ciuitatem adquirere uel ingeniare potuerit per se uel per alios, concordi uoce ei urbem dono *b* concedamus.' Qui omnino prohibuerunt, et denegauerunt dicentes: 'Nemini dimittetur haec ciuitas, sed omnes aequaliter habebimus illam. Sicut aequalem habuimus laborem, sic inde aequalem

---

a DX *omit* omnes
b DX *omit* dono

[1] Raymond d'Agiles calls him a 'Turcatus', i.e. a Christian renegade. This would make his betrayal of the city rather more comprehensible (*P.L.*, CLV, 608).

and so lucky that he managed to keep all the paths barred and blocked against the Turks until Antioch was taken.

I cannot tell you all the things which we did before the city fell, for there is in this land neither clerk nor layman who could write down the whole story or describe it as it happened, but I will tell you a little of it.

[xx] There was a certain amir of Turkish race called Firuz,[1] who had struck up a great friendship with Bohemond. Bohemond used often to send messengers to him, sounding him as to whether he would receive him, in friendship's name, into the city, and promising in return that he would willingly have Firuz christened, and would cause riches and great honour to be bestowed on him. Firuz agreed, and accepted the promised benefits, saying, 'I am warden of three towers, which I freely promise to Bohemond, and I will receive him into them at whatever time he shall choose.' So when Bohemond was sure that he could enter the city he was glad, and came coolly, looking pleased with himself, to the council of leaders, and said to them jokingly, 'Most gallant knights, you see that we are all, both great and less, in dire poverty and misery, and we do not know whence better fortune will come to us. If, therefore, you think it a good and proper plan, let one of us set himself above the others, on condition that if he can capture the city or engineer its downfall by any means, by himself or by others, we will all agree to give it to him.' The other leaders all refused and denied him, saying, 'This city shall not be granted to anyone, but we will all share it alike; as we have had equal toil, so

habeamus honorem.' Itaque Boamundus auditis his uerbis, paulominus subridens protinus recessit.

Non multo post audiuimus nuntios de exercitu hostium nostrorum, Turcorum, Publicanorum, Agulanorum,[a] Azimitarum,[1] et aliarum plurimarum nationum; statimque adunauerunt se omnes maiores nostri simul, tenueruntque concilium dicentes, quoniam 'si Boamundus potuerit adquirere ciuitatem aut per se aut per alios, nos una libenti corde ultro ei donamus, eo tenore ut si imperator uenerit nobis in adiutorium, et omnem conuentionem nobis sicut promisit et iurauit attendere uoluerit, nos ei eam iure reddemus. Sin autem, Boamundus eam in suam habeat potestatem.' Mox itaque Boamundus coepit humiliter amicum suum cotidiana deprecari petitione, promittendo humillima, maxima, et dulcia, in hunc modum: 'Ecce uere tempus modo habemus idoneum, in quo possumus operari quicquid boni uolumus, ergo adiuuet me nunc amicus meus Pirrus.' Qui satis gauisus de nuntio, ait se illum adiuuare omnino sicut agere deberet. Nocte itaque ueniente proxima, misit caute filium suum pignus[b] Boamundo, ut securior fieret de introitu urbis. Misit quoque ei uerba in hunc modum, ut in crastinum omnem Francorum gentem summoneri faciat, et quasi in[c] Saracenorum terram depredari uadat dissimulet, ac deinde celeriter reuertatur per dextram montaneam[2]: 'Ego uero,' ait, 'ero intentione erecta prestolans illa agmina, eaque recipiam in turres quas in mea habeo potestate ac custodia.' Dein Boamundus iussit celeriter ad se uocari quendam ser-

[a] DX *omit* Agulanorum
[b] Pyrrus DX
[c] DX *omit* in

[1] A Greek word used to describe those who used unleavened bread in the Communion. It refers here to the Armenians.

let us have equal honour.' When Bohemond heard these words he looked less pleased, and went straight off.

Not long afterwards we heard news of an army of our enemies, drawn from the Turks, Paulicians, Agulani, Azymites[1] and many other peoples. All our leaders came together at once and held a council, saying, 'If Bohemond can take this city, either by himself or by others, we will thereafter give it to him gladly, on condition that if the emperor come to our aid and fulfil all his obligations which he promised and vowed, we will return the city to him as it is right to do. Otherwise Bohemond shall take it into his power.' So Bohemond now began to send a tactful request to his friend every day, making the most flattering, extensive and tempting promises, saying, 'See, now we have a chance of doing whatever good deed we want to do, so now, friend Firuz, give me your help.' Firuz was pleased by the message, and said that he would give Bohemond all the help that he was bound to provide, and the next night he secretly despatched his son to Bohemond, as a pledge to give him greater confidence that he should enter the city. He also sent word that on the morrow the whole Frankish army should be summoned, and should pretend to go out and plunder the land of the Saracens, but that afterwards it should return quickly by the western mountain.[2] 'And I,' he said, 'will watch out for these troops very carefully, and I will admit them into the towers which I have in my power and keeping.' Then Bohemond sent quickly for one of his followers,

---

[2] The towers held by Firuz were near St George's Gate, and would therefore be on the right-hand side of the city from the viewpoint of the Crusaders' camp.

uientem suum uidelicet Malam Coronam, eique precepit
ut quasi preco commoneret Francorum maximam gentem, quatinus fideliter prepararet*a* se in Saracenorum
itura terram. Factumque est ita. Credidit itaque Boamundus hoc consilium duci Godefrido, et Flandrensi
comiti, comiti quoque de Sancto Egidio, atque*b* Podiensi
episcopo, dicens quia: 'Dei fauente gracia, hac nocte
tradetur nobis Antiochia'.

Ordinata sunt denique haec omnia. Milites tenuerunt plana*c* et pedites montaneam, tota nocte equitauerunt et ambulauerunt usque prope auroram, ac deinceps coeperunt appropinquare ad turres quas ille uigil*d*
custodiebat. Confestim descendit Boamundus et precepit omnibus, dicens: 'Ite securo animo et felici concordia, et ascendite per scalam in Antiochiam, quam
statim habebimus si Deo placet in nostra custodia.'
Venerunt illi usque ad scalam quae iam erat erecta et
fortiter ligata ad ciuitatis moenia, et ascenderunt per
illam homines fere sexaginta ex nostris; ac diuisi sunt
per turres quas ille obseruabat.*e* Videns hoc Pirrus quod
tam pauci ascendissent ex nostris, coepit pauere, timens
sibi et nostris, ne in manus Turcorum inciderent, dixitque: 'Micró Francos echomé (hoc est: paucos Francos
habemus). Vbi est acerrimus Boamundus? Vbi est ille
inuictus?' Interim descendit quidam seruiens Longo-
bardus deorsum, et cucurrit quantocius ad Boamundum,
dicens: 'Quid hic stas*f* uir prudens? Quamobrem huc
uenisti? Ecce nos iam tres turres habemus!' Motus est
ille cum aliis, et omnes gaudentes peruenerunt usque ad
scalam. Videntes itaque illi qui iam erant in turribus,

a preparet DX	*b* et DX
c planam DX	*d* peruigil DX
e custodiebat DX	*f* agis DX

nick-named 'Bad-crown', and told him to go out as a herald to summon a great force of Franks to make faithful preparations to go into the land of the Saracens, and this Bad-crown did. Bohemond confided his plan to Duke Godfrey and the count of Flanders, the count of St Gilles and the bishop of Le Puy, telling them, 'God willing, this night shall Antioch be betrayed to us.'

All the preparations were thus made. The knights went by the plain and the foot-soldiers by the mountain, and they rode and marched all night until towards dawn, when they began to approach the towers of which Firuz, who had been watching all night, was warden. Then Bohemond dismounted at once and said to his men, 'Go on, strong in heart and lucky in your comrades, and scale the ladder into Antioch, for by God's will we shall have it in our power in a trice.' The men came to the ladder, which was already set up and lashed firmly to the battlements of the city, and nearly sixty of them went up it and occupied the towers which Firuz was guarding. But when Firuz saw that so few of our men had come up, he began to be afraid, fearing lest he and they should fall into the hands of the Turks and he said (in Greek), 'Μικροὺς φράγκους ἔχομεν' (which means 'We have few Franks'). 'Where is the hero Bohemond? Where is that unconquered soldier?' Meanwhile a certain soldier from southern Italy went back down the ladder and ran as fast as he could to Bohemond, crying out, 'Why are you standing here, sir, if you have any sense? What did you come to get? Look! We have taken three towers already!' Bohemond and the others bestirred themselves, and they all came rejoicing to the ladder. When those who were in the towers saw them, they began to call out

coeperunt iocunda uoce clamare: 'Deus uult!' Nos
uero idem clamabamus. Nunc*a* coeperunt ilico mirabiliter ascendere, ascenderunt tamen, et cucurrerunt
festinanter in alias turres. Quos illic inueniebant, morti
tradebant, fratrem quoque Pirri occiderunt. Interea
forte rupta est scala, per quam noster erat ascensus, unde
inter nos orta est immensa angustia et tristitia. Quamquam autem scala fuisset fracta, tamen quaedam porta
erat iuxta nos clausa in sinistra parte, quae quibusdam
manebat incognita. Nox namque erat, sed tamen pal-
pando et inquirendo inuenimus eam, omnesque cucur-
rimus ad illam, et ipsa fracta intrauimus per eam.[1]

Tunc innumerabilis fragor mirabiliter resonabat per
totam urbem. Non adquieuit Boamundus his, sed ilico
imperauit honorabile uexillum deferri sursum coram
castello in quodam monte. Omnes uero pariter stride-
bant in ciuitate. Summo autem diluculo audientes illi
qui foris erant in tentoriis uehementissimum rumorem
strepere per ciuitatem, exierunt festinantes et uiderunt
uexillum Boamundi sursum in monte, celerique cursu
properantes, uenerunt omnes, et per portas intrauerunt
in urbem; et interfecerunt Turcos et Saracenos quos ibi
reppererunt, extra illos qui fugerant sursum in castrum.
Alii uero Turcorum per portas exierunt, et fugientes uiui
euaserunt. Cassianus[2] uero dominus illorum timens
ualde gentem Francorum dedit se omnimodo fugae, cum
aliis multis qui erant cum eo; et fugiendo peruenit in
Tancredi terram non longe a ciuitate. Fatigati uero

---

a tunc DX

[1] The Author was in this party, and is therefore a first-hand authority
for the events of the attack.

[2] Yaghi Siyan had been appointed governor of Antioch by Tutush
about 1090. After the death of Tutush at the battle of Rayy in 1095 he had
tried to play off the two sons of Tutush, Rudwan of Aleppo and Duqaq of

cheerfully, 'God's will!' and we called back the same words. Now an amazing number of men began to climb; they went up and ran quickly to the other towers. Whomsoever they found there they put to death at once, killing the brother of Firuz among them. Meanwhile the ladder, up which our men had climbed, happened to break, so that we were plunged in great despair and grief. However, although the ladder was broken, there was a gate not far from us to the left, but it was shut and some of us did not know where it was, for it was still dark. Yet by fumbling with our hands and poking about we found it, and all made a rush at it, so that we broke it down and entered.[1]

At this moment the shrieks of countless people arose, making an amazing noise throughout the city. Bohemond did not waste time on this account, but ordered his glorious banner to be carried up to a hill opposite the citadel. All the people in the city were screaming at once. At dawn, our men who were outside in the tents heard an overpowering din break out in the city, so they hurried out and saw Bohemond's banner aloft on the hill. They all came running as fast as they could and entered the city gates, killing all the Turks and Saracens whom they found there except for those who fled up to the citadel. Some other Turks got out through the gates and saved their lives by flight. Yaghi Siyan,[2] their leader, who was much afraid of the Franks, took to flight headlong with many companions, and as they fled they came into Tancred's land not far from the city. Their horses were tired out, so they

---

Damascus, against one another. This probably explains why neither of them made a whole-hearted attempt to raise the siege of Antioch.

erant equi eorum, miseruntque se in quoddam casale et mersi sunt in unam domum. Cognouerunt ergo eum habitatores illius montaneae, scilicet Surani, et Hermenii; et confestim apprehenderunt eum, truncaueruntque caput illius, et tulerunt ante Boamundi presentiam, ut inde mererentur libertatem accipere. Balteum quoque eius et uaginam appretiauerunt sexaginta bizanteis.

Haec omnia gesta sunt tertia die*a* intrante mense Iunio, quinta feria, III nonas Iunii. Omnes namque plateae ciuitatis iam undique erant plenae cadaueribus mortuorum, ita ut nemo posset sufferre*b* ibi esse prae nimiis foetoribus. Nullus uero poterat ire per semitam ciuitatis, nisi super cadauera mortuorum.[1]

[*Explicit liber VIII. Incipit liber IX.*]

a DX *omit* tertia die
b DX *omit* sufferre

[1] Although the usual doxology is omitted, the MS makes it clear that Book VIII ends at this point.

entered one of the villages and hid in a house. When the people who lived in that mountain (they were Syrians and Armenians) knew who the fugitive was, they captured him at once and cut off his head, which they took to my lord Bohemond as the price of their freedom. His belt and scabbard were worth sixty bezants.

All this happened on the third of June, which was a Thursday. All the streets of the city on every side were full of corpses, so that no-one could endure to be there because of the stench, nor could anyone walk along the narrow paths of the city except over the corpses of the dead.[1]

Here ends the eighth book, and the ninth book begins.

IX

[xxi] Curbaram[1] princeps militiae soldani Persiae[2]
dum adhuc esset Corrozanum, quantocius[a] Cassianus
ammiralius Antiochiae legationem ei misit, quo sibi
succurreret in tempore oportuno, quoniam gens fortis-
sima Francorum eum impeditum grauiter obsidebat in
Antiochia; et si adiutorium ei impenderet, urbem An-
tiochenam illi traderet, aut eum maximo munere ditaret;
cumque iam habuisset maximum exercitum Turcorum,
ex longo collectum tempore, et licentiam Christianos
occidendi accepisset a Calipha illorum apostolico,[3] ilico
inchoauit iter longae uiae Antiochiae. Hierosolimitanus
ammiralius[4] in adiutorium cum suo exercitu uenit. Rex
Damasci[5] illuc uenit, cum maxima gente. Idem uero
Curbaram congregauit innumeras gentes paganorum,[6]
uidelicet Turcos, Arabas, Saracenos, Publicanos, Azi-
mitas, Curtos, Persas, Agulanos, et alias multas gentes
innumerabiles. Et Agulani fuerunt numero tria milia;
qui neque lanceas neque sagittas neque ulla arma timebant, quia omnes erant undique cooperti ferro et equi
eorum, ipsique nolebant in bellum ferre arma nisi solummodo gladios.

---

[a] quotiens ED; X *has* quantocius, *but after* Antiochiae

[1] Amir of Mosul. He was the first commander to be sent by the sultan
in an attempt to cut through the local rivalries of the Muslim rulers in
Syria and Palestine, and to stamp out the crusade. His intervention was
therefore far more dangerous than anything the crusaders had experienced
hitherto, since it was backed up by the official leader of the whole Turkish
army.
[2] Barkyaruq, son of Malikshah
[3] The Abbassid khalif of Baghdad was recognised by orthodox Muslims
as their spiritual leader.

IX

[xxi] Now Karbuqa[1] was commander-in-chief of
the army of the sultan of Persia.[2] While he was still in
Khorasan, Yaghi Siyan the amir of Antioch had
instantly sent him an envoy asking for timely help
(since a very strong army of Franks held him closely
besieged in Antioch) and promising to give him either
the city of Antioch or very great riches if he would
bring aid. Since Karbuqa had with him a great army
of Turks whom he had been assembling for a long time,
and had been given leave by the khalif (who is the pope
of the Turks[3]) to kill Christians, he set out, there and
then, on the long journey to Antioch. The amir of
Jerusalem[4] came to his help with an army, and the
king of Damascus[5] brought a great number of men.
So Karbuqa collected an immense force of pagans[6]—
Turks, Arabs, Saracens, Paulicians, Azymites, Kurds,
Persians, Agulani and many other people who could
not be counted. The Agulani numbered three thousand;
they fear neither spears nor arrows nor any other
weapon, for they and their horses are covered all over
with plates of iron. They will not use any weapons
except swords when they are fighting.

---

[4] Sukman-ibn-Ortuq
[5] Duqaq
[6] The Author uses the word in a vague sense, as some of the people
whom he mentions were not pagans but heretics. He did not really know
what was going on in Karbuqa's camp and draws freely upon his imagin-
ation, supplemented by the rumours which were being passed round in the
Frankish army. Consequently, the Karbuqa passages tell us a good deal
more about the contemporary Frankish idea of Karbuqa than about the
man himself.

Isti omnes uenerunt in obsidionem Antiochiae, ad dispergendum Francorum collegium. Et cum appropinquassent urbi, uenit obuiam illis Sensadolus filius Cassiani ammiralii Antiochiae, et continuo cucurrit ad Curbaram lacrimabiliter rogans eum et dicens: 'Inuictissime princeps te supplex precor, quatinus modo mihi succurras, quoniam Franci undique obsident me in Antiocheno oppido, urbemque in suo tenent imperio; nosque alienare a regione Romaniae siue Syriae, adhuc autem et Corrozani,[a] cupiunt. Omnia patrauere quae uoluerunt, patrem occidere meum, nichil aliud superest nisi ut me et te et omnes alios ex genere nostro interficiant. Ego namque iamdudum tuum exspecto auxilium, ut mihi succurras in hoc periculo.' Cui ait ille: 'Si uis ut ex toto corde in tuo sim proficuo, tibique fideliter in hoc succurram periculo, illud oppidum in meam trade manum; et tunc uidebis qualiter in tuo ero proficuo, idque faciam custodire meos homines.'[b] Ait illi Sensadolus: 'Si potes omnes Francos occidere, michique capita eorum tradere, tibi dabo oppidum tibique faciam hominium, et in tua fidelitate[1] custodiam illud oppidum.' Cui Curbaram: 'Non ita' inquit 'erit; sed continuo in meam manum committe castrum.' Tandem uolens siue nolens commisit illi castrum.

Tertia uero die postquam intrauimus ciuitatem,[2] eorum precursores ante urbem precurrerunt. Exercitus autem illorum ad pontem Farreum castrametatus est; et expugauerunt turrim, et occiderunt omnes quos illic inuenerunt; et nemo euasit uiuus nisi dominus illorum

---

[a] Corozana D, Corozanae X
[b] meis hominibus DX

[1] This use of contemporary Frankish terms indicates that the conversation, like virtually all conversations in medieval chronicles, was fictitious, although it may rest on a basis of historical truth.
[2] 5 June 1098

All these men came to raise the siege of Antioch, so that they might scatter the company of the Franks, and when they had approached the city there met them Shems-ed-Daula, son of Yaghi Siyan the amir of Antioch, and he ran straight up to Karbuqa weeping, entreating him and saying, 'Most victorious prince, I am a suppliant begging you for help, for the Franks are besieging me on all sides in the citadel of Antioch, and they have got the city in their power, and they want to drive us out of Rum and Syria and even from Khorasan. They have accomplished everything they planned, and have killed my father, and the next thing will be that they will kill me and you and all the rest of our people. I have waited a long time for assistance, so that you may help me in this peril.' Karbuqa answered, 'If you want my sincere help, I will faithfully give you assistance in this peril, but you must first surrender the citadel to me, and I will put my own men in to guard it. Then you shall see how much I can help you.' Then said Shems-ed-Daula, 'If you can kill all the Franks and send me their heads, I will give you the citadel, and do homage to you, and hold it as your liege man.'[1] 'That will not do at all,' replied Karbuqa, 'you must surrender the citadel into my hands at once.' So Shems-ed-Daula gave him the citadel willy-nilly.

On the third day after we entered the city[2] Karbuqa's vanguard came up before the walls, for his main army was encamped at the Orontes bridge, where it stormed one of the towers on the bridge and killed all the garrison in it. None of our men there survived except the leader, whom we found, bound in iron chains, when we

quem inuenimus ligatum in uinculis ferreis, facto maiore
bello. Crastina uero die moto exercitu paganorum
appropinquauerunt urbi, et castrametati sunt inter duo
flumina,[1] steteruntque ibi per duos dies. Recepto itaque
castro, Curbaram conuocauit unum ammiralium ex suis,
quem sciebat ueracem, mitem et pacificum, et ait illi:
'Volo ut intres in fidelitatem meam custodire hoc castrum, quoniam ex longissimo tempore scio te fidelissi-
mum, ideoque precor te ut summa cautela hoc serues
oppidum.' Cui ait ammiralius: 'Tibi unquam de tali
nollem obedire officio.[a] Sed tamen hoc faciam, illo
tenore, ut si Franci eiecerint uos de mortali prelio et
uicerint, eis continuo tradam hoc castrum.' Dixitque
illi Curbaram: 'Tam honestum et prudentem te cogno-
sco, ut omne quicquid boni uis agere ego consentiam.'

Reuersus est itaque Curbaram ad suum exercitum;
et protinus Turci[b] deludentes Francorum collegium,
detulerunt ante conspectum Curbaram quemdam uilis-
simum ensem rubigine tectum, et deterrimum[c] arcum
ligneum, et lanceam nimis inutilem, quae abstulerant
nuper pauperibus peregrinis; dixeruntque: 'Ecce arma,
quae attulerunt Franci obuiam nobis ad pugnam.' Tunc
Curbaram coepit surridere, palam dicens omnibus:
'Haec sunt arma bellica et nitida, quae attulerunt
Christiani super nos in Asiam, quibus putant nos et
confidunt expellere ultra confinia Corrozanae, et delere
omnia nostra ultra Amazonia flumina; qui propulerunt
omnes parentes nostros a Romania,[2] et Antiochia urbe

---

[a] tibi unquam nollem (numquam uellem X) de tali officio (re X)
obedire DX
[b] DX *omit* Turci
[c] teterrimum DX

[1] The Orontes and the Qara-su
[2] A reference to the wars of Nicephorus Phocas and John Tzimisces in
the tenth century. These were, however, Byzantine enterprises for which
the Franks could claim no credit.

had fought the Great Battle. Next day the main army of the pagans moved up and approached the city, encamping between the two rivers,[1] where it stayed for two days. When Karbuqa had received the surrender of the citadel he called one of his amirs, whom he knew to be a truthful, kindly and peaceable man, and said to him, 'I want you to hold this citadel as my liege man, for I have known for a very long time that you are most worthy of trust. Therefore I beg you to keep it with extreme care.' The amir replied, 'I would prefer never to do such a thing for you, but I will do it on this condition, that if the Franks drive you back and defeat you in mortal combat, I may surrender the citadel to them at once.' Then Karbuqa said to him, 'I know that you are such an honourable and brave man that I will agree to anything you think fit.'

After this Karbuqa went back to his army, and immediately the Turks, making mock of the Frankish troops, brought him a very poor sword all covered with rust, and a thoroughly bad wooden bow, and a spear which was quite useless, all of which they had just stolen from the poor pilgrims, and they said, 'Look at the arms which the Franks have brought to fight against us!' Then Karbuqa began to chuckle, and said to all those who were present, 'Are these the warlike and splendid weapons which the Christians have brought into Asia against us, and with these do they confidently expect to drive us beyond the furthest boundaries of Khorasan, and to blot out our names beyond the rivers of the Amazons? Are these the people who drove all our forefathers out of Rum[2] and from the royal city of Antioch, which is the honoured capital of all

regia quae est honorabile caput totius Syriae?' Mox
conuocauit suum notarium, et ait: 'Scribe cito plures
cartas quae in Corrozania *a* sint legendae[1]; uidelicet
Caliphae nostro apostolico, ac nostri regi domino Sol-
dano militi fortissimo, atque omnibus prudentissimis
Corrozanae militibus, salus et immensus honor. Satis
sint leti et gauisi iocunda concordia, et satisfaciant
uentribus, imperent et sermocinent per uniuersam regionem illam, ut omnino dent sese ad petulantiam et
luxuriam, multosque filios patrare congaudeant, qui
contra Christianos fortiter pugnare preualeant; et libenter suscipiant haec tria arma, quae olim abstulimus a
Francorum turma, et discant modo quae arma attulerunt *b* super nos gens Francigena. Adhuc quoque sciant
omnes, quoniam ego cunctos Francos intus in Antiochia
conclusos habeo, et castrum in mea libera teneo uolun-
tate, illi uero deorsum sunt in ciuitate. Habeo etiam
omnes illos iam in mea manu, eosque faciam aut capitalem subire sententiam, aut deduci in Corrozanam in
captiuitatem nimiam, eo quod minantur nos suis armis
propulsare et expellere ab omnibus finibus nostris; ceu
eiecerunt omnes parentes nostros a Romania siue Syria.
Amodo iuro uobis per Machomet et per omnia deorum
nomina,[2] quoniam ante uestram non ero rediturus presentiam, donec regalem urbem Antiochiam et omnem
Suriam siue Romaniam atque Bulgariam[3] usque in
Apuliam[4] adquisiero mea forti dextera, ad deorum

a Corozane DX
b attulit DX

[1] In this letter, and in the speeches attributed to Karbuqa and his
mother, the Author tries to reproduce the bombastic style generally attributed by contemporary Christians to Muslims, but he tends to slip back at
intervals into his own simple words. I have tried to reproduce the peculiar
result as well as I can. I cannot agree with M. Bréhier's theory that these
passages are interpolations written by a clerk. See Introduction, p. xv.

Syria?' Then he called his scribe and said, 'Be quick and write many letters which may be read in Khorasan, in these words[1]: "To the khalif our pope and the lord sultan our king, that most valiant warrior, and to all the most gallant knights of Khorasan, greeting and boundless honour! Enjoy yourselves, rejoicing with one accord, and fill your bellies, and let commands and injunctions be sent throughout the whole country that all men shall give themselves up to wantonness and lust, and take their pleasure in getting many sons who shall fight bravely against the Christians and defeat them. And receive, with my good wishes, these three weapons which we have already taken from the Frankish rabble, and learn what kind of arms the Franks have brought against us. Know also that I have got all the Franks shut up in Antioch, and I hold the citadel in my power while they are down below in the city. I have them all in my hands, and I will have them either executed or led into Khorasan in most bitter captivity, because they threaten to repulse us by their weapons and to drive us out of all our lands, as they drove our forefathers out of Rum and Syria. Moreover I swear to you by Mohammed and by all the names of our gods[2] that I will not appear again before your face until I have conquered, by the strength of my right arm, the royal city of Antioch and all Syria, Rum, Bulgaria[3] and even as far as Apulia,[4] to the glory of the Gods and of you and

---

[2] The Author always assumes that the Muslims are polytheists.

[3] Used here in the general sense of 'the Balkans', as it appears to have been used in France in the thirteenth century to denote the birthplace of the Manichean heresy

[4] The Author, a follower of Bohemond, had probably been born and bred in southern Italy. Hence he makes the conquest of Apulia the supreme vaunt of the Muslim leader.

honorem et uestrum, et omnium qui sunt ex genere
Turcorum.' Sic fecit finem dictis.

[xxii] Mater uero eiusdem Curbaram quae erat in
Aleph ciuitate, denuo uenit ad eum, dixitque illi lacrimabiliter: 'Fili, suntne uera quae audio?' Cui ait ille:
'Quae?' Et dixit illa: 'Audiui quia bellum uis com-
mittere cum Francorum gente.' Ait ille: 'Verum omnino
scias.' Dixit illa: 'Contestor te, fili, per omnium deorum
nomina,ᵃ et per tuam magnam bonitatem, ne bellum
cum Francis committas, quoniam tu es miles inuictus,
et te e campo ab aliquo uictore fugientem quisquam
minime inuenit. Diffamata est tua militia ubique,
omnesque prudentes milites audito tuo nomine con-
tremiscunt. Satis scimus, fili, quoniam tu es bellipotens
et fortis, nullaque gens Christianorum uel paganorum
ante tuum conspectum aliquam uirtutem habere potuit;
sed fugiebant solummodo audito tuo nomine, sicut oues
ante leonis furorem fugiunt, ideoque obsecro te karissime
fili ut meis adquiescas consiliis, et ne unquam in tuo
hesites animo, aut in tuo inueniatur consilio, ut bellum
uelis incipere cum Christianorumᵇ gente.' Tum Curbaram materna audiens monita feroci respondit sermone:
'Quid est hoc mater quod mihi refers? Puto quod in-
sanis, aut furiis es plena. Enimuero mecum habeo plures
ammiralios, quam Christiani sintᶜ sive maiores sive
minores.' Respondit ei mater sua: 'O dulcissime fili,
Christiani nequeunt uobiscum bellare, scio namque quod
non ualent uobis pugnam inferre, sed deus eorum pro
ipsis cotidie pugnat, eosque die noctuque sua protectione
defendit, et uigilat super eos sicut pastor uigilat super

ᵃ numina DX
ᵇ Christiana DX
ᶜ sunt DX

of all who are sprung from the race of the Turks.'"
This was the end of the letter.

[xxii] It happened that the mother of Karbuqa,
who was in the city of Aleppo, came at once to him,
and said to him, 'My son, are these things true, which
I hear?' 'What things?' said he, and she answered,
'I have heard that you desire to join battle with the
people of the Franks.' 'Know,' said he, 'that this is
quite true.' She cried, 'I beseech you, my son, by the
names of all the Gods and by your own great excellence,
not to join battle with the Franks, for you are an unconquered warrior and no man has ever seen you fleeing
from the battlefield before any victor. Your prowess
is renowned, and brave soldiers tremble, wherever they
may be, at the mere sound of your name. Surely we
know well enough, my son, that you are a mighty warrior
and a man of valour, so that no people, Christian or
pagan, can show any courage in your sight—men flee
before you when they have but heard your name, as
sheep before a raging lion. Therefore I implore you,
beloved son, listen to my counsels and never let the
idea of making war with the Christians occupy your
mind or find a place in your counsels.' When Karbuqa
heard his mother's warnings he replied furiously,
'What sort of tale are you telling me, mother? I think
you are mad or possessed by the furies—why, I have
more amirs in my following than the whole of the
Christians, both great and small.' 'O sweetest son,'
replied his mother, 'the Christians alone cannot fight
with you—indeed I know that they are unworthy to
meet you in battle—but their god fights for them every
day, and keeps them day and night under his protection,
and watches over them as a shepherd watches over his

gregem suam*; et non permittit eos laedi nec* conturbari
ab ulla gente, et quicumque uolunt eis obsistere, idem
eorum deus conturbat illos, sicut ait ipse per os David
prophetae: "Dissipa gentes quae bella uolunt".¹ Et
alibi: "Effunde iram tuam in gentes quae te non
nouerunt, et in regna quae nomen tuum non inuoca-
uerunt."² Antequam uero preparati sint ad incipiendum bellum, eorum deus omnipotens et bellipotens simul
cum sanctis suis omnes inimicos iam habet deuictos;
quanto magis modo faciet circa uos qui eius estis inimici,
et qui preparastis uos eis obsistere tota uirtute? Hoc
autem, karissime, in rei ueritate scias, quoniam isti
Christiani filii Christi³ uocati sunt; et prophetarum ore
filii adoptionis et promissionis,⁴ et secundum apostolum
heredes Christi⁵ sunt, quibus Christus hereditates repro-
missas iam donauit, dicendo per prophetas: "A solis ortu
usque ad occasum erunt termini uestri, et nemo stabit
contra uos."⁶ Et quis potest his dictis contradicere uel
obstare?* Certe si hoc bellum contra illos incoeperis,
maximum tibi erit dampnum ac dedecus, et multos
fideles tuos milites perdes, et uniuersa spolia quae apud
te habes amittes, et nimio pauore fugiendo euerteris. Tu
autem in hoc bello non morieris modo, sed tamen in
hoc anno,⁷ quoniam ipse deus non statim iudicat offen-
dentem se exerta ira, sed quando uult punit eum mani-
festa uindicta, ideoque timeo ne te iudicet poenali

ª suum DX
ᵇ uel DX
ᶜ obsistere DX

¹ Psalm 67:31 ² Psalm 78:6
³ Theologically inexact. The X MSS correct it to 'sons of God'.
⁴ A rather confused recollection of Romans 9:8 and Galatians 4:5
⁵ Romans 8:17, quoted incorrectly
⁹ A rather confused recollection either of Deuteronomy 11:24-25 or of
Joshua 1:4-5. The use of texts suggests that the Author was a devout

flock, and suffers no people to hurt or vex them, and if
anyone wishes to fight them, this same god of theirs
will smite them, as he says by the mouth of David the
prophet, "Scatter the people that delight in war"[1] and
again, "Pour out thine anger upon the people that have
not known thee, and upon the kingdoms that have not
called upon thy name."[2] Before they are even ready to
join battle, their god, mighty and powerful in battle,
together with his saints, has already conquered all their
enemies, and how much more will he do to you who
are his own enemy, and have prepared with all your
might to resist? Beloved, know also the truth of this,
that those Christians are called "sons of Christ"[3] and,
by the mouth of the prophets, "sons of adoption and
promise"[4] and the apostle says that they are "heirs of
Christ",[5] to whom Christ has even now given the
promised inheritance, saying by the prophets, "From
the rising of the sun to the going down thereof shall be
your bounds, and no man shall stand against you."[6]
Who can contradict these words or resist them? I tell
you truly that if you join battle with these men you will
suffer very great loss and dishonour, and lose many of
your faithful soldiers, and you will leave behind all the
plunder which you have taken, and escape as a panic-
stricken fugitive. You will not die now in this battle,
but yet in this very year,[7] for this same god, when his
wrath is roused, does not punish the offender at once,
but when he wills he punishes him with manifest ven-
geance, and therefore I fear that he will condemn you

layman, quoting familiar scriptural passages from a good but not completely accurate memory.
[7] Karbuqa died some time between 26 October 1101 and 14 October
1102. The confidence of the prophecy suggests that the Author wrote it in
the summer of 1098, after the Great Battle of Antioch.

tristitia. Non morieris, inquam, modo, uerumtamen
perditurus es inpresentiarum habita.'

Curbaram denique ualde dolens intimis uisceribus,
auditis maternis sermonibus, respondit: 'Mater karissima, quaeso te quis dixit tibi ista*a* de gente Christiana,
quod deus eorum tantum eos amet, et quod ipse pugnandi uirtutem in se retinet maximam, et quod illi
Christiani uincent nos in Antiochena prelia,*b* et quod
ipsi capturi sunt nostra spolia, nosque persecuturi magna
uictoria; et quod in hoc anno moriturus sum morte
subitanea?' Tunc respondit ei mater sua dolens: 'Fili
karissime, ecce sunt plus quam centum annorum tempora, de quibus inuentum est in nostra pagina et in
gentilium uoluminibus, quoniam gens Christiana super
nos foret uentura, et nos ubique uictura, ac super paganos regnatura; et nostra gens illis ubique erit subdita.
Sed ignoro, utrum modo, an in futuro sint haec euentura.
Ego utique*c* misera sum te secuta ab Aleph urbe pul-
cherrima, in qua speculando atque ingeniose rimando
respexi in caelorum astra, et sagaciter scrutata sum pla-
netas, et duodecim signa, siue sortes innumeras. In eis
omnibus repperi quoniam*d* gens Christiana nos ubique
est deuictura, ideoque de te ualde timeo nimis maesta,
ne ex te remaneam orbata.'

Dixit illi Curbaram: 'Mater karissima, dic michi
omnia quae in corde meo sunt incredula.' Quae ait:
'Hoc, karissime, libenter faciam, si sciero ea quae tibi
sunt incognita.' Cui ille dixit: 'Non sunt igitur Boamundus et Tancredus Francorum dii, et non eos liberant

a talia DX   *b* Antiocheno prelio DX
c itaque DX   *d* quod DX

to a heavy sentence. You will not, as I say, die at once, but nevertheless you will lose all that you now have.'

Then Karbuqa, when he had heard his mother's words, was bitterly grieved to the depths of his heart, and he replied, 'Mother dearest, I desire to know who told you these things about the Christian people, how their god loves them so dearly, and how he has in himself such great might in battle, and how these Christians shall conquer in the battle of Antioch and take our spoils and pursue us, gaining a great victory, and how I am doomed to sudden death this very year.' His mother answered sorrowfully, 'Beloved son, more than a hundred years ago it was discovered in our Koran, as well as in the books of the infidel, that the Christian people was destined to come upon us and to defeat us in every place, and that it should rule over the pagans, and that our people should be subject to these men wherever they are; but I do not know whether these things will come to pass now or in the future. Therefore I, wretched woman that I am, have followed you from Aleppo the fairest of cities, where by my observations and careful calculations I have looked into the stars of the sky, and studied the planets and the twelve signs of the Zodiac and all kinds of omens. In all of them I found prognostications that the Christian people is fated to defeat us utterly, and therefore I fear terribly for you, with bitter grief, for I may live to be bereft of you.'

Karbuqa said to her, 'Mother dearest, tell me the truth about certain things which my heart will not let me believe.' 'Willingly, beloved,' said she, 'if you will tell me what you do not understand.' He answered, 'Are not Bohemond and Tancred the gods of the Franks,

de inimicis suis? et quod *ipsi manducant in uno quoque
prandio duo milia uaccas et quatuor milia porcos?'
Respondit mater: 'Fili karissime, Boamundus et Tancredus mortales sunt sicut alii omnes, sed deus eorum
ualde diligit eos prae omnibus aliis, et uirtutem preliandi
dat eis prae ceteris. Nam deus illorum, est *Omnipotens
nomen eius, qui fecit caelum et terram et fundauit maria
et omnia quae in eis sunt[1]; cuius sedes in caelo parata in
aeternum, cuius potestas ubique est metuenda.' Ait
filius: 'Si ita est causa, cum eis preliari non desinam.'
Itaque audiens mater eius quod nullo modo adquiesceret
consiliis suis, maestissima recessit retrorsum in Aleph,
deferens secum cuncta spolia quae conducere potuit.

[xxiii] Tertia uero die armauit se Curbaram et
maxima pars Turcorum cum eo, ueneruntque ad ciuitatem ex illa parte in qua erat castrum.[2] Nos autem
putantes resistere posse illis, parauimus bellum contra
eos. Sed tam magna fuit uirtus illorum, quod nequiuimus illis resistere, sicque coacti intrauimus in ciuitatem, quibus fuit tam mirabiliter arta et angusta porta, ut
illic fuerint multi mortui oppressione aliorum. Interea
alii pugnabant extra urbem, alii intus in quinta feria[3]
per totum diem usque ad uesperam. Inter haec Willelmus de Grentamenilg,[c4] et Albricus frater eius, et Wido
Trursellus,[d5] et Lambertus Pauper,[6] isti omnes timore perterriti de hesterno bello quod durauerat usque ad uesperam, nocte latenter demissi sunt per murum, fugientes

---

[a] non DX
[b] DX *omit* est
[c] Grentemaisnil D, Grentemaisnelo X
[d] Trossellus D, Trussellus X (*which adds* et Wilhelmus de Archis)

[1] Exodus 20:11, quoted incorrectly
[2] On the south, at the highest point of the city walls
[3] 10 June 1098   [4] Grandmesnil near Lisieux
[5] Lord of Montlhéry near Paris   [6] Count of Clermont near Liège

and do they not deliver them from their enemies? And do they not eat two thousand cows and four thousand pigs at a single meal?' 'Beloved son,' said his mother, 'Bohemond and Tancred are mortal, like all other men, but their god loves them exceedingly beyond all others, and therefore he grants them excelling courage in battle. For their god—almighty is his name—is he who made the heaven and earth, the sea and all that in them is[1]; whose throne in heaven is prepared from all eternity, whose power is everywhere to be feared.' 'Be it so,' said her son, 'yet will I not turn aside from battle with them.' So when his mother heard that he would pay no heed to her counsels, she was exceedingly sad; but she went back to Aleppo taking with her everything on which she could lay her hands.

[xxiii] On the third day after his arrival at Antioch Karbuqa prepared for battle, and a great force of Turks came with him and approached the city from the side on which the citadel stood.[2] We, thinking that we could resist them, prepared to fight, but their power was such that we could not withstand them, so we were forced back into the city. The gate was so terribly strait and narrow that many of the people were trampled to death in the crowd. All through that day (which was Thursday),[3] until the evening, some of our men were fighting outside the walls and others within. While this was going on, William of Grandmesnil,[4] Aubré his brother, Guy Trousseau[5] and Lambert the Poor,[6] who were all scared by the battle of the previous day, which had lasted until evening, let themselves down from the wall secretly during the night and fled

pedibus contra mare, ita ut neque in manibus neque in
pedibus* remaneret aliquid nisi solummodo ossa. Multi-
que alii fugerunt cum illis, quos nescio.* Venientes
igitur ad naues qui erant ad Portum Sancti Symeonis,
dixerunt nautis: 'Quid hic miseri statis? Omnes nostri
mortui sunt, et nos mortem uix euasimus, quia exercitus
Turcorum undique obsident alios in urbe.' At illi
audientes talia, stabant stupefacti, ac timore perterriti
cucurrerunt ad naues et miserunt* se in mare. Deinde
superuenientes Turci quos inuenerunt occiderunt, et
naues quae in alueo fluminis remanserant, combusserunt
igni et apprehenderunt spolia eorum.

Nos denique qui remansimus nequiuimus sufferre
pondus armorum illorum, fecimusque murum inter nos
et illos, quem custodiebamus diu noctuque. Interea
tanta oppressione fuimus oppressi, ut equos et asinos
nostros manducaremus.

[xxiiii] Quodam uero die stantibus nostris maioribus
sursum ante castellum tristibus ac dolentibus, uenit
quidam sacerdos[1] ante eos et dixit: 'Seniores, si uobis
placet audite rem quamdam, quam in uisione uidi. Cum
nocte una iacerem in ecclesia Sanctae Mariae matris
Domini nostri Iesu Christi, apparuit mihi Saluator mundi
cum sua genitrice et beato Petro apostolorum principe;
stetitque ante me et dixit mihi: Agnoscis me? Cui
respondi: Non. His dictis, ecce apparuit integra crux
in capita eius.[2] Iterum ergo interrogauit me Dominus
dicens: Agnoscis me? Cui dixi: Te alio modo non

---

* DX *add* eorum
* ignoro DX
* D *omits all after* miserunt se, *as far as page* 71, non est Boa(mundi)

[1] His name was Stephen, and he had taken refuge in the church during
a Turkish attack 'wishing to have God as witness of his death' (Raymond
d'Agiles, *P.L.*, CLV, 612).
[2] Christ was generally depicted in eleventh-century carvings with a
nimbus surrounding a cross (e.g. on the Romsey rood and at Chichester).

on foot to the sea, so that both their hands and their feet were worn away to the bone. Many others, whose names I do not know, fled with them. When they reached the ships which were in St Simeon's Port they said to the sailors, 'You poor devils, why are you staying here? All our men are dead, and we have barely escaped death ourselves, for the Turkish army is besieging the others in the city.' When the sailors heard this they were horrified, and rushed in terror to their ships and put to sea. At that moment the Turks arrived and killed everyone whom they could catch. They burned those ships which were still in the mouth of the river and took their cargoes.

As for us who stayed in Antioch, we could not defend ourselves against the attacks from the citadel, so we built a wall between us and it, and patrolled it day and night. Meanwhile we were so short of food that we were eating our horses and asses.

[xxiiii] One day, when our leaders were standing in the upper city before the citadel, grieving and troubled, there came to them a certain priest,[1] and he said, 'Gentlemen, may it please you to listen to the account of a certain vision which I have seen. One night, as I lay prostrate in the church of St Mary the Mother of our Lord Jesus Christ, the Saviour of the world appeared to me with his Mother and St Peter, Prince of the Apostles, and he stood before me and said, "Knowest thou me?" "No," said I. When I had said this, behold, an unbroken cross appeared behind his head,[2] and the Lord asked me a second time, saying, "Knowest

agnosco, nisi quia crucem in capite tui*ᵃ* cerno sicut
Saluatoris nostri. Qui dixit: Ego sum. Statim cecidi
ad pedes eius, rogans humiliter ut subueniret nobis in
oppressione illa quae super nos erat. Respondit Dominus: Bene adiuui uos, et amodo adiuuabo. Ego permisi
uos habere Niceam ciuitatem, et omnia deuincere bella,
et conduxi uos huc usque, et condolui uestrae miseriae
quam passi fuistis in obsidione Antiochiae. Ecce in
auxilio oportuno, misi uos sanos et incolumes in ciuitatem, et ecce multam prauamque dilectionem operantes
cum Christianis et prauis paganis mulieribus, unde immensus foetor ascendit in caelum. Tunc alma Virgo et
beatus Petrus ceciderunt ad pedes eius, rogantes eum et
deprecantes, ut suum in hac tribulatione adiuuaret
populum. Dixitque beatus Petrus: Domine, per tot
tempora tenuit paganorum gens domum meam,[1] in qua
multa et ineffabilia mala fecerunt. Modo uero expulsis
inimicis inde, Domine, letantur angeli in caelis. Dixitque mihi Dominus: Vade ergo et dic populo meo, ut
reuertatur ad me, et ego reuertar ad illum, et infra
quinque dies mittam ei magnum adiutorium; et cotidie
decantet responsorium *Congregati sunt*,[2] totum cum uersu.
Seniores, si hoc non creditis esse uerum, sinite modo me
in hanc scandere turrim, mittamque me deorsum; si
uero fuero incolumis, credatis hoc esse uerum, sin autem
ullam lesionem fuero passus, decollate me, aut in ignem
proicite me.'

Tunc Podiensis episcopus iussit ut adferentur euan-
gelia et crux, quatinus iuraret ille si hoc esset uerum.

ᵃ tuo X

[1] The cathedral at Antioch was dedicated to St Peter.
[2] Psalm 47:5

THE DEEDS OF THE FRANKS

thou me?" I answered, "I should not know you,
except that I see about your head a cross like that of
our Saviour." He answered, "I am he." So I fell
down at his feet, humbly beseeching him to help us in
the trouble which had come upon us. The Lord
replied, "I have given you great help, and I will help
you hereafter. I granted you the city of Nicea, and
victory in all your battles, and I have led you hither
and suffered with you in all the troubles which you
have endured in the siege of Antioch. Behold, I gave
you timely help and put you safe and sound into the
city of Antioch, but you are satisfying your filthy lusts
both with Christians and with loose pagan women, so
that a great stench goes up to Heaven." Then the
gracious Virgin and blessed Peter fell at his feet, praying
and beseeching him to help his people in this trouble,
and blessed Peter said, "Lord, the pagans have held
my house[1] for so long, and have done many unspeakable
evil deeds therein. Now, O Lord, if thine enemies be
driven out, there will be rejoicing among the angels in
Heaven." And the Lord said to me, "Go and say to
my people that they shall return unto me, and I will
return unto them, and within five days I will send
them a mighty help. Let them sing each day the
response 'For lo, the kings were assembled',[2] together
with the doxology." Gentlemen, if you do not believe
this to be true, let me climb up this tower and throw
myself down from it; if I am unhurt, believe that I
speak the truth, but if I suffer any injury, then behead
me or throw me into the fire.'

Then the bishop of Le Puy gave orders that the
Gospels and a crucifix were to be brought, on which
the man could swear to the truth of his story; and all

Consiliati sunt omnes maiores nostri in illa hora, ut iurarent omnes sacramentum quod nullus illorum fugeret neque pro morte neque pro uita, quamdiu uiui essent. Primus dicitur iurasse Boamundus, deinde comes Sancti Egidii, et Rotbertus Nortmannus, ac dux Godefridus, et comes Flandrensis.[a] Tancredus uero iurauit ac promisit tali modo, quia quamdiu secum quadraginta milites haberet, non solum ex illo bello sed etiam ab Hierosolimitano itinere non esset recessurus. Nimis autem exsultauit Christiana congregatio, hoc audiens sacramentum.

[xxv] Erat autem ibi quidam peregrinus de nostro exercitu cui nomen Petrus,[1] cui antequam ciuitatem intraremus apparuit sanctus Andreas apostolus dicens: 'Quid agis, bone uir?' Cui ille respondit: 'Tu quis es?' Dixit ei apostolus: 'Ego sum Andreas apostolus. Agnoscas fili, quia dum uillam intraueris, uadens ad ecclesiam beati Petri ibi inuenies lanceam saluatoris nostri Iesu Christi, ex qua in crucis pendens patibulo uulneratus fuit.' Haec omnia dicens apostolus, continuo recessit.

Ipse autem timens reuelare consilium apostoli, noluit indicare nostris peregrinis. Estimabat autem se uisum uidere. Et dixit ad eum: 'Domine quis hoc crediderit?' In illa uero hora accepit eum sanctus Andreas, et portauit eum usque ad locum ubi lancea erat recondita in terra.

Iterum cum essemus ita ut superius diximus, uenit sanctus Andreas rursus dicens ei: 'Quare non abstulisti

---

[a] Egidii comesque nobilis Normannie Rotbertus et comes Flandrensis et dux Godefridus X

[1] Peter, called Bartholomew, was a poor pilgrim in the Provençal army. According to Raymond d'Agiles he had five visions of St Andrew, and revealed the exact spot where the Holy Lance had been buried. Raymond himself helped to dig out the relic (*P.L.*, CLV, 610-14). According to Fulcher

our leaders took counsel together at that hour that they should all swear an oath that none of them, while he lived, would flee, either from fear of death or from hope of life. It is said that Bohemond took the oath first, and after him the count of St Gilles, Robert the Norman, Duke Godfrey and the count of Flanders. But Tancred swore and vowed that so long as he had forty knights to follow him, he would not turn aside either from this battle or from the march to Jerusalem. When the Christians heard of this oath they were greatly encouraged.

[xxv] There was in our army there a certain pilgrim whose name was Peter.[1] Before we took the city of Antioch, St Andrew the Apostle appeared to him, saying, 'Friend, what doest thou?' He answered 'Who are you?' The Apostle answered him, 'I am Andrew the Apostle. Know, my son, that if thou goest to the church of blessed Peter, when thou enterest the city, thou wilt find there the lance with which our Saviour Jesus Christ was pierced when he was hanging on the cross.' Saying this, the Apostle disappeared.

Peter was afraid to reveal the words of the Apostle, so he would not tell our pilgrims, for he thought that he had seen an apparition, and he said to the saint, 'Lord, who will believe this?' In that same hour St Andrew took him and carried him to the place where the lance was hidden in the ground.

Later on, when we were in the straits which I have just described, St Andrew appeared again, saying to

---

of Chartres (who was not present at Antioch) he was a humbug (*P.L.*, CLV, 843-4) who died in 1099 as a direct result of an ordeal taken to prove that the lance was genuine. Whether an authentic relic or not, the lance revived the flagging spirits of the Frankish army.

lanceam de terra ut ego tibi precepi? Scias reuera, quia
quicunque hanc lanceam portauerit in bello, nunquam
ab hoste superabitur.' Petrus uero continuo reuelauit
mysterium apostoli hominibus nostris. Populus autem
non credebat, sed prohibebat dicens: 'Quomodo possumus hoc credere?' Omnino enim erant pauentes, et
protinus mori putabant. Accessit itaque ille,[1] et iurauit
hoc totum ueracissimum esse; quoniam ei sanctus Andreas bis in uisione apparuerat, eique dixerat: 'Surge,
uade, et dic populo Dei ne timeat, sed firmiter toto corde
credat in unum uerum Deum; eruntque ubique uicturi,
et infra quinque dies mandabit eis Dominus talem rem,
unde laeti et gauisi manebunt; et si certare uoluerint,
mox ut exierint unanimiter ad bellum, omnes inimici
eorum uincentur, et nemo stabit contra illos.' Audientes
itaque quod inimici eorum ab eis omnino essent uin-
cendi, protinus coeperunt sese uiuificare, et confortabant
se adinuicem dicentes: 'Expergiscimini, et estote ubique
fortes ac prudentes, quoniam in proximo erit nobis Deus
in adiutorium, et erit maximum refugium populo suo
quem respicit in merore manentem.'

[xxvi] Turci denique qui erant seorsum[a] in castello,
undique tam mirabiliter coangustabant nos, ut quadam
die incluserint tres milites ex nostris in turrim quae erat
ante castellum. Exierant namque gentiles et irruerant
super illos tam acriter, ut nequirent sufferre pondus
eorum. Duo ex militibus exierunt de turri uulnerati, et
tertius per totum diem uiriliter defendebat se de Tur-

[a] sursum X

[1] Presumably to the council of leaders. He had previously spoken of it
to the rank and file ('hominibus nostris'). Raymond d'Agiles says that he
had seen visions of St Andrew since December 1097, and had been unwilling
to reveal them.

Peter, 'Why hast thou not taken the lance from the earth, as I bade thee? Know of a truth that he who carries this lance in battle shall never be overcome by the enemy.' Then at once Peter revealed to our men the mystery told to him by the Apostle, but they did not believe him, and turned him away saying, 'How can we believe a thing like this?' for they were all terrified, thinking that they were at death's door. So Peter came[1] and swore that the whole story was quite true, since St Andrew had twice appeared to him in a vision, and had said to him, 'Arise, go and tell the people of God to have no fear, but to trust surely with their whole hearts in the One True God, and they shall be victorious everywhere, and within five days God will send them such a sign as shall fill them with joy and confidence, so that if they will fight, their enemies shall all be overcome as soon as they go out together to battle, and no-one shall stand against them.' When our men heard that their enemies were destined to be altogether defeated, their spirits revived at once, and they began to encourage one another, saying, 'Let us arise, and be strong and brave, for God will soon come to our help, and he will be a mighty refuge for his people, on whom he has looked in the time of their affliction.'

[xxvi] Meanwhile the Turks who were up in the citadel attacked us so fiercely at all points that on one day they trapped three of our knights in a tower which stood in front of the fortress, for the pagans had sallied out and made such a sharp attack that our forces could not bear the brunt of it. Two of the knights were wounded and came out from the tower, but the third defended himself manfully all day from the Turkish

corum inuasione, tam prudenter ut in ipsa die duos
Turcos strauerit super aditum muri caesis hastis. Nam
tres hastae detruncatae sunt illi illa die in manibus suis.
Illi uero acceperunt capitalem sententiam. Erat nomen
illi Hugo Insanus,¹ de exercitu Gosfredi² de Monte
Scabioso.ᵃ

Videns autem uir uenerabilisᵇ Boamundus quia
nullatenus posset conducere gentes sursum in castellum
ad bellum — nam qui erant inclusi in domibus timebant
alii fame alii timore Turcorum — iratus est ualde iussitque confestim mitti ignem per urbem, in illa parte in
qua erat Cassiani palatium. Quod uidentes illi qui erant
in ciuitate, dereliquerunt domos et omnia quae habebant
fugiebantque alii in castellum, alii ad portam comitis
Sancti Egidii,³ alii ad portam ducis Godefridi,⁴ unusquisque ad suam gentem. Tunc nimia tempestas uenti
subito surrexit, ita ut nemo posset se regere rectum.
Boamundus itaque uir sapiens contristatus est ualde,
timens pro ecclesia sancti Petri et sanctae Mariae aliisque
ecclesiis.ᶜ Haec ira durauit ab hora tertia usque in
mediam noctem, fueruntque crematae fere duo milia
ecclesiarum et domorum. Veniente autem media nocte,
statim omnis feritas ignis cecidit.

Itaque Turci habitantes in castello, intra urbem
bellabant nobiscum die noctuque, et nichil aliud dis-
separabat nos nisi arma. Videntes hoc nostri, quod non
possent diu haec pati, quoniam qui habebat panem non
licebat ei manducare, et qui habebat aquam non licebat

ᵃ Scaioso E
ᵇ X *omits* uenerabilis
ᶜ X *omits all this sentence in praise of Bohemond.*

¹ Or 'Mad Hugh'. However, there was a strong Viking strain in the
Normans, and it sounds as if Hugh had simply reverted to the ancient
Scandinavian tradition of blind fury in battle.

attack, and fought so bravely that he overthrew two Turks at the approach to the wall, breaking his own spears. On that day three spears were broken in his hands, but both the Turks were killed. He was called Hugh the Berserk,[1] and he belonged to the band of Godfrey[2] of Monte Scaglioso.

When the honoured Bohemond saw that he could by no means induce his followers to come up to the citadel to fight (for they stayed in the houses cowering, some for hunger and some for fear of the Turks) he was very angry, and gave immediate orders that the part of the city containing Yaghi Siyan's palace should be set on fire. When the men in the city saw this they left the houses and all their possessions and fled, some towards the citadel, some towards the gate held by the count of St Gilles,[3] others to that held by Duke Godfrey[4] —every man to his own people. At this moment a great storm of wind arose suddenly, so that no-one could direct his course aright. The valiant Bohemond was very anxious, fearing for the safety of St Peter's and St Mary's and the other churches. The danger lasted from the third hour until midnight, and nearly two thousand churches and houses were burnt, but at midnight all the violence of the fire suddenly died down.

In this way the Turks who held the citadel fought within the city against our men day and night, and it was only our arms which kept them off us. When our men saw that they could bear this no longer (for a man with food had no time to eat, and a man with

[2] Or Humphrey. See pp. 8, 21.
[3] The Bridge Gate, opposite the fortified mosque
[4] This gate lay to the east of the Bridge Gate.

bibere, fecerunt murum inter nos et ipsos petra et calce, et edificauerunt castellum et machinas, ut securi essent. Pars autem Turcorum remansit in castello agendo nobiscum bellum, alia uero pars hospitata erat prope castellum in una ualle.

Nocte quippe superueniente, ignis de caelo apparuit ab occidente ueniens, et appropinquans cecidit intra Turcorum exercitus. Vnde mirati sunt et nostri et Turci. Mane autem facto, tremefacti Turci fugerunt omnes pariter pro ignis timore, ante domini Boamundi portam, illicque hospitati sunt. Pars uero quae erat in castello, agebat bellum cum nostris die noctuque, sagittando, uulnerando, occidendo. Alia autem pars undique obsedit ciuitatem, ita ut nullus nostrorum ciuitatem auderet exire aut intrare, nisi nocte et occulte. Ita uero eramus obsessi et oppressi ab illis, quorum numerus fuit innumerabilis. Isti autem prophani et inimici Dei ita tenebant nos inclusos in urbe Antiochiae, ut multi mortui fuerint fame, quoniam paruus panis uendebatur uno bisantio. De uino non loquar. Equinas namque carnes aut asininas manducabant, et uendebant. Vendebant quoque gallinam quindecim solidis, ouum duobus solidis, unam nucem uno denario; omnia enim ualde erant cara.[1] Folia fici et uitis et cardui, omniumque arborum coquebant et manducabant, tantam famem immensam habebant. Alii coria caballorum et camelorum et asinorum atque boum seu bufalorum sicca decoquebant, et manducabant. Istas et multas anxietates ac angustias quas nominare nequeo passi sumus pro Christi nomine et Sancti Sepulchri uia deliberanda. Tales quoque tribu-

---

[1] Some idea of these prices may be gained from the fact that in England about 1136 the allowance for a man's daily ration of food in the king's household seems to have been three halfpence. ('Constitutio Domus Regis', ed. C. Johnson, *Dialogus de Scaccario* (Nelson's Medieval Texts, 1950), p. 133.)

water no time to drink) they built a wall of stones and mortar between the Turks and us, and set up a tower and catapults, so that they might be safe. One band of the Turks was holding the citadel, attacking us, and another was encamped in a valley near the citadel.

That very night there appeared a fire in the sky, coming from the west, and it approached and fell upon the Turkish army, to the great astonishment of our men and of the Turks also. In the morning the Turks, who were all scared by the fire, took to flight in a panic and went to my lord Bohemond's gate, where they encamped; but those who were in the citadel fought with our men day and night, shooting arrows and wounding or killing them. The rest of the Turks besieged the city on all sides, so that none of our men dared to go out or come in except by night and secretly. Thus we were besieged and afflicted by those pagans, whose number was beyond counting, These blasphemous enemies of God kept us so closely shut up in the city of Antioch that many of us died of hunger, for a small loaf cost a bezant, and I cannot tell you the price of wine. Our men ate the flesh of horses and asses, and sold it to one another; a hen cost fifteen shillings, an egg two, and a walnut a penny. All things were very dear.[1] So terrible was the famine that men boiled and ate the leaves of figs, vines, thistles and all kinds of trees. Others stewed the dried skins of horses, camels, asses, oxen or buffaloes, which they ate. These and many other troubles and anxieties, which I cannot describe, we suffered for the Name of Christ and to set free the road to the Holy Sepulchre; and we endured

lationes et fames ac timores passi sumus per uiginti sex dies.

[xxvii] Imprudens[a] itaque Stephanus Carnotensis comes quem omnes nostri maiores elegerant ut esset ductor nostrorum, maxima finxit se deprimi infirmitate priusquam Antiochia esset capta, turpiterque recessit in aliud castrum, quod uocatur Alexandreta. Nos itaque cotidie prestolabamur eum quatinus subueniret nobis in adiutorio qui eramus inclusi in urbe, salutifero carentes auxilio. At ille postquam audiuit gentem Turcorum circumcingentem et obsidentem nos, latenter ascendit super proximam montaneam quae stabat prope Antiochiam uiditque innumerabilia tentoria, uehementique captus timore recessit, fugitque festinanter[b] cum suo exercitu. Veniens autem in suum castrum, exspoliauit illud, et celeri cursu retro uertit iter. Postquam uero uenit obuiam imperatori ad Philomenam,[c][1] seorsum uocauit eum secreto dicens: 'Scias reuera quoniam capta est Antiochia, et castrum minime captum est; nostrique omnes graui oppressione obsessi sunt et, ut puto, a Turcis modo interfecti sunt. Reuertere ergo retro quam citius potes, ne et ipsi inueniant te et hanc gentem quam tecum ducis.'[d] Tunc imperator timore perterritus, clam uocauit Widonem fratrem Boamundi[2] et quosdem alios, et ait illis: 'Seniores, quid faciemus? Ecce omnes nostri districta obsessione impediti sunt, et forsitan in hac hora

---

[a] *Corrected to* impudens *in* E, *and so the Madrid MS*
[b] X *adds* ut formidolosus
[c] X *adds* qui cum suo exercitu in auxilium properabat Christianorum
[d] X *adds* Willelmus denique de Archis, dudum monachus egregius, tunc uero miles acerrimus, quem superius memorauimus se per murum cum aliis noctu latenter demisisse, quique se in fuga comiti Stephano sociauerat, affirmare cepit sub iureiurando dicens imperatori quia, si Antiochiam pergeret, quo ire festinabat, caput sine dubio amitteret; sic enim Boamundum iurasse cum sacramento firmabat. His auditis imperator *etc* (*omitting* tunc)

this misery, hunger and fear for six-and-twenty days.

[xxvii] Now it happened that, before Antioch was captured, that coward Stephen, count of Chartres, whom all our leaders had elected commander-in-chief, pretended to be very ill, and he went away shamefully to another castle which is called Alexandretta. When we were shut up in the city, lacking help to save us, we waited each day for him to bring us aid. But he, having heard that the Turks had surrounded and besieged us, went secretly up a neighbouring mountain which stood near Antioch, and when he saw more tents than he could count he returned in terror, and hastily retreated in flight with his army. When he reached his camp he took all his goods and retraced his steps as fast as he could. Afterwards, when he met the emperor at Philomelium,[1] he asked for a private interview and said, 'I tell you truly that Antioch has been taken, but that the citadel has not fallen, and our men are all closely besieged, and I expect that by this time they have been killed by the Turks. Go back, therefore, as fast as you can, in case they find you and the men who are following you.' Then the emperor was much afraid, and he called to a secret council Guy, Bohemond's brother,[2] and certain other men, and said to them, 'Gentlemen, what shall we do? All our allies are closely besieged, and perhaps at this very moment they

---

[1] Near Iconium (Konieh). The Emperor was preparing to relieve Antioch (*Alexiad*, xi, 6).

[2] Actually his half-brother, who had taken service with Alexius as a mercenary. Bréhier and Cahen both regard this story as an interpolation, written after 1105, in support of Bohemond. It is, however, written in the Author's characteristic style, and seems to be an imaginary scene such as that of Karbuqa's conversation with his mother. The rough outlines of the story probably reached the Crusaders during the period July-October 1098.

omnes a Turcorum manibus mortui sunt, aut in captiuitatem ducti, sicut iste infelix comes turpiter fugiens
narrat. Si uultis reuertamur retro celeri cursu, ne et nos
moriamur repentina morte quemadmodum et illi mortui
sunt.'

Cum Wido miles honestissimus talia audisset, cum
omnibus statim coepit plorare, atque uehementissimo
ululatu plangere; unaque uoce omnes dicebant: 'O
Deus uerus, trinus et unus, quamobrem haec fieri permisisti? Cur populum sequentem te in manibus inimicorum incidere permisisti et uiam tui itineris tuique
Sepulchri liberare uolentes tam cito dimisisti? Certe si
uerum est hoc uerbum quod ab istis nequissimis audiuimus, nos et alii Christiani derelinquemus te; nec te
amplius rememorabimur, et unus ex nobis non audebit
ulterius inuocare nomen tuum.' Et fuit hic sermo ualde
mestissimus in tota militia, ita ut nullus illorum siue
episcopus siue abbas, seu clericus seu laicus, auderet
inuocare Christi nomen per plures dies. Nemo namque
poterat consolari Widonem plorantem et ferientem se
manibus suosque frangentem digitos[1] et dicentem: 'Heu
mihi domine mi Boamunde honor et decus totius mundi,
quem omnis mundus timebat et amabat! Heu mihi
tristis! Non merui dolens tuam uidere honestissimam
speciem, qui nullam rem magis uidere desiderabam.
Quis mihi det ut ego moriar pro te, dulcissime amice et
domine? Cur ego ex utero matris meae exiens, non
statim mortuus fui? Cur ad hanc lugubrem diem per-
ueni? Cur non demersus fui in mare? Cur non ex
equo cecidi fracto collo, ut recepissem repentinum in-

---

[1] Entirely proper conduct for a knight who had lost his lord or his
friend. Tancred, on hearing a report of the death of his overlord (whom he
disliked) 'began to weep for great sorrow and grief, and so did all who were
present' (*P.L.*, CLV, 875).

have died or been led into captivity at the hands of
the Turks, according to the tale of this wretched count
who has fled in such a shameful way. If you agree, let
us retire quickly, lest we also suffer sudden death, even
as they have died.'

When Guy, who was a very honourable knight, had
heard these lies, he and all the others began to weep
and to make loud lamentation, and all of them said, 'O
true God, Three in One, why hast thou allowed this to
be? Why hast thou permitted the people who followed
thee to fall into the hands of thine enemies, and forsaken
so soon those who wished to free the road to thy Holy
Sepulchre? By our faith, if the word which we have
heard from these scoundrels is true, we and the other
Christians will forsake thee and remember thee no more,
nor will one of us henceforward be so bold as to call
upon thy Name.' This rumour seemed so grievous to
the whole army that none of them, bishop, abbot, clerk
or layman, dared to call upon the Name of Christ for
many days. Moreover no-one could comfort Guy, who
wept and beat his breast and wrung his hands,[1] crying,
'Woe's me, my lord Bohemond, honour and glory of
the whole world, whom all the world feared and loved!
Woe's me, sorrowful as I am! I have not even been
found worthy, to my grief, to see your most excellent
countenance, although there is nothing that I desire
more. Who will give me a chance to die for you, my
sweetest friend and lord? Why did I not die at once
when I came out of my mother's womb? Why have I
lived to see this accursed day? Why did I not drown in
the sea, or fall off my horse and break my neck so that

teritum? Vtinam tecum recepissem felix martyrium,
ut cernerem te gloriosissimum suscepisse finem!' Cumque omnes cucurrissent ad eum quatinus consolarentur
eum, ut iam finem daret planctui, in se reuersus ait:
'Forsitan creditis huic semicano imprudenti militi.
Vnquam uere non audiui loqui de militia aliqua, quam
idem fecisset. Sed turpiter et inhoneste recedit, sicut
nequissimus et infelix, et quicquid miser nuntiat, sciatis
falsum esse.'

Interea iussit imperator suis hominibus dicens: 'Ite
et conducite omnes homines istius terrae in Bulgariam,[1]
et explorate et deuastate uniuersa loca, ut cum uenerint
Turci, nichil possint hic reperire.' Voluissent noluissent
nostri reuersi sunt retrorsum, dolentes amarissime usque
ad mortem; fueruntque mortui multi ex peregrinis lan-
guentes nec ualentes fortiter militiam sequi; remanebant-
que morientes in uia. Omnes uero alii reuersi sunt
Constantinopolim.

[xxviii] Nos igitur auditis sermonibus illius qui nobis
Christi reuelationem retulit per uerba apostoli, statim
festinantes peruenimus ad locum in sancti Petri ecclesia,
quem ille demonstrauerat. Et foderunt ibi tredecim[a]
homines a mane usque ad uesperam, sicque homo ille
inuenit lanceam[2] sicut indicauerat. Et acceperunt illam
cum magno gaudio et timore, fuitque orta immensa
laetitia in tota urbe.[3] Ab illa hora accepimus inter nos
consilium belli. Porro statuerunt omnes maiores nostri

---

[a] duodecim X

[1] Used generally of those parts of the Empire which lay in Europe.
[2] Raymond of Agiles adds the detail that he himself kissed the point of
the lance while the haft was still embedded in the ground (*P.L.*, CLV, 614).
Fulcher of Chartres, however, suspects that the lance was 'planted' (invenit
lanceam fallaciter occultatam forsitan, *P.L.*, CLV, 843).
[3] Whatever the origin of the lance—and the more intelligent contemporary churchmen suspected it of being a false relic—it clearly had an

I might have died at once? O that I had been so lucky
as to suffer martyrdom with you, that I might behold
your glorious death!' And when everyone ran to
comfort him, so that he might cease from his lamentation, he controlled himself and said, 'Perhaps you
believe this cowardly old fool of a knight? I tell you
that I have never heard of any knightly deed which he
has done. He has retreated shamefully and indecently,
like a scoundrel and a wretch, and whatever the knave
says, you may be sure that it is a lie.'

Meanwhile the emperor issued orders to his army,
saying, 'Go and escort all the people of this country into
Bulgaria.¹ Seek out and destroy everything in the land,
so that when the Turks come they may find here nothing
at all.' So, willy-nilly, our friends retreated, grieving
very bitterly even to death, and many of the sick
pilgrims died because they had not the strength to
follow the army, so they lay down to die by the wayside.
All the others went back to Constantinople.

[xxviii] Now we, who heard the words of the man
who brought us the message of Christ through the
words of his Apostle, hurried at once to the place in
St Peter's church which he had described, and thirteen
men dug there from morning until evening. And so
that man found the lance,² as he had foretold, and they
all took it up with great joy and dread, and throughout
all the city there was boundless rejoicing.³ From that
hour we decided on a plan of attack, and all our leaders

---

immense effect in restoring the morale of the army. The crusaders who,
a few days earlier, had been skulking in the houses of Antioch until Bohemond had been forced to drive them out by fire, now sent an audacious
challenge to Karbuqa and followed it up by defeating him in battle.

concilium, quatinus nuntium mitterent ad inimicos
Christi Turcos, qui per aliquem interpretem interrogaret
eos securo eloquio dicens quamobrem superbissime in
Christianorum introissent terram, et cur castrametati
sint, et quare Christi seruos occidant et conquassent.
Cumque iam finis esset dictis, inuenerunt quosdam
uiros, Petrum scilicet Heremitam et Herluinum, illisque
dixerunt haec omnia: 'Ite ad execratum Turcorum
exercitum, et diligenter narrate eis haec omnia, inter-
rogantes eos, cur audacter et superbissime introierint
terram Christianorum et nostram.'

His dictis, recesserunt nuntii, ueneruntque ad pro-
phanum collegium, dicentes omnia missa uerba Curbaram et aliis, ita: 'Satis multumque mirantur nostri
maiores et seniores, quamobrem temere ac superbissime
in Christianorum introistis terram et illorum. Putamus
forsitan et credimus, quia ideo huc uenistis, quoniam
per omnia uultis effici Christiani; aut propterea igitur
huc uenistis,ᵃ ut per omnia Christianos afficiatis?
Rogant uos igitur omnes pariter nostri maiores, ut
uelociter recedatis a terra Dei et Christianorum, quam
beatus Petrus apostolus iam dudum predicando ad
Christi culturam conuertit. At illi permittunt adhuc
uobiscum deduci omnia uestra, scilicet equos et mulos,
et asinos et camelos; oues quoque et boues, et omnia
alia ornamenta permittunt uobiscum quocumque uol-
ueritis ferre.'

Tunc Curbaram princeps militiae Soldani Persidis,
cum omnibus aliis, pleni superbia feroci responderunt
sermone: 'Deum uestrum et uestram christianitatem nec

ᵃ E *and the Madrid MS omit* quoniam ... uenistis

forthwith held a council and arranged to send a messenger to Christ's enemies the Turks, so that he might
question them through an interpreter, asking confidently why they had been so vainglorious as to enter
into the Christians' land and encamp there, and why
they were killing and bullying the servants of Christ.
When they had ended their council they found certain
men, Peter the Hermit and Herluin, and said to them,
'Go to the accursed army of the Turks and give them
this whole message in full, asking them why they have
been so rash and vainglorious as to enter the land which
belongs to the Christians and to us.' When they had
received this message, our envoys went off and came to
that blasphemous company, where they delivered all
their message to Karbuqa and the others in these
words: 'Our leaders and commanders are shocked to
see that you have been so bold and vainglorious as to
enter this land, which belongs to the Christians and to
them. Perhaps (as we think and believe) you have
come hither with the full intention of being christened?
Or have you come to make yourselves a nuisance to the
Christians in any way you can? In any case our leaders,
as one man, require you to take yourselves off quickly
from the land which belongs to God and the Christians,
for the blessed Peter converted it long ago to the faith
of Christ by his preaching. But they give you per-
mission to take away all your goods, horses and mules,
asses and camels, and to take with you all your sheep
and oxen and other possessions whithersoever you may
choose.'

Then Karbuqa, commander-in-chief of the army of
the sultan of Persia, with all his counsellors, was filled
with pride, and he answered fiercely, 'We neither want

optamus nec uolumus, uosque cum illis omnino re-
spuimus. Huc usque iam uenimus eo, quod ualde
miramur quamobrem seniores ac maiores quos memo-
ratis, cur[a] terram quam abstulimus effeminatis gentibus
illi uocant esse suam. Vultis namque scire quid uobis
dicimus? Reuertimini ergo quantocius, et dicite uestris
senioribus, quia si per omnia cupiunt effici Turci,[1] et
deum uestrum quem uos inclini colitis abnegare uolunt
et leges uestras spernere, nos illis hanc et satis plus
dabimus de terra, et ciuitates et castella adhuc autem
quod nemo uestrorum remanebit pedes, sed erunt omnes
milites sicut et nos sumus; et habebimus semper eos in
summa amicitia. Sin autem, sciant se per omnia capitalem subire sententiam, aut deducti in uinculis Corfo-
zanam in captiuitate perpetua seruient nobis nostrisque
infantibus per sempiterna tempora.'

Nuntii uero nostri uelociter reuersi sunt retrorsum,
referentes omnia quae respondisset eis gens crudelissima.
Fertur Herluinus utramque scisse linguam, fuitque inter-
pres Petro Heremitae. Interea[2] exercitus noster in
utraque tremefactus parte, ignorabat quid faceret. Ex
una enim parte coangustabat eos cruciabilis fames, in
alia constringebat timor Turcorum.

[xxix] Tandem triduanis expletis ieiuniis, et pro-
cessionibus celebratis, ab una ecclesia in aliam, de
peccatis suis confessi sunt et absoluti, fideliterque corpori
et sanguini Christi communicauerunt, datisque elemo-

---

[a] X omits cur

[1] In the sense of becoming Muslims
[2] The chronology of the Author is vague at this point. The lance was
discovered on 14 June and the great battle of Antioch was fought on 28
June. Since Karbuqa's army was encamped outside the walls of Antioch
the embassy could hardly have taken more than one day. (For further dis-
cussions on this point, see Bréhier, *Histoire Anonyme*, pp. 147-51 and also

nor like your god and your Christendom, and we spit
upon you and upon them. We have come here because
we are scandalised to think that those leaders and
commanders whom you name should lay claim to the
land which we have conquered from an effeminate
people. Do you want to know our answer? Then go
back as fast as you can, and tell your leaders that if
they will all become Turks,[1] and renounce the god
whom you worship on bended knee, and cast off your
laws, we will give them this land and more besides,
with cities and castles, so that none of you shall remain
a foot-soldier, but you shall all be knights as we are:
and tell them that we will count them always among
our dearest friends. Otherwise, let them know that
they shall all be slain or led in chains to Khorasan,
where they shall serve us and our children for all time,
in everlasting captivity.'

Our messengers came back quickly and reported all
the things which this most cruel people had said to them.
(It is reported that Herluin knew both languages, and
that he acted as interpreter for Peter the Hermit.)
While all this was happening[2] our men did not know
what to do, for they were afraid, being caught between
two perils, the torments of hunger and the fear of the
Turks.

[xxix] At last, after three days spent in fasting and
in processions from one church to another, our men
confessed their sins and received absolution, and by
faith they received the Body and Blood of Christ in
communion, and they gave alms and arranged for

Grousset, 1, 102-03. Grousset's date of 27 June for this embassy to Karbuqa
seems too late, since the three days of fasting came after it, and Karbuqa
apparently was not expecting an attack on 28 June.)

sinis fecerunt celebrari missas. Deinde stabilitae sunt
sex acies ex eis, intra ciuitatem. In prima uero acie in
primo uidelicet capite fuit Hugo Magnus, cum Franci-
genis et Flandrensi comite.ᵃ In secunda dux Godefridus
cum suo exercitu. In tertia uero fuit Rotbertus Nortmannus cum suis militibus.ᵇ In quarta fuit Podiensis
episcopus, portans secum lanceam Saluatoris cum sua
gente, et cum exercitu Raimundi comitis Sancti Egidii;
qui remansit sursum custodire castellum pro timore
Turcorum, ne descenderent in ciuitatem. In quinta
acie fuit Tancredus, cum sua gente. In sexta fuit Boamundus, cum sua militia.¹ Episcopi nostri et presbyteri
et clerici ac monachi, sacris uestibus induti, nobiscum
exierunt cum crucibus, orantes et deprecantes Dominum,
ut nos saluos faceret et custodiret et ab omnibus malis
eriperet. Alii stabant super murum portae, tenentes
sacras cruces in manibus suis, signando et benedicendo
nos. Ita nos ordinati et signo crucis protecti, exiuimus
per portam quae est ante machomariam.

Postquam Curbaram uidit Francorum acies tam
pulchre ordinatas exire unam post aliam, dixit: 'Sinite
eos exire, ut melius eos habeamus in potestate nostra.'²
Postquam uero fuerunt foris de urbe, uiditque Curbaram
ingentem Francorum gentem, ualde timuit.³ Mox mandauit suo ammiralio qui omnia habebat in custodia, ut
si ille uideret ignem accensum in capite hostis, protinus

ᵃ et Flandrensis comes cum suis X
ᵇ fuit miles fortis Robertus comes Normannie cum suis electis militibus X

¹ Smail (*Crusading Warfare*, p. 173) accepts the statement of Raymond
d'Agiles that the Franks came out in four divisions. Since, however, Raymond was a notably unwarlike priest and the Anonymous a knight who
actually fought in the battle, I think the latter's statement carries more
weight.
² Fulcher of Chartres reports a story that Karbuqa was playing chess
when the Franks moved into position (*P.L.*, CLV, 845)

masses to be celebrated. Then six lines of battle were drawn up from those who were in the city. In the first line (the vanguard) were Hugh the Great, with the French troops, and the count of Flanders; in the second Duke Godfrey and his men; in the third Robert the Norman with his knights; in the fourth the bishop of Le Puy, bearing the lance of our Saviour, and he had with him both his own men and those of Raymond, count of St Gilles, who stayed behind on the hill to guard the citadel, for fear lest the Turks should come down into the city; in the fifth Tancred with his men; in the sixth Bohemond with his army.[1] Our bishops and priests and clerks and monks put on their holy vestments and came out with us, carrying crosses, praying and beseeching God to save us and keep us and rescue us from all evil, while others stood above the gate with holy crosses in their hands, making the Sign of the Cross and blessing us. So we closed our ranks, and protected by the Sign of the Cross we went out by the gate which is over against the mosque.

When Karbuqa saw the Frankish squadrons, so well drawn up, coming out one after the other, he said, 'Let them come, so that we may have them the more surely in our power.'[2] But after they were all outside the city, and he saw how great was the force of the Franks, he was much afraid,[3] so he told the amir who had charge of the host that if he saw a fire lighted in the vanguard he should immediately cause the whole

---

[3] As representative of the sultan, he seems to have been suspicious, not without reason, of the loyalty of Muslim forces drawn from Syria and Damascus (Grousset, I, 103-04)

preconari faceret, omnem exercitum redire, sciens Turcos amisisse bellum.

Continuo Curbaram coepit paulatim redire retro,
contra montaneam[1]; nostrique paulatim persequebantur
illos. Denique diuisi sunt Turci; una pars iuit contra
mare,[2] et alii steterunt illic, putantes nostros includere
inter se. Videntes hoc nostri, fecerunt similiter. Illic
fuit ordinata acies septena, ex acie ducis Godefridi et
comitis Nortmanniae, et caput illius fuit comes Rainaldus.[a][3] Hanc miserunt obuiam Turcis, qui ueniebant
a mari. Turci autem preliati sunt cum illis, et sagittando
multos occiderunt ex nostris. Aliae autem turmae
ordinatae sunt a flumine usque ad montaneam, quod
distat per duo miliaria. Coeperunt uero turmae ex
utraque parte exire, nostrosque undique circumcingere,
iaculando, sagittando, uulnerando.

Exibant quoque de montaneis innumerabiles exercitus, habentes equos albos, quorum uexilla omnia erant
alba. Videntes itaque nostri hunc exercitum, ignorabant
penitus quid hoc esset et qui essent; donec cognouerunt
esse adiutorium Christi, cuius ductores fuerunt sancti,
Georgius, Mercurius et Demetrius.[4] Hec uerba credenda
sunt, quia plures ex nostris uiderunt.

Turci autem qui stabant in parte maris uidentes
quod non possent sufferre amplius, miserunt ignem in
herbam, ut uidentes illi qui erant in tentoriis fugerent.

---

[a] illius extitit Reinaldus de Beluaco X

[1] North-west of the city
[2] South-west
[3] Called in the Escorial MS, and by the thirteenth-century reviser,
'Rainald of Beauvais'. William of Tyre describes him as 'a knight from
Toul'.
[4] All these were soldier saints, who might be expected to help a soldier
in his extremities. St George was particularly honoured as the patron saint
of knights, while St Mercurius and St Demetrius seem often, in the Greek

army to be summoned to retreat, for he would know that the Turks had lost the battle.

Without delay Karbuqa began to withdraw a little way towards the mountain,[1] and our men followed him. Then the Turkish army divided into two; one wing moved towards the sea[2] and the other stayed in position, for they hoped to surround our men. When our leaders saw this they did likewise, and improvised a seventh line from the forces of Duke Godfrey and the count of Normandy. Count Rainald[3] was put in command of this squadron, which they sent to face the Turks who were coming up from the direction of the sea. The Turks joined battle with them and killed many of our men with their arrows. Meanwhile other Turkish forces were drawn up between the river and the mountain, which is two miles away, and troops began to come out on each wing, surrounding our men, throwing darts, shooting arrows, and wounding them.

Then also appeared from the mountains a countless host of men on white horses, whose banners were all white. When our men saw this, they did not understand what was happening or who these men might be, until they realised that this was the succour sent by Christ, and that the leaders were St George, St Mercurius and St Demetrius.[4] (This is quite true, for many of our men saw it.)

Meanwhile the Turks who were on the wing stretching towards the sea, realising that they could no longer withstand us, set fire to the grass, so that their fellows who were in the camp might see it and flee. They

church, to have represented a Christianised version of Castor and Pollux. In all cases the legends are obscure.

At illi cognoscentes illud signum, arripuerunt omnia honorabilia spolia, et fugerunt. Nostri uero paulatim militabant ubi maxima uirtus eorum erat, scilicet ad tentoria illorum. Dux Godefridus, et Flandrensis comes, et Hugo Magnus, equitabant iuxta aquam, ubi uirtus illorum erat. Isti primitus signo crucis muniti, unanimiter inuaserunt illos. Videntes hoc aliae acies, simili modo inuaserunt illos. Exclamauerunt autem Persae et Turci. Nos[1] itaque, inuocantes Deum uiuum et uerum, equitauimus contra illos; et in nomine Iesu Christi et Sancti Sepulchri incepimus bellum, et Deo iuuante deuicimus eos.

Turci uero tremefacti arripuerunt fugam, nostrique illos persequebantur iuxta tentoria. Itaque milites Christi magis amabant persequi illos, quam ulla spolia quaerere. Et persecuti sunt eos usque ad pontem Farreum, ac deinde usque ad castellum Tancredi. Illi uero dimiserunt ibi papiliones suos, et aurum, et argentum, multaque ornamenta; oues quoque et boues, equos et mulos, camelos et asinos, frumentum et uinum, farinam et alia multa quae nobis erant necessaria.

Hermenii et Surani qui habitabant in illis partibus, audientes nos superasse Turcos, cucurrerunt ad montaneam obuiantes illis; et quantos comprehenderunt ex illis interfecerunt. Nos autem reuertentes ad ciuitatem cum magno gaudio, laudauimus et benediximus Deum, qui uictoriam dedit populo suo.

Ammiralius itaque qui castellum custodiebat, uidens Curbaram et omnes alios fugientes e campo ante Francorum exercitum, magis timuit. Statim uero cum

---

[1] The Author fought in Bohemond's division.

recognised the signal, seized all their valuables, and took to flight. Our men were gradually fighting their way forwards towards the main Turkish army at the camp. Duke Godfrey, the count of Flanders and Hugh the Great rode along the river bank, where the strongest Turkish force was stationed, and, defended by the Sign of the Cross, were the first to make a concerted attack upon the enemy. When our other troops saw this, they attacked likewise, and the Persians and Turks began to cry out. Then we[1] called upon the true and living God and rode against them, joining battle in the name of Jesus Christ and of the Holy Sepulchre, and by God's help we defeated them.

The Turks fled in terror and we pursued them right up to their camp, for the knights of Christ were more eager to chase them than to look for any plunder, and the pursuit continued as far as the Orontes bridge, and in the other direction as far as Tancred's castle. The enemy left his pavilions, with gold and silver and many furnishings, as well as sheep, oxen, horses, mules, camels and asses, corn, wine, flour and many other things of which we were badly in need.

The Armenians and Syrians who lived in those lands, hearing that we had overcome the Turks, rushed towards the mountain to cut off their retreat, and killed any of them whom they caught. We returned to the city with great rejoicing, praising and blessing God who had given victory to his people.

When the amir who was in charge of the citadel saw Karbuqa and all the others fleeing from the battlefield before the Frankish army, he was much afraid, and he

magna festinatione petebat Francorum uexilla.[1] Comes
igitur Sancti Egidii qui illic astabat ante castellum,
iussit ei portari suum uexillum. Ille autem accepit
illud, et diligenter misit in turrim. Statim dixerunt
Longobardi, qui illic stabant: 'Hoc uexillum non est
Boamundi.'[a] Interrogauit ille et dixit: 'Cuius est?'
Qui dixerunt: 'Sancti Egidii comitis.' Accessit ille, et
apprehenso uexillo reddidit comiti. Ipsa uero hora
uenit uir uenerabilis Boamundus, deditque illi suum
uexillum. Ille autem illud accepit cum magno gaudio;
et iniit pactum cum domino Boamundo, ut pagani qui
uellent Christianitatem recipere essent cum eo, et qui
uellent abire, sanos et absque ulla laesione abire permitteret. Consensit ille quicquid ei[b] ammiralius postu-
lauit, et continuo misit suos seruientes in castellum. Non
post multos dies baptizatus est ammiralius, cum illis qui
Christum recognoscere maluerunt. Illos uero qui suas
uoluerunt tenere leges, fecit dominus Boamundus conduci in Saracenorum terram.

Hoc bellum factum est in[c] IIII kalendas Iulii,
uigilia apostolorum Petri et Pauli; regnante domino
nostro Iesu Christo, cui est honor et gloria in sempiterna
secula. Amen.[2]

[*Explicit liber IX. Incipit liber X.*]

---

[a] *With this word* D *resumes*
[b] DX *omit* ei
[c] DX *omit* in

---

[1] As a sign that the citadel had surrendered and was no longer 'lawful
prize'. For a banner as a sign of protection, see below p. 92.
[2] The ninth book ends at this point.

came in a great hurry to ask for a Frankish banner.[1] The count of St Gilles, who was there keeping watch outside the citadel, ordered his own banner to be delivered to the amir, who took it and was careful to display it upon his tower. Some men from southern Italy, who were standing by, said at once, 'This is not Bohemond's banner.' The amir questioned them, saying, 'Whose is it?' and they replied, 'It belongs to the count of St Gilles.' The amir came and took the banner and gave it back to the count, and just then the noble Bohemond came up and gave him his own banner, which he accepted with great joy. He made an agreement with my lord Bohemond that those pagans who wished to be christened might join his band, and that he would allow those who wished to depart to go away safe and uninjured. Bohemond agreed to the amir's terms and put his followers into the citadel at once. Not many days afterwards the amir was christened, with those who preferred to accept Christ, and my lord Bohemond caused those who wished to adhere to their own laws to be escorted into the land of the Saracens.

This battle was fought on 28 June, the vigil of the Apostles Peter and Paul, in the reign of our Lord Jesus Christ, to whom be honour and glory for ever and ever. Amen.[2]

Here ends the ninth book, and the tenth book begins.

X

[xxx] Et[a] cum iam essent omnes inimici nostri (Deo trino et uno summoque dignas referimus grates) per omnia deuicti huc illucque fugientes, alii semiuiui, alii uulnerati, in uallibus et in nemoribus et in aruis et in uiis deficiebant mortui. Populus uero Christi uictores scilicet peregrini, reuersi sunt gaudentes felici triumpho deuictis hostibus in ciuitatem. Statim omnes nostri seniores, uidelicet dux Godefridus, comes Sancti Egidii Raimundus, Boamundus, et comes Nortmanniae,[b] comesque Flandrensis, et alii omnes miserunt nobilissimum militem Hugonem Magnum imperatori Constantinopolim, ut ad recipiendam ciuitatem ueniret, et conuentiones quas erga illos habebat expleret. Iuit, nec postea rediit.

Postquam uero haec omnia facta[c] sunt, congregati omnes[d] nostri maiores ordinauerunt concilium, quemadmodum hunc feliciter ualerent conducere et regere populum, donec peragerent iter Sancti Sepulchri, pro quo hucusque multa erant passi pericula. Inuentum est in concilio, quia nondum auderent intrare in paganorum terram, eo quod ualde in aestiuo tempore est arida et inaquosa; ideoque acceperunt terminum attendendum ad kalendas Nouembris. Denique diuisi sunt seniores, et unusquisque profectus est in terram suam, donec esset prope[e] terminus eundi. Feceruntque principes preconari per urbem uniuersam, ut si forte aliquis egens illic adesset et auro argentoque careret, conuen-

---

[a] DX *omit* et   [b] DX *add* dominus Rotbertus
[c] gesta DX   [d] DX *omit* omnes
[e] DX *omit* prope

X

[xxx] When all our enemies had been resoundingly defeated (high praise be to God Almighty, the Three in One) they fled hither and thither, some of them half dead, others wounded, and they fell down and died in the valleys and woods and fields and by the roadside. Christ's people, the conquering pilgrims, went back into the city after their enemies had been defeated, exulting in their joyful triumph. Without delay all our leaders, Duke Godfrey, Raymond, count of St Gilles, Bohemond, the count of Normandy and the count of Flanders, and all the others, sent the high-born knight Hugh the Great to the emperor at Constantinople, asking him to come and take over the city and fulfil the obligations which he had undertaken towards them. Hugh went, but he never came back.

After all these things were done, all our leaders assembled and held a council to decide how best to guide and lead the people until they should complete their journey to the Holy Sepulchre, for which they had already suffered so many perils. In this council they decided that they dared not yet enter into the land of the pagans, because in summer it is very dry and waterless, and that they would therefore wait until the beginning of November. So our leaders separated and each went off into his own territory until it should be time to resume the march. They had it announced throughout the city that if there were any poor man,

tione facta cum illis remanere[a] si uellet, ab eis cum gaudio retentus esset.

Erat autem ibi quidam miles de exercitu comitis Sancti Egidii, cui nomen Raimundus Piletus.[1] Hic plurimos retinuit homines, milites ac pedites. Egressus est ille cum collecto exercitu ut uiriliter introiit in Saracenorum terram, et profectus est ultra duas ciuitates et peruenit ad quoddam castrum cui nomen Talamania. Habitatores castri, scilicet Suriani, confestim sua sponte se tradiderunt ei. Cumque omnes essent ibi fere per octo dies, nuntii uenerunt ad eum dicentes quoniam hic prope nos est castrum Saracenorum multitudine plenum. Ad hoc castrum ilico ierunt Christi milites peregrini, et undique inuaserunt illud,[b] quod continuo ab illis captum est Christi adiutorio. Apprehenderunt igitur omnes illius loci colonos, et qui christianitatem recipere noluerunt, occiderunt; qui uero Christum recognoscere maluerunt,[c] uiuos conseruauerunt. Reuersi sunt itaque hoc peracto nostri Franci cum magno gaudio ad prius castrum. Tertia uero die exierunt et uenerunt ad quamdam urbem cui nomen Marra,[2] quae illic erat prope illos. Erant autem ibi multi Turci congregati, et Saraceni ab Aleph ciuitate, et ab omnibus urbibus et castris quae circa illam sunt. Exierunt ergo barbari contra illos ad bellum, nostrique aestimantes luctari cum illis preliando, coegerunt eos in fugam; et tamen reuersi per totum diem inuadebant nostros adinuicem, et usque ad uesperam perdurauit illa inuasio. Aestus namque erat immensus. Nequibant iam nostri sufferre tantam sitim, quoniam nullatenus ibi ad bibendum inuenire aquam

---

[a] DX *omit* remanere
[b] DX *omit* illud
[c] uoluerunt DX

[1] From Limousin. The text suggests that the Author accompanied him

lacking gold and silver, who wished to take service with them and stay on, they would gladly enrol him.

There was in the army of the count of St Gilles a certain knight whose name was Raymond Pilet.[1] He took into his service many knights and foot-soldiers, and set out boldly, with the army which he had collected, into the land of the Saracens. He passed by two cities and came to a castle named Tell-Mannas. The occupants of this castle, who were Syrians, surrendered it to him at once, and when his men had all been there for eight days messengers came to him, saying, 'There is a castle full of Saracens near at hand.' The knights and pilgrims of Christ went straight to that castle and besieged it on all sides, and by Christ's help they took it at once. They captured all the peasants of the district and killed those who would not be christened, but those who preferred to acknowledge Christ they spared. When this was done, our Franks came back with great joy to the first castle. On the third day they set out and came to a city named Marra[2] which was not far off, in which were assembled many Turks and Saracens from the city of Aleppo and from all the cities and castles round about. The barbarians came out to fight with our men who, resolving to do battle with them, put them to flight, yet the enemy rallied and went on attacking our men all through the day, and their onslaught lasted until the evening. The heat was unspeakable, and our men could not endure such fearful thirst, for they could find no water to

---

on this expedition, which must have been his first experience of service under a man of Count Raymond's army. He did not, however, attach himself to Raymond Piletus during the march south or the siege of Jerusalem.

[2] Ma'arat, on the road from Hamah to Aleppo

poterant; uoluerunt tamen ad illorum castrum secure
redire. Pro illorum enim peccatis Suriani et minuta
gens nimio pauore correpti, mox coeperunt uiam carpere
retrorsum. Vt autem Turci uiderunt illos retrocedentes,
statim coeperunt illos persequi, et uictoria illis ministra-
bat uires. Multi namque ex ipsis reddiderunt animas
Deo, cuius amore illic congregati fuerant. Haec occisio
facta est quinto die in mense Iulio. Reuersi sunt autem
Franci illi qui remanserant in suum castrum; et fuit ibi
Raimundus cum sua gente per plures dies.

Alii uero qui in Antiochia remanserant steterunt in
ea cum gaudio et laetitia magna, quorum rector et pastor
extitit Podiensis episcopus. Qui nutu Dei graui aegri-
tudine captus est; et ut Dei uoluntas fuit migrauit ab hoc
saeculo, et in pace requiescens obdormiuit in Domino,
in solempnitate scilicet sancti Petri quae dicitur Ad
Vincula.[1] Vnde magna angustia et tribulatio immensus-
que dolor fuit in tota Christi militia, quia ille erat sus-
tentamentum pauperum, consilium diuitum, ipseque
ordinabat clericos, predicabat et summonebat milites,
dicens quia: 'Nemo ex uobis saluari potest nisi honóri-
ficet pauperes et reficiat, uosque non potestis saluari
sine illis, ipsique uiuere nequeunt[a] sine uobis. Oportet
igitur ut ipsi cotidiana supplicatione pro uestris orent
delictis Deum, quem in multis cotidie offenditis. Vnde
uos rogo ut pro Dei amore eos diligatis, et in quantum
potestis eos sustentetis.'

[xxxi] Non post multum uero temporis uenit uir
uenerabilis Raimundus comes de Sancto Egidio, et
intrauit in Saracenorum terram, et peruenit ad quamdam urbem quae uocatur Albara, quam inuasit una

---

drink, so they wanted to get back safely to their castle. The Syrians and poor pilgrims, for their sins, got into a blind panic and began to retreat in a hurry. When the Turks saw them drawing back, they began to pursue them, and victory increased their strength, so that many of our people gave up their souls to God, for love of whom they had come thither. This massacre took place on 5 July. The surviving Franks withdrew into the castle, and Raymond with his men stayed there for several days.

The other crusaders, who remained in Antioch, stayed there with joy and great gladness, having the bishop of Le Puy as their ruler and shepherd. But, as God would have it, he fell very sick, and by God's will he departed from this world, and resting in peace he fell asleep in the Lord on the feast of St Peter's Chains.[1] Therefore there was grief and sorrow and great mourning throughout the whole army of Christ, for the bishop was a helper of the poor and a counsellor of the rich, and he used to keep the clergy in order and preach to the knights, warning them and saying, 'None of you can be saved if he does not respect the poor and succour them; you cannot be saved without them, and they cannot survive without you. They ought every day to pray that God will show mercy towards your sins, by which you daily offend him in many ways, and therefore I beseech you, for the love of God, to be kind to them, and to help them as much as you can.'

[xxxi] Not long afterwards the noble Raymond, count of St Gilles, came and entered into the land of the Saracens and reached a city called al-Bara, which

---

[1] 1 August 1098

cum suo exercitu, eamque continuo cepit; et occidit
omnes Saracenos et Saracenas, maiores et minores, quos
ibi repperit. Quam postquam suo continuit imperio,
ad Christi reuocauit fidem; quaesiuitque consilium a
suis sapientissimis uiris, ut episcopum in hac urbe
deuotissime preordinari faceret, qui illam ad Christi
cultum*a* fideliter reuocaret, et de domo diabolica[1]
templum Deo uiuo et uero et oracula sanctorum con-
secraret. Nouissime elegerunt quemdam honorabilem
ac sapientissimum[2] uirum et duxere illum in Antiochiam
ad consecrandum. Factumque est ita. Alii autem qui
in Antiochia remanserant, fuerunt ibidem cum gaudio
et laetitia.

Appropinquante uero termino uidelicet festo Omnium Sanctorum, regressi sunt omnes maiores nostri in
unum, in Antiochiam, omnesque simul coeperunt quaerere qualiter Sancti Sepulchri iter ualerent peragere,
dicentes, quoniam appropinquauerat eundi terminus,
nulla erat hora conturbandum*b* amplius. Boamundus
autem quaerebat cotidie conuentionem quam omnes
seniores olim habuerant ei in reddendam ciuitatem; sed
comes Sancti Egidii ad nullam conuentionem uolebat se
emollire erga Boamundum, eo quod timebat se peierare
erga imperatorem. Tamen sepe fuerunt congregati in
ecclesia sancti Petri, ad faciendum quod iustum erat.
Boamundus recitauit suam conuentionem, suumque
ostendit compotum. Comes Sancti Egidii similiter sua
patefecit uerba, et iusiurandum quod fecerat imperatori,
per consilium Boamundi. Episcopi, et dux Godefridus,

---

a ad fidem Christi cultumque DX
b conturbandi D; X *writes* quoniam eundi terminus appropinquauit,
nulla mora est differendum amplius

[1] The mosque
[2] Peter of Narbonne

he attacked with his army and captured at once. He
killed all the Saracens whom he found in it, both men
and women, great and small, and after he had established his power there he restored the town to the
Christian faith, and took counsel with his most trustworthy advisers as to how he might, with due devotion,
have a bishop set up in the city, to recall it to the
worship of Christ, and to consecrate the house of the
devil[1] to be a temple of the true and living God, and a
church dedicated to his saints. Eventually they chose
an honourable and learned man[2] and took him to
Antioch to be consecrated, and this was done. The
rest of the army, which was in Antioch, stayed there
with joy and gladness.

When the appointed day (the feast of All Saints)
approached, all our leaders returned together to
Antioch and began to discuss how they should continue
their journey to the Holy Sepulchre, for, said they,
'The appointed day is at hand, and it is no time for
any further quarrels', for Bohemond had been asking
every day for the recognition of the agreement by
which all the leaders had formerly promised to give
him the city, but the count of St Gilles would make no
agreement and did not want to give way to Bohemond,
because he was afraid of breaking his oath to the
emperor. Many meetings were held in the church of
St Peter in order to come to a just conclusion. Bohemond recited his agreement and showed a list of his
expenses, and likewise the count of St Gilles repeated
the words and the oath which he had sworn to the
emperor on Bohemond's advice. The bishops, with

Flandrensisque comes, et comes de Nortmannia, aliique
seniores diuisi sunt ab aliis, et intrauerunt ubi est
cathedra sancti Petri, ut ibi iudicium inter utrumque
discernerent. Postea uero timentes ne Sancti Sepulchri
uia proturbaretur,ᵃ noluerunt aperte dicere iudicium.
Ait denique comes Sancti Egidii: 'Priusquam uia Sancti
Sepulchri remaneat, si Boamundus nobiscum uenire
uoluerit, quicquid nostri pares uidelicet dux Godefridus
et Flandrensis comes et Rotbertus Nortmannus, aliique
seniores laudauerint, ego fideliter consentiam, salua
fidelitate imperatoris.'¹ Hoc totum laudauit Boamundus, et promiserunt ambo in manibus episcoporum,
quod nullo modo per se uia Sancti Sepulchri deturbaretur.
Tunc accepit Boamundus consilium cum suis hominibus,
quomodo muniret castrum de alta montanea, hominibus
et uictu. Similiter comes Sancti Egidii accepit consilium cum suis, quomodo muniret palatium Cassiani
ammiralii, et turrim quae est super portam pontis qui
est ex parte portus sancti Symeonis, muniret inquam
hominibus et uictu qui non deficeret longo tempore.

[xxxii] *Status Urbis*.² Haec urbs Antiochia scilicet
ualde est pulchra et honorabilis, quia infra muros eius
sunt quatuor montaneae maximae et nimis altae. In
altiori quoque est castellum aedificatum mirabile, et
nimis forte. De deorsum est ciuitas honorabilis et conueniens, omnibusque ornata honoribus, quoniam multae

---

ᵃ perturbaretur DX

¹ It seems to have been about this time that the Author transferred his
allegiance from Bohemond to Raymond of Toulouse

² Bréhier relegates this description to an appendix. It does, however,
appear in the MSS at this point and its style is in no way inconsistent with
that of the Author. The capital 'H' of 'Hec' is omitted, presumably because the scribe meant to illuminate it. The first line of the Description is
written in *Capitalis Rustica*.

Duke Godfrey, the counts of Flanders and Normandy
and the other leaders, went apart from the rest, and
entered that part of the church where stands St Peter's
chair, so that they might give judgement between the
two parties; but afterwards, fearing lest the journey to
the Holy Sepulchre might be interrupted, they would
not give a clear judgement. Then said the count of
St Gilles, 'Rather than abandon the journey to the
Holy Sepulchre, and provided that Bohemond will
come with us, I will faithfully promise to do whatever
is approved by our peers, Duke Godfrey and the count
of Flanders and Robert the Norman and the other
leaders, saving the faith which I owe to the emperor.[1]
Bohemond agreed to all this, and the two of them
promised, putting their hands into those of the bishops,
that the journey to the Holy Sepulchre should in no
wise be interrupted by them. Then Bohemond took
counsel with his men as to how he could garrison and
victual the citadel on top of the mountain. Likewise
the count of St Gilles took counsel with his men as to
how he could garrison and victual the palace of Yaghi
Siyan the amir, and the tower which is over the Bridge
Gate (which lies on the side of the city nearest to St
Simeon's Port), so that it could hold out for a long time.

[xxxii] *Description of the city of Antioch.*[2] The city of
Antioch is a very fine and distinguished place. Within
its walls are four great mountains which are exceedingly
high. The citadel, a wonderful building which is
exceedingly strong, stands on the highest of them.
Down below lies the city, which is impressive and well-
planned, adorned with all kinds of splendid buildings,

ecclesiae sunt in ea aedificatae. Tercenta et sexaginta
monasteria in se continet. Sub suo iugo continet
patriarcha centum quinquaginta tres episcopos.[1]

Clauditur ciuitas duobus muris. Maior quoque
ualde est altus et mirabiliter latus, magnisque lapidibus
compositus; in quo sunt ordinatae quater centum et
quinquaginta turres; modisque omnibus est ciuitas for-
mosa. Ab oriente, clauditur quatuor magnis montaneis.
Ab occidente, secus muros urbis fluit quoddam flumen,
cui nomen Farfar. Quae ciuitas magnae auctoritatis
est. Nam eam prius septuaginta quinque reges con-
stituerunt, quorum fuit caput Antiochus rex, a quo
dicitur Antiochia.[2] Istam ciuitatem tenuerunt Franci
obsessam, per octo menses et unum diem. Postea
fuerunt intus inclusi per tres ebdomadas a Turcis et ab
aliis paganis quorum numero nunquam fuit maior congregatio hominum, uel Christianorum uel paganorum.
Tamen adiutorio Dei et Sancti Sepulchri deuictis illis
a Christianis Dei, requieuimus[3] cum gaudio et letitia
magna in Antiochia, per quinque menses et octo dies.

[xxxiii] Quibus expletis, mense Nouembrio discessit
Raimundus comes Sancti Egidii cum suo exercitu ab
Antiochia, uenitque per unam ciuitatem, quae uocatur
Rugia, et per aliam quae dicitur Albaria. Quarto uero
die exeunte Nouembrio peruenit ad Marram ciuitatem,
in qua maxima multitudo Saracenorum et Turcorum et
Arabum aliorumque paganorum est congregata, ipseque
comes in crastinum[a] inuasit eam. Non post multum

---

[a] crastino DX

[1] Bréhier takes this to be the number of bishoprics dependent upon the
metropolitan see in the latter half of the sixth century, but I personally
think that the Author was simply trying to say 'a very large number' (see
John 21:11).
[2] The Author knew Antioch well but had no map of it. Hence his

for there are many churches, and three hundred and
sixty monasteries. Its patriarch is metropolitan over a
hundred and fifty-three bishops.[1]

This city is surrounded by two walls, the greater of
which is very high and amazingly broad, built of great
stones, and there are set upon it four hundred and fifty
towers. Everything about this city is beautiful. On
the east it is shut in by four great mountains, on the
west, beside the city walls, runs a river called the
Orontes. This city is the centre of great authority, for
it was formerly established by seventy-five kings, of
whom the chief was King Antiochus, from whom it gets
its name of Antioch.[2] The Franks besieged this city
for eight months and a day, and thereafter they themselves were besieged for three weeks by the Turks and
other pagans, in greater number than have ever before
been gathered together, whether of Christian men or
pagans. Finally, by the help of God and the Holy
Sepulchre, they were defeated by the Christians, and
we[3] rested in Antioch, with joy and gladness, for five
months and eight days.

[xxxiii] When this time came to an end, Raymond
count of St Gilles set out from Antioch with his army
in the month of November, and came to a city called
Riha and thence to one called al-Bara. On 28 November he reached the city of Marra, in which was assembled
a great number of Saracens, Turks, Arabs and other
pagans, and the count attacked it next day. Bohemond

---

mistakes. The mountains lie to the south-east and the river to the north-
west. The seventy-five kings are apocryphal, but the city did become the
capital of the Seleucid ruler Antiochus Soter in or about 280 B.C. St Paul
preached there (Acts 11:26) and the city became the seat of one of the five
patriarchs.
    [3] This appears to be personal testimony to the authorship of the passage.

uero temporis Boamundus cum suo exercitu secutus est
comites, et applicitus est cum eis in die dominica.
Secunda uero feria nimis fortiter inuaserunt undique
ciuitatem, et tam acriter tamque fortiter, ut scalae
starent erectae ad murum. Sed tam maxima uirtus
paganorum erat, quod illa die nichil eos offendere aut
nocere potuerunt. Videntes autem seniores quia nichil
agere poterant, et frustra laborabant, facit Raimundus
comes de Sancto Egidio fieri quoddam ligneum castrum
forte et altum. Quod castrum ingeniatum et aedificatum
erat super quatuor rotas; super quod stabant plures
milites, et Eurardus Venator tubam fortiter sonans.
Subter uero erant armati milites, qui deduxerunt castrum usque prope urbis murum iuxta turrim quamdam.
Quod uidens gens pagana, statim fecerunt instrumentum
quo iactabant maximos lapides super castrum, ita ut
pene nostros milites occiderent. Iaciebant quoque grecos ignes super castrum, putantes illud ardere et de-
uastari.ª Sed Deus omnipotens noluit ut castrum arderet
hac uice. Supereminebat uero omnes muros ciuitatis.
Milites igitur nostri qui erant in superiori solario, uidelicet Willelmus de Monte Pislerio et alii multi, iactabant
immensos lapides super illos qui stabant in muro urbis,
et ita percutiebant eos super clipeos, ut clipeus et inimicus caderent deorsum in ciuitatem in mortem. Ita
faciebant isti, alii uero tenebant in hastis honorabilia
signa,[1] et cum lanceis et hamis ferreis putabant eos
trahere ad se, et sic preliati sunt usque ad uesperam.
Retro castrum stabant presbyteri, clerici, sacris uestibus
induti, orantes et obsecrantes Deum ut suum defenderet

ª deuastare DX

[1] I do not understand the significance of these spears.

and his army followed the other counts soon afterwards, and joined forces with them on a Sunday. On the Monday they attacked the town very bravely from all sides, and pressed on with such eagerness and courage that scaling-ladders were set up against the wall, but such was the power of the pagans that on that day it was not possible to come to grips with them or to do them any harm. When our leaders saw that they could do nothing, and that they were labouring in vain, Raymond count of St Gilles caused a wooden siege-tower to be built, and it was strong and lofty, so engineered and constructed that it ran upon four wheels. On the top storey stood many knights and Everard the Huntsman, who blew loud blasts on his horn, and underneath were armed knights who pushed the tower up to the city wall, over against one of its towers. When the pagans saw this they immediately made an engine by which they threw great stones upon our siege-tower, so that they nearly killed our knights. Moreover they threw Greek fire upon the siege-tower, hoping to burn and destroy it, but this time Almighty God would not let the siege-tower burn, and it was higher than all the walls of the city. Our knights who were on its upper storey (William of Montpellier and many others) threw great stones down upon those who stood on the city wall, and struck them upon their shields; so that shield and man fell backward into the city, and the man was killed. While they were doing this others held in their hands spears adorned with pennants,[1] and tried to pull the enemy towards them with lances and hooks of iron. Thus they fought until the evening. Behind the siege-tower stood the priests and clerks, clad in their holy vestments, praying and beseeching God

populum, et Christianitatem exaltaret, ac paganismum deponeret.[1]

In alia uero parte certabant nostri milites cotidie cum illis, erigentes scalas ad murum urbis, sed uirtus paganorum erat tanta, ut nichil proficere nostri possent. Tamen Gulferius de Daturre[2] primus ascendit per scalam in murum, sed statim fuit fracta scala pro[a] multitudine aliorum; tamen ascendit ipse cum aliquantis supra murum. Illi autem qui ascenderant, expediebant circa illos murum. Alii quoque inuenerunt aliam scalam, erexeruntque eam festinanter ad murum, et ascenderunt per eam multi milites et pedites, statimque ascenderunt super murum. Saraceni igitur tam robuste inuaserunt illos per murum et per terram, sagittando et spiculando comminus cum suis lanceis; ut multi ex nostris timore[b] perterriti demitterent se per[c] murum. Tamdiu uero illi prudentissimi uiri qui remanserant in muro sufferebant illorum persecutionem, quamdiu alii qui subter castrum erant foderunt murum urbis. Videntes uero Saraceni quod nostri fodissent murum, statim timore perterriti inierunt fugam in ciuitatem. Hoc totum factum est in die sabbati ad horam uesperi occidente sole, undecima die intrante Decembri.

Boamundus igitur fecit per interpretem loqui Saracenis maioribus, ut ipsi cum suis mulieribus et infantibus aliisque substantiis mitterent se in unum palatium quod est supra portam, ipseque defenderet eos de mortali sententia. Intrauerunt uero omnes nostri in ciuitatem, et quicquid boni inuenerunt in domibus et in foueis, hoc unusquisque ad suum continebat proprium. Facto

---

[a] pre DX
[b] DX *omit* timore
[c] se per] super DX

to defend his people, and to exalt Christendom and cast down idolatry.[1]

On the other side of the city our knights were fighting every day with the enemy, putting up scaling-ladders against the city wall, but the might of the pagans was such that they could gain no advantage. At last Geoffrey of Lastours[2] was the first to get up the ladder on to the wall; the ladder broke at once under the weight of the crowd who followed him, but nevertheless he and some others succeeded in reaching the top of the wall. Those who had gone up cleared a space around them on the wall. Others found a fresh ladder and put it up quickly, and many knights and foot-soldiers went up it at once, but the Saracens attacked them so fiercely, from the wall and from the ground, shooting arrows and fighting hand-to-hand with spears, that many of our men were terrified and jumped off the wall. While those very gallant men who stayed on the wall were resisting the enemy attack, others, protected by the siege-tower, were undermining the defences of the city. When the Saracens saw that our men had undermined the wall they were panic-stricken and fled into the city. (This all happened on a Saturday, at the hour of vespers, when the sun was setting. It was 11 December.)

Then Bohemond sent an interpreter to the Saracen leaders to tell them that if they, with their wives and children and goods, would take refuge in a palace which lies above the gate he would save them from death. Our men all entered the city, and each seized his own share of whatever goods he found in houses or

---

[1] The Muslims were not, of course, idolaters, but the author thought that they were. This seems, therefore, a fair translation.
[2] Lord of Lastours near Nexon (Haute-Vienne)

autem die, ubicunque reperiebant quemquam illorum
siue masculum siue feminam, occidebant. Nullus angulus
ciuitatis deerat uacuus Saracenorum cadaueribus, uix-
que poterat aliquis per uias ire ciuitatis, nisi calcando
super Saracenorum cadauera. Boamundus denique illos
quos iusserat in palatium intrare apprehendit, illisque
abstulit omnia quae habebant, uidelicet aurum, argentum, aliaque ornamenta; alios uero fecit occidi, alios
autem iussit conduci ad uendendum Antiochiae.

Mora autem Francorum fuit in illa urbe, per unum
mensem et quatuor dies; in qua fuit mortuus Oriensis
episcopus. Fuerunt ibi ex nostris qui illic non inuenerunt
sicuti opus eis erat, tantum ex longa mora, quantum ex
districtione famis, quia foris nequiuerant aliquid inuenire ad capiendum, sed scindebant corpora mortuorum, eo quod in uentribus eorum inueniebant bisanteos
reconditos; alii uero caedebant carnes eorum per frusta,
et coquebant ad manducandum.

[xxxiiii] Boamundus autem[a] non potuit apud comitem Sancti Egidii concordari super id quod petebat,
iratusque reuersus est Antiochiam. Comes igitur[b]
Raimundus non diu moratus mandauit per suos legatos
Antiochiae, duci Godefrido et Flandrensi comiti ac
Rotberto Nortmanno et Boamundo, ut ipsi uenirent ad
Rugiam ciuitatem loqui cum eo. Veneruntque illuc
omnes seniores feceruntque concilium quomodo honeste
possent tenere uiam Sancti Sepulchri pro qua moti sunt
et huc usque peruentum sit. Nequiuerunt concordare
Boamundum cum Raimundo, nisi Raimundus comes
redderet Antiochiam ei. Noluit comes ad hoc assentire,
pro fiducia quam fecerat imperatori. Comites denique

---

[a] DX *omit* autem
[b] autem DX

cellars, and when it was dawn they killed everyone, man or woman, whom they met in any place whatsoever. No corner of the city was clear of Saracen corpses, and one could scarcely go about the city streets except by treading on the dead bodies of the Saracens. Then Bohemond took those whom he had ordered to enter the palace, and stripped them of all their belongings, gold, silver and other valuables, and some of them he caused to be killed, others to be taken to Antioch and sold as slaves.

The Franks stayed in that city for one month and four days, during which time the bishop of Orange died. While we were there some of our men could not satisfy their needs, either because of the long stay or because they were so hungry, for there was no plunder to be had outside the walls. So they ripped up the bodies of the dead, because they used to find bezants hidden in their entrails, and others cut the dead flesh into slices and cooked it to eat.

[xxxiiii] Bohemond could not reach an agreement about his claims with the count of St Gilles, so he was angry and went back to Antioch. Count Raymond, without much delay, sent messengers to Antioch, asking Duke Godfrey and the count of Flanders and Robert the Norman and Bohemond to come and hold a conference with him at Riha. All the leaders came thither, and took counsel as to how they should continue on their way to the Holy Sepulchre, for which they had set out and towards which they had marched until this time, but they could not reconcile Bohemond with Raymond, unless Count Raymond would surrender Antioch to Bohemond, and this the count was unwilling to do. because of the oath which he had sworn

et dux reuersi sunt in*a* Antiochiam una cum Boamundo.
Comes uero Raimundus reuersus est ad Marram, ubi
peregrini erant. Mandauit quoque suis militibus hone-
stare palatium et castellum quod erat supra portam
pontis ciuitatis.*b*

Videns autem Raimundus quod nullus seniorum
uoluisset causa eius ire in uiam Sancti Sepulchri, exiuit
nudis pedibus de Marra[1] decima tertia die intrante
Ianuario, et peruenit usque Capharda, fuitque ibi per
tres dies. Illic adiunxit se comes Normanniae*c* comiti
Raimundo. Rex autem Caesareae[2] multotiens man-
dauerat per suos nuntios comiti Marrae et Caphardae
quod cum eo pacem uellet habere, et de suo precium ei
daret; et Christianos peregrinos diligeret, fiduciamque
faceret quia quantum continet eius imperium, peregrinis
non esset offendiculum; et mercatum de equis et de
corporalibus alimentis daret gaudenter. Exierunt autem
nostri et uenerunt hospitari iuxta Caesaream, super
fluuium Farfar. Cumque uidisset rex Caesareae con-
tubernium Francorum tam prope ciuitatem hospitatum
esse, doluit animo, et iussit illis deuetari mercatum, nisi
discederent a ciuitatis confinio. Crastina uero die misit
cum illis duos Turcos suos uidelicet nuntios, qui eis
monstrarent fluminis uadum, eosque conducerent ubi
inuenire possent ad capiendum. Denique uenerunt in
uallem quamdam subter quoddam castrum, ibique depredati sunt plus quam quinque animalium milia, et

---

a DX *omit* in
b *The first hand of* E *writes* pontis *over* ciuitatis *as an alternative*
c nobilissimus comes Normanniae Ro(t)bertus DX

[1] Raymond of Agiles says that he put himself at the head of a popular
uprising of 'poor pilgrims' who were dissatisfied with the dilatory behaviour
of their leaders (*P.L.*, CLV, 629-30)
[2] Shaizar at this time was governed by an independent Arab amir,
Ali ibn Munqidh, who had remained on good terms with the Christians.

to the emperor. Then the other counts and the duke returned to Antioch with Bohemond, but Count Raymond returned to Marra, where the poor pilgrims were, and he ordered his knights to fortify the palace, and the castle which was above the gate by the city bridge.

When Raymond saw that he was the cause why none of the other leaders would set out on the way to the Holy Sepulchre, he went out barefoot from Marra[1] on the thirteenth of January and reached Kafartab, where he stayed for three days and the count of Normandy joined him. The king of Shaizar[2] had sent many messengers to Count Raymond while he was at Marra and Kafartab, because he wanted a treaty of peace, and he swore to pay an indemnity, and to be kind to the Christian pilgrims, so that while they were within his territory they should not suffer the least offence, and he said that he would be glad to sell them horses and food. So our men went out and came to encamp near Shaizar, on the river Orontes. When the king of Shaizar saw the Frankish camp so near to the city he was anxious, and ordered merchandise to be withheld from them unless they moved further off from the city boundary. Next day he sent two Turks, his messengers, to go with them and show them the ford over the river, and to lead them where they could find booty, so they came into a valley guarded by a castle, and seized there more than five thousand animals and plenty of corn

---

His grandson Usama wrote memoirs which gave a most interesting account of the relations between Franks and Arabs in the first half of the twelfth century (see H. A. R. Gibb, *The Damascus Chronicle*, pp. 18-19, and Potter, *The Autobiography of Ousama*).

satis frumenti atque alia bona, unde ualde fuit refecta
tota Christi militia.   Tamen illud castrum reddidit se
comiti, eique dedit equos et aurum purissimum; et
iurauerunt sua lege quod peregrinis nil exinde fieret
mali.   Fuimusque ibi per quinque dies.   Egressi etenim
inde peruenimus gaudentes hospitari ad quoddam
Arabum^a castrum.   Exiuit igitur dominus castri, et
concordatus est cum comite.   Exeuntes uero inde, peruenimus ad quamdam ciuitatem pulcherrimam et omnibus bonis refertam, in quadam ualle sitam, nomine
Kephaliam.[1]   Habitatores uero illius audientes Francos
uenisse dimiserunt urbem, et ortos plenos oleribus, et
domos plenas alimentis corporalibus, et fugerunt.   Tertia
die egressi ab illa urbe, transiuimus^b per altam et immensam montaneam,[2] et intrauimus in uallem de Sem[3];
in qua erat maxima ubertas omnibus bonis^c; fuimusque
ibi per dies fere quindecim.   Hic prope nos erat quoddam castrum, in quo erat congregata maxima paganorum multitudo.   Quod castrum aggressi sunt nostri,
idque fortiter superassent, nisi Saraceni iactassent foras
immensas turmas animalium.   Reuersi sunt nostri, deferentes omnia bona ad sua tentoria.   Summo autem
diluculo collegerunt nostri suos papiliones, et uenerunt
obsidere idem castrum, ibique putabant extendere tentoria; sed genus pagana omnino dedit sese fugae, ac
dimiserunt castrum uacuum.   Intrantes autem nostri
inuenerunt ibi omnem abundantiam frumenti, uini,
farinae, olei, et quicquid eis opus erat.   Illic deuotissime
celebrauimus festiuitatem purificationis sanctae Mariae,

^a DX *omit* Arabum
^b DX *omit* transiuimus
^c omnium bonorum DX

[1] Formerly called Raphania
[2] The Ansarieh range

and other goods, which were a great refreshment to the whole army of Christ. The garrison of the castle surrendered to the count, and gave him horses and refined gold, and swore on the Koran that they would do no harm to the pilgrims. We stayed there for five days, and when we set out we came rejoicing and took up our quarters in a castle belonging to Arabs, for its lord came out and made an agreement with the count. After leaving this place we reached a city which was very beautiful and full of all kinds of good things; it was called Kephalia[1] and stood in a valley. Its inhabitants, on hearing of the approach of the Franks, left the city, and their gardens full of vegetables and houses full of food, and took to flight. On the third day we left this city and crossed a mountain[2] which was very high and broad, and entered the valley of Sem,[3] which was extremely fertile, and there we stayed for nearly fifteen days. Not far off there was a castle, in which a great multitude of pagans had assembled. Our men attacked it, and would have taken it by force if the Saracens had not turned out of the gates an immense number of beasts, so that our men returned to the camp with all the good things which they had captured. At dawn our men struck their tents and came to besiege that castle, proposing to encamp there, but the pagans had fled and left the castle empty. Our men entered and found plenty of corn, wine, oil, flour and whatever they needed, so we celebrated the feast of Candlemas there with great devotion. While we were there messengers came from the city of La Cham-

---

[3] The name of this place obviously caused confusion in the twelfth century. MS Vatican Reginensis 641 has the reading 'in uallem densam'. The place is generally identified with al-Boukeia.

ueneruntque illic nuntii de Camela ciuitate.[1] Rex namque illius mandauit[a] comiti equos, aurum, et pactus est
cum eo quod Christianos nullomodo offenderet, sed eos
diligeret et honoraret. Rex autem Tripolis[2] mandauit
comiti, quoniam cum eo fideliter pactum iniret et amicitiam haberet, si ei placeret, misitque illi equos decem
et quatuor mulas et aurum. Sed comes ait nullomodo
cum eo pacem se recipere, nisi ille Christianus efficeretur.

Exeuntes autem de optima ualle, peruenimus ad
quoddam castrum quod dicitur Archae,[3] in die lunae
scilicet secunda feria mediante Februario[4]; circa quod
tentoria tetendimus. Quod castrum plenum erat in-
numerabili gente paganorum, uidelicet Turcorum, Saracenorum, Arabum, Publicanorum, et mirabiliter muni-
erant castrum illud et defendebant se fortiter. Tunc
exeuntes quatuordecim ex nostris militibus, ierunt contra
Tripolim urbem, quae erat secus nos. Isti quatuordecim
inuenerunt circa sexaginta Turcos, et alios quosdam;
qui habebant ante se collectos homines,. et animalia plus
quam mille quingenta. Qui signo crucis muniti inuaserunt eos, et Deo iuuante mirabiliter superauerunt
illos, et occiderunt sex ex illis, apprehenderuntque sex
equos.

De exercitu uero Raimundi comitis exierunt Raimundus Piletus, et Raimundus uicecomes de Tentoria,[b5]
ueneruntque ante Tortosam ciuitatem,[6] et fortiter aggre-
diuntur illam. Quae nimis erat munita multitudine

---

[a] misit D, transmisit X
[b] Tentoriis DX

[1] Homs, which was governed by Janah al-Dawla, atabek of Rudwan of
Aleppo. The Franks, for some reason unknown, called it 'She-Camel'.
[2] Tripoli was an independent Arab principality under the rule of
Fakhr al-Mulk ibn Ammar (Grousset, I, 131-2).
[3] This place lies near the coast, north-east of Tripoli.
[4] 14 February 1099

elle,[1] the king of which sent to the count horses and gold, and made an agreement with him that he would not do the Christians the least harm, but that he would be kind to them and respect them. Also the king of Tripoli[2] sent to the count, proposing to make a faithful treaty of friendship with him, if he agreed, and he sent ten horses and four mules and some gold; but the count said that he would make no treaty at all with him, unless he would be christened.

When we left that valley (which was a very good place) we came on Monday in the second week in February[4] to a castle which is called Arqa[3] and pitched our tents around it. This castle was full of an immense horde of pagans, Turks, Saracens, Arabs and Paulicians, who had made its fortifications exceedingly strong and defended themselves bravely. While we were there fourteen of our knights rode over to the city of Tripoli, which was quite near, and found about sixty Turks and others who had rounded up men and beasts to the number of more than fifteen hundred. Our men made the Sign of the Cross and attacked them, killing six men and capturing six horses, and by God's help they won a marvellous victory.

Raymond Pilet and Raymond vicomte of Turenne[5] left the main army of Count Raymond and came to the city of Tortosa,[6] which they attacked bravely, for

---

[5] From Turenne in Limousin. The word 'vicomte' is untranslatable, and does not approximate to the English 'viscount'. It signifies a man who ranked below the count, and sometimes (as in Normandy) performed duties not unlike those of the English sheriff. The closest possible translation here would probably be 'baron'.

[6] A port lying north of Tripoli

paganorum. Sero autem iam facto, secesserunt in quemdam angulum, ibique hospitati sunt; feceruntque innumerabiles ignes, ita ut[a] tota hostis esset ibi. Pagani
uero timore perterriti nocte latenter fugerunt, et dimiserunt ciuitatem plenam omnibus bonis, quae etiam
ualde optimum portum secus mare in se retinet. Crastina
autem die uenerunt nostri, ut undique inuaderent illam
inueneruntque illam[b] uacuam. Et intrantes habita-
uerunt[c] in ea usque dum obsessio[d] esset ante urbem
Archae. Est prope istam alia urbs, quae dicitur Maraclea. Amiralius qui eam regebat pactus est cum nostris,
et misit nostros in ciuitatem, nostraque uexilla.

[xxxv] Dux quoque Godefridus et Boamundus,
Flandrensisque comes, uenerunt usque ad Lichiam ciuitatem.[1] Disseparauit enim se Boamundus ab eis, et
reuersus est Antiochiam. Illi uero uenerunt, et obsederunt quandam urbem cui nomen Gibellum.[2] Audiens
itaque Raimundus comes de Sancto Egidio quod innumerabilis paganorum gens rueret super nos ad certum
bellum, ilico consilium habuit cum suis ut mandet[e]
senioribus qui sunt in obsidione Gibelli, quatinus eis
subuenirent. Quod illi audientes, statim pacti sunt cum
amiralio, facientes pacem cum eo, et acceperunt[f] equos,
et aurum; dimiseruntque urbem uenientes ad nos in
adiutorium; sed illi[g] non uenerunt ad bellum contra nos.
Itaque comites predicti hospitati sunt ultra flumen,
ibique obsederunt castrum illud.

Non multo post equitauerunt nostri contra Tripolim,
inueneruntque extra ciuitatem Turcos, Arabes, et Sara-

[a] ita ut] quasi DX   [b] DX *omit* illam
[c] hospitati sunt DX   [d] obsidio DX
[e] mandaret DX   [f] D *adds* ab eo, X ab illo
          [g] X *adds* de quibus audieramus

it was garrisoned by many of the pagans. When night fell they withdrew into a corner where they encamped and lit many fires, so that it might appear that the whole host was there. The pagans were terrified and fled secretly in the night, leaving the city full of provisions. (It has also an excellent harbour.) Next morning our men came and attacked it from all sides, but they found it empty, so they entered it and stayed there until the siege of Arqa began. There is another city, called Marakia, not far from this one; the amir who governed it made a treaty with our men, admitted them to the city, and put up our banner.

[xxxv] Meanwhile Duke Godfrey, Bohemond and the count of Flanders came to the city of Laodicea,[1] where Bohemond broke away and went back to Antioch. The others came and laid siege to a city called Gibel.[2] But when Raymond count of St Gilles heard that an immense force of pagans was speeding towards us, determined to fight, he took counsel with his followers and decided to summon those of our leaders who were besieging Gibel to come to his aid. When they heard this news they made a treaty with the amir at once, and agreed with him on terms of peace, receiving a tribute of horses and gold, and so they left the city and came to our help; but the threatened attack did not come, so the said counts encamped on the other side of the river and took part in the siege of Arqa.

Not long afterwards our men rode against Tripoli, and came upon Turks, Arabs and Saracens outside the

---

[1] Latakieh, sometimes called by the crusaders 'La Liche'. This attack was made by way of the coast from Antioch.

[2] Djibleh, between Laodicea and Tortosa. It was nominally dependent upon Tripoli (Grousset, I, 134).

cenos, quos inuaserunt nostri, et miserunt eos in fugam;
et occiderunt maximam partem nobilium urbis. Tanta
fuit paganorum occisio, et sanguinis effusio, ut etiam
aqua quae in ciuitate fluebat, uideretur rubere et fluere
in cisternas eorum, unde ualde fuerunt tristes alii dolentesque. Iam uero erant tanto timore perterriti, ut nullus
eorum auderet exire extra ciuitatis portam.

Alia uero die equitauerunt nostri ultra de Sem, et
inuenerunt boues et oues et asinos, multaque animalia,
camelos quoque depredati sunt fere tria milia. Obsedimus uero castrum supra dictum per tres menses,
minus una die; ibique pascha Domini celebrauimus
IIII idus Aprilis. Naues quippe nostrae[1] uenerunt
prope nos in quendam portum, quamdiu fuimus in illa
obsidione deferentes maximum mercatum, scilicet frumentum, uinum et carnem et caseum, et ordeum, et
oleum, unde maxima ubertas fuit in tota expeditione.
In illa denique obsidione feliciter acceperunt martyrium
plures ex nostris, uidelicet Anselmus ·de Riboatmont,[a2]
Willelmus Picardus, et alii plures[b] quos ignoro. Rex
quoque Tripolis sepe nuntios mittebat senioribus ut
dimitterent castrum, et cum eo concordarentur. Audientes itaque nostri hoc, scilicet dux Godefridus, et Raimundus comes Sancti Egidii, ac Rotbertus Normannus,
Flandrensisque comes, uidentesque nouos fructus pro-
perasse, quia in medio Martio comedebamus nouellas
fabas, medio quoque Aprili frumentum, consiliati sunt
nostri dicentes, bonum ualde esse Hierosolimitanum iter
explere cum nouis fructibus.

[xxxvi] Discessimus igitur a castro, et peruenimus
Tripolim in sexta feria, XIII[mo] die intrante Maio, ibique

---
[a] Ribodimonte DX
[b] DX *omit* plures

city. Our men scared them off and put them to flight, killing many of the leading men of the city. So great were the slaughter of pagans and the bloodshed that even the stream which flowed into the city ran red and stained the water in the citizens' tanks, for which reason they were full of grief and lamentation, and so frightened that none of them dared to go outside the city gate.

Another day our men rode over beyond Sem and found oxen, sheep, asses and many other beasts, and they also carried off nearly three thousand camels. We went on besieging Arqa for three months, all but one day, and celebrated Easter there on 10 April. While the siege was going on our ships[1] put into a port near at hand, and they were laden with plenty of provisions, corn, wine, meat, cheese, barley and oil, so that the whole army was very well supplied. Many of our men, including Anselm of Ribemont,[2] William the Picard and many others whose names I do not know, suffered blessed martyrdom in the course of this siege. The king of Tripoli sent frequent messengers to our leaders, asking them to raise the siege and make a treaty with him. When Duke Godfrey and Raymond, count of St Gilles, and Robert the Norman and the count of Flanders heard this, and saw that the season of harvest was come, for we were eating spring beans in the middle of March and corn in the middle of April, they took counsel together and decided that it would be a very good thing to finish the journey to Jerusalem while the harvest was being gathered in.

[xxxvi] Therefore we left the castle and came to Tripoli on Friday the thirteenth of May, and there we

---

[1] The Genoese fleet which had previouly put in to St Simeon's Port.
[2] Lord of Ribemont near St Quentin

fuimus per tres dies. Tandem concordatus est rex
Tripolis cum senioribus, illisque continuo dissoluit plus
quam trecentos peregrinos, qui illic capti erant; deditque illis quindecim milia bisanteos, et quindecim equos
magni precii. Dedit etiam nobis magnum mercatum
equorum, asinorum, omniumque bonorum, unde nimis
ditata est omnis Christi militia. Pactus est uero cum
illis, quia si bellum quod eis amiralius Babiloniae[1] para-
bat possent deuincere, et Hierusalem apprehendere, ille
Christianus efficeretur, terramque ab eis recognosceret,
atque tali modo factum est placitum.

Nos autem discessimus ab urbe in secunda feria
mensis Maii, transiuimusque per uiam artam et arduam
tota die et nocte[a] et peruenimus ad castrum cui nomen
Bethelon[2]; deinde ad urbem quae dicitur Zebari secus
mare,[3] in qua passi sumus nimiam sitim, et sic defessi
peruenimus ad flumen cui nomen Braym.[4] Deinde
transiuimus nocte ac die ascensionis Domini per montem, in quo est uia nimis angusta, et illic putauimus
inimicos insidiantes nobis inuenire, sed Deo annuente
nullus eorum audebat properare ante nos. Nostri denique milites precedentes nos[5] liberauerunt ante nos uiam
illam, et applicuimus ad ciuitatem iuxta mare quae
dicitur Baruth, et inde uenimus ad aliam urbem quae
uocatur Sagitta,[6] dehinc ad aliam, quae dicitur Sur,[7]

---

[a] tota nocte DX

[1] Al-Afdal, commander-in-chief of the Fatimid forces in Egypt. He
had profited by the diversion caused by the Frankish attack in Syria to
capture Jerusalem from the Turkish house of Ortuq in July 1098 (H. A. R.
Gibb, *Damascus Chronicle*, p. 45).
   [2] Batrun   [3] The classical Byblos, now called Djebail
   [4] The Nahr Ibrahim. To the south of it lay a dangerous place where
the narrow path crossed the Nahr al-Kalb, known by the Crusaders as the
Dog's River. An army on the main route south could easily be ambushed
here, as was that of Baldwin I in 1100. (Fulcher of Chartres, *P.L.*, CLV,
862-4.)

stayed for three days. The king of Tripoli finally made an agreement to set free at once more than three hundred pilgrims who had been captured there, and to give us fifteen thousand bezants and fifteen horses of great value. He also sold us plenty of horses, asses and provisions, so that the whole army of Christ was well supplied. The treaty also stated that if we could defeat the army which the amir of Cairo[1] was preparing against our men, and could take Jerusalem, then the king of Tripoli would be christened and hold his land from our leaders. This was the lawful agreement.

We departed from the city one Monday in the month of May and travelled all that day and night, by a narrow and steep path, until we came to a castle called Bethelon,[2] and thence to a city on the coast called Gibelon,[3] where we suffered badly from thirst, so that we were exhausted by the time that we reached the river called Braym.[4] After this we spent the night and the following day (which was Ascension Day) in crossing a cliff where the path is very narrow, and we expected to find our enemies lying in ambush, but by God's grace none of them dared to come near us. Then our knights went on ahead of us,[5] clearing the way, and we reached a city called Beyrut which lies on the coast. From thence we came to another city called Sagitta,[6] and so to another called Sur,[7] and from Sur to Acre.

---

[5] This has been taken to indicate that the Author had now lost his knightly status and become one of the poor pilgrims. The conclusion seems to me doubtful. In leaving Bohemond and joining Raymond of Toulouse he had obviously forfeited the advantages of 'good lordship' and he may have lost his horse at Antioch. Knighthood, however, was indelible, and the mention of tributes of horses paid by the Arab states suggests that the army was now well supplied. He may simply mean that Raymond sent out his own knights in the vanguard.

[6] The classical Sidon, now called Saida   [7] The classical Tyre

et de Sur ad Acram ciuitatem. De Acra uero uenimus
ad castrum cui nomen Cayphas, ac deinceps hospitati
sumus iuxta Caesaream, ibique celebrauimus Pente-
costen, tertia die exeunte Maio. Denique uenimus ad
urbem Ramola,[1] quam Saraceni dimiserant uacuam
propter metum Francorum. Iuxta quam erat honorabilis ecclesia in qua requieuit preciosissimum sancti
Georgii corpus, quia illic a perfidis paganis pro Christi
nomine feliciter martyrium suscepit. Ibi consiliati sunt
nostri maiores, ut illic[a] eligerent episcopum,[2] qui hanc
custodiret et erigeret[b] ecclesiam. Cui suas dederunt
decimas, et auro argentoque ditauerunt, et equis ac
animalibus aliis, quo deuote et honeste uiueret cum illis
qui cum eo essent.

[xxxvii] Remansit ipse illic cum gaudio, nos autem
letantes et exultantes, usque ad ciuitatem Hierusalem
peruenimus feria tertia, VIII idus Iunii,[3] eamque mirabiliter obsedimus. Rotbertus namque Normannus eam
obsedit[c] a septentrione, iuxta sancti Stephani protho-
martyris ecclesiam, ubi lapidatus est pro nomine Christi.
Iuxta Rotbertum Flandrensis comes.[d] Ab occidente uero
obsedit eam dux Godefridus et Tancredus. A meridie
obsedit eam comes Sancti Egidii, scilicet in monte Sion
circa ecclesiam sanctae Mariae matris Domini, ubi
Dominus cum suis cenauit discipulis.[4]

Tertia uero die ex nostris, scilicet Raimundus Piletus
et Raimundus de Taurina et alii plures[e] causa preliandi

---

[a] DX *omit* illic
[b] regeret DX
[c] piissimus electusque miles Rotbertus uir nobilissimus Normannorum
(Normannie X) comes cum suo preclaro exercitu obsedit eam DX
[d] iuxta quem Rotbertus Flandrensis comes (comes *not in* D) obsedit eam
(illam obsedit X) DX
[e] DX *adds* ex nostris

From Acre we came to a castle named Haifa, and afterwards we encamped near Caesarea, where we celebrated Whit Sunday on 30 May. Thence we came to the city of Ramleh,[1] which the Saracens had evacuated for fear of the Franks. Near Ramleh is a church worthy of great reverence, for in it rests the most precious body of St George, who there suffered blessed martyrdom at the hands of the treacherous pagans for the name of Christ. While we were there our leaders took counsel together to choose a bishop[2] who might protect and build up this church, and they paid him tithes and endowed him with gold and silver, horses and other animals, so that he and his household might live in a proper and religious manner.

[xxxvii] He stayed there gladly, but we, rejoicing and exulting, came to the city of Jerusalem on Tuesday 6 June[3] and established a very thorough siege. Robert the Norman took up his station on the north, next to the church of St Stephen the Protomartyr, who was stoned there for the name of Christ, and Robert count of Flanders was next to him. Duke Godfrey and Tancred besieged the city from the west. The count of St Gilles was on the south, that is to say on Mount Sion, near the church of St Mary the Mother of the Lord, where the Lord shared the Last Supper with his disciples.[4]

On the third day some of our men—Raymond Pilet, Raymond of Turenne and many others—went

---

[1] On the road from Jaffa to Jerusalem, at a point where the main route from Egypt came in. Later Frankish kings of Jerusalem had to fight repeated battles against the Egyptians at this spot.

[2] Robert of Rouen

[3] In this year Tuesday actually fell on 7 June.

[4] The steep descent to the Kedron valley made it impossible to besiege the city from the east.

sequestrauerunt se ab exercitu inueneruntque bis centum
Arabes, et preliati sunt Christi milites contra illos incredulos; et Deo adiuuante[a] fortiter illos superauerunt,
et occiderunt multos ex eis, et apprehenderunt triginta
equos. Secunda uero ueniente feria,[1] aggredimur for-
tissime ciuitatem, tam mirabiliter, ut si scalae fuissent
paratae, in nostra fuisset ciuitas manu. Tamen mino-
rem strauimus murum, et unam scalam ereximus ad
maiorem murum. Super quam ascendebant nostri
milites, et comminus percutiebant Saracenos suis ensibus
et lanceis, et defensores ciuitatis. Fueruntque mortui
multi ex nostris, sed plures ex illis. In illa autem obsidione panes ad emendum inuenire non poteramus fere
per spatium dierum decem, donec uenit nuntius nostrarum nauium.[2] Et in nimia pressura sitis detenti
fuimus, ita ut per nimium terrorem et pauorem per sex
milia nostros potaremus equos, et alia animalia. Syloa
namque fons qui est ad radicem montis Syon, sustinebat
nos; sed tamen cara uendebatur aqua inter nos.

Postquam enim uenit nuntius nostrarum nauium,
acceperunt inter se nostri seniores consilium, quemadmodum mitterent milites qui fideliter custodirent homines et naues in portu Iaphie. Summo autem diluculo,
exierunt centum milites de exercitu Raimundi, comitis
Sancti Egidii, Raimundus Piletus et Achardus de Mommellou,[b] et Willelmus de Sabra,[c] et ibant cum fiducia
ad portum. Diuiserunt denique se triginta milites ex
nostris ab aliis, et inuenerunt septingentos Arabes et
Turcos[3] ac[d] Saracenos de exercitu ammirauisi[e4]. Quos

[a] iuuante DX
[b] Monlou D
[c] X *adds* et alii
[d] et DX
[e] DX *do not accept this form, but always replace it by their normal* admiralius

off to fight, and found two hundred Arabs. The knights of Christ fought against these misbelievers, and by God's help bravely defeated them, killing many and capturing thirty horses. On the Monday[1] we pressed upon the city in such a vigorous assault that if our scaling-ladders had been ready we should have taken it. We did indeed destroy the curtain-wall, and against the great wall we set up one ladder, up which our knights climbed and fought hand-to-hand with the Saracens and those who were defending the city, using swords and spears. We lost many men, but the enemy lost more. During this siege we could not buy bread for nearly ten days, until a messenger arrived from our ships,[2] and we suffered so badly from thirst that we had to take our horses and other beasts six miles to water, enduring great terror and apprehension on the way. The pool of Siloam, at the foot of Mount Sion, kept us going, but water was sold very dearly in the army.

After the messenger from our ships arrived, our leaders took counsel and decided to send knights who might provide a faithful guard for the men and ships who were in the harbour of Jaffa. At dawn a hundred knights set out from the army of Raymond, count of St Gilles. They included Raymond Pilet, Achard of Montmerle and William of Sabran, and they rode confidently towards the port. Then thirty of our knights got separated from the others, and fell in with seven hundred Arabs, Turks[3] and Saracens from the army of the amir.[4] The Christian knights attacked

---

[1] 13 June 1099

[2] A Genoese fleet (Heyd, tr. Furcy-Renaud, *Histoire du commerce du Levant*, I, 134-5)

[3] Probably the Author's formula for 'enemies'. The presence of Turks (except perhaps for a few mercenaries) in an Egyptian army in 1099 would be most unlikely.   [4] Al-Afdal

inuaserunt fortiter Christi milites, sed tam magna fuit
uirtus illorum super nostros, ut undique circumcingerent
illos. Et occiderunt Achardum de Mommellou, et
pauperes homines pedites. Cum autem tenerent nostros
iam inclusos, qui omnes putabant mori, uenit aliis
quidam nuntius, dicens Raimundo Pileto: 'Quid hic
astas^a cum his militibus? Ecce omnes nostri in nimia
districtione Arabum et Turcorum ac Saracenorum sunt;
et forsitan in hac hora omnes mortui sunt. Succurrite
ergo illis, succurrite!' Audientes nostri haec, statim
cucurrerunt celeri cursu, et festinanter peruenerunt usque ad illos preliando. Paganorum uero gens uidens
Christi milites, diuisit se; et fecerunt duo agmina. Nostri
autem inuocato Christi nomine, tam acriter inuaserunt
illos incredulos, ut quisque miles prosterneret suum.
Videntes uero illi quod non possent stare ante Francorum
fortitudinem, timore nimio perterriti, uerterunt scapulas
retro. Quos nostri persequentes fere per spatia quatuor
milium, occiderunt multos ex eis, unumque retinuerunt
uiuum, qui noua eis per ordinem diceret; retinuerunt
quoque centum et tres equos.

In eadem obsidione tanta oppressione sitis fuimus
grauati, ut sueremus coria boum et bufalorum, in quibus
deferebamus aquas fere per spatium sex miliariorum.
Ex illis quippe uasculis foetida utebamur aqua, et
quantum ex olida aqua et ordeaceo pane in nimia
districtione et afflictione eramus cotidie. Saraceni namque in cunctis fontibus et aquis latentes, insidiabantur
nostris, eosque ubique occidebant et dilaniabant, animalia quoque secum in suas cauernas et speluncas
deducebant.

[xxxviii] Tunc seniores nostri ordinauerunt quomodo

---

^a stas DX

them bravely, but they were such a mighty force in comparison with ours that they surrounded our men and killed Achard of Montmerle and some poor foot-soldiers. While our men were thus surrounded and all expecting death, a messenger reached the others, saying to Raymond Pilet, 'Why are you staying here with your knights? Look! All our men are trapped by the Arabs and Turks, and perhaps at this very moment they are all dead, so bring help, bring help!' When our men heard this they rode at once as hard as they could, and came quickly to where the others were fighting. When the pagans saw the Christian knights they split up into two bands, but our men called upon the Name of Christ and charged these misbelievers so fiercely that every knight overthrew his opponent. When the enemy saw that they could not stand up to the brave attack of the Franks they turned tail, panic-stricken, and our men pursued them for the space of nearly four miles, killing many of them, but they spared the life of one so that he could give them information. They also captured one hundred and three horses.

During this siege, we suffered so badly from thirst that we sewed up the skins of oxen and buffaloes, and we used to carry water in them for the distance of nearly six miles. We drank the water from these vessels, although it stank, and what with foul water and barley bread we suffered great distress and affliction every day, for the Saracens used to lie in wait for our men by every spring and pool, where they killed them and cut them to pieces; moreover they used to carry off the beasts into their caves and secret places in the rocks.

[xxxviii] Our leaders then decided to attack the

ingeniare[1] possent ciuitatem, ut ad adorandum nostri Salvatoris intrarent Sepulchrum. Feceruntque duo lignea castra, et alia plura machinamenta. Dux Godefridus suum fecit castrum cum machinis, et Raimundus comes similiter; quibus de longinquis terris attrahebant ligna. Saraceni igitur uidentes nostros facientes has machinas, mirabiliter muniebant ciuitatem, et turres nocte accrescebant. Videntes autem nostri seniores ex qua parte esset ciuitas magis languida, illuc in quadam nocte sabbati[2] deportauerunt nostram machinam et ligneum castrum in orientalem partem. Summo autem diluculo erexerunt ea, et aptauerunt et ornauerunt castrum, in prima et secunda ac tertia feria. Comes namque Sancti Egidii, a meridiana plaga reficiebat suam machinam. Interea in tanta pressura sitis fuimus districti, ut unus homo non posset pro uno denario ad sufficientiam habere aquam, aut exstinguere sitim suam.

Nocte uero ac die in quarta et quinta feria mirabiliter aggredimur ciuitatem, ex omni parte; sed antequam inuaderemus eam, ordinauerunt episcopi et sacerdotes predicando et commonendo omnes, ut processionem Deo in circuitu Hierusalem celebrarent, et orationes ac elemosinas et ieiunia fideliter facerent.[3] Sexta uero feria summo mane undique aggredimur urbem, et nichil ei nocere potuimus, eramusque omnes stupefacti ac in nimio pauore. Appropinquante autem hora scilicet in qua Dominus noster Iesus Christus dignatus est pro nobis sufferre patibulum crucis, nostri milites fortiter pugnabant in castello, uidelicet dux Godefridus, et comes Eustachius frater eius. Tunc ascendit quidam

---

[1] With siege-towers, battering rams, catapults and balistas
[2] 9 July 1099. The defenders were not expecting an attack from the east, because of the steepness of the rocks.
[3] The processions took place on 8 July.

city with engines,[1] so that we might enter it and worship at our Saviour's Sepulchre. They made two wooden siege-towers and various other mechanical devices. Duke Godfrey filled his siege-tower with machines, and so did Count Raymond, but they had to get the timber from far afield. When the Saracens saw our men making these machines, they built up the city wall and its towers by night, so that they were exceedingly strong. When, however, our leaders saw which was the weakest spot in the city's defences, they had a machine and a siege-tower transported round to the eastern side one Saturday night.[2] They set up these engines at dawn, and spent Sunday, Monday and Tuesday in preparing the siege-tower and fitting it out, while the count of St Gilles was getting his engine ready on the southern side. All this time we were suffering so badly from the shortage of water that for one penny a man could not buy sufficient to quench his thirst.

On Wednesday and Thursday we launched a fierce attack upon the city, both by day and by night, from all sides, but before we attacked our bishops and priests preached to us, and told us to go in procession round Jerusalem to the glory of God, and to pray and give alms and fast, as faithful men should do.[3] On Friday at dawn we attacked the city from all sides but could achieve nothing, so that we were all astounded and very much afraid, yet, when that hour came when our Lord Jesus Christ deigned to suffer for us upon the cross, our knights were fighting bravely on the siege-tower, led by Duke Godfrey and Count Eustace his brother. At

miles ex nostris Laetholdus*¹ nomine super murum urbis. Mox uero ut ascendit, omnes defensores ciuitatis fugerunt per muros et per ciuitatem, nostrique subsecuti persequebantur eos occidendo et detruncando usque ad Templum Salomonis.² Ibique talis occisio fuit, ut nostri in sanguine illorum pedes usque ad cauillas mitterent.

At Raimundus comes a meridie conduxit suum exercitum et castellum usque prope murum, sed inter castellum et murum erat quaedam fouea nimis profunda. Tunc consiliati sunt nostri ut implerent foueam, feceruntque preconari, ut si aliquis*ᵇ in illam foueam portasset*ᶜ tres petras, unum haberet denarium. Perdurauit uero*ᵈ haec impletio per tres dies et noctes. Tandem plena fouea conduxerunt castellum iuxta murum. Illi autem qui intus erant mirabiliter preliabantur cum nostris, igne et lapidibus. Audiens itaque comes quod Franci essent in urbe, suis dixit hominibus: 'Quid tardatis? Ecce omnes Francigenae iam sunt in urbe.' Amiralius itaque qui erat in Turri David, reddidit se comiti, eique aperuit portam ubi peregrini persoluere solebant tributa.³ Intrantes autem nostri ciuitatem peregrini, persequebantur et occidebant Saracenos usque ad Templum Salomonis. In quo congregati, dederunt nostris maximum bellum per totum diem, ita ut sanguis illorum per totum templum flueret. Tandem superatis paganis, apprehenderunt nostri masculos et feminas sat in templo, et occiderunt quos uoluerunt, et quos uoluerunt retinuerunt uiuos. Super Templum uero Salomonis erat maxima

---

ᵃ Letoldus DX   *ᵇ* quis DX
ᶜ deportaret DX   *ᵈ* DX *omit* uero

¹ Of Tournai   ² The Mosque of Omar
³ The gate which opened on to the Jaffa road

that moment one of our knights, called Lethold,[1] succeeded in getting on to the wall. As soon as he reached it, all the defenders fled along the walls and through the city, and our men went after them, killing them and cutting them down as far as Solomon's Temple,[2] where there was such a massacre that our men were wading up to their ankles in enemy blood.

Count Raymond was bringing up his army and a siege-tower from the south to the neighbourhood of the wall, but between the wall and the tower there was a deep pit. Our leaders discussed how they should fill the pit, and they had it announced that if anyone would bring three stones to cast into that pit he should have a penny. It took three days and nights to fill the pit, and when it was full they took the siege-tower up to the wall. The defenders fought against our men with amazing courage, casting fire and stones. But when the count heard that the Franks were in the city he said to his men, 'Why are you so slow? Look! All the other Franks are in the city already!' Then the amir who held David's Tower surrendered to the count, and opened for him the gate where the pilgrims used to pay their taxes,[3] so our men entered the city, chasing the Saracens and killing them up to Solomon's Temple, where they took refuge and fought hard against our men for the whole day, so that all the temple was streaming with their blood. At last, when the pagans were defeated, our men took many prisoners, both men and women, in the temple. They killed whom they chose, and whom they chose they saved alive. On the roof of the Temple of Solomon were crowded great numbers of pagans of both sexes, to

paganorum congregatio utriusque sexus, quibus Tancredus et Gaston de Beert dederunt sua uexilla.

Mox cucurrerunt per uniuersam urbem, capientes
aurum et argentum, equos et mulos, domosque plenas
omnibus bonis. Venerunt autem omnes nostri gaudentes et prae nimio gaudio plorantes ad nostri Saluatoris
Iesu sepulchrum adorandum, et reddiderunt ei capitale
debitum.ᵃ Mane autem facto ascenderunt nostri caute
supra tectum templi, et inuaserunt Saracenos masculos
et feminas, decollantes eos nudis ensibus. Alii uero
dabant se precipites e templo. Hoc uidens Tancredus
iratus est nimis.[1]

[xxxix] Tunc nostri tenuerunt concilium, ut unusquisque faceret elemosinas cum orationibus, quatinus
sibi Deus eligeret quem uellet regnare super alios et
regere ciuitatem. Iusserunt quoque Saracenos mortuos
omnes eici foras, prae nimio foetore; quia omnis urbs
fere plena erat illorum cadaueribus. Et uiui Saraceni
trahebant mortuos ante portarum exitus, et ordinabant
montes ex eis,ᵇ quasi essent domos. Tales occisiones de
paganorum gente nullus unquam audiuit nec uidit;
quoniam pyrae erant ordinatae ex eis sicut metae, et
nemo scit numerum eorum nisi solus Deus. Fecit uero
comes Raimundus conduci amiralium et alios qui cum
eo erant, usque Scalonam,ᶜ sanos et illaesos.

Octauo autem die quo ciuitas fuit capta, elegerunt
ducem Godefridum[2] principem ciuitatis, qui debellaret

ᵃ tributum DX
ᵇ et faciebant montes (inde aggeres X) DX
ᶜ Ascalonam D, *as always*

[1] The Author is clearly unaware of any incongruity in this passage.
[2] The election was disputed; the clergy wished to elect the patriarch
before the lay ruler. Godfrey took the title of 'Advocate of the Holy
Sepulchre', thus suggesting that the Latin kingdom was a theocracy. His

whom Tancred and Gaston of Bearn gave their banners.

After this our men rushed round the whole city, seizing gold and silver, horses and mules, and houses full of all sorts of goods, and they all came rejoicing and weeping from excess of gladness to worship at the Sepulchre of our Saviour Jesus, and there they fulfilled their vows to him. Next morning they went cautiously up on to the Temple roof and attacked the Saracens, both men and women, cutting off their heads with drawn swords. Some of the Saracens threw themselves down headlong from the Temple. Tancred was extremely angry when he saw this.[1]

[xxxix] Our leaders then took counsel and ordered that every man should give alms and pray that God would choose for himself whomsoever he wished, to rule over the others and to govern the city. They also commanded that all the Saracen corpses should be thrown outside the city because of the fearful stench, for almost the whole city was full of their dead bodies. So the surviving Saracens dragged the dead ones out in front of the gates, and piled them up in mounds as big as houses. No-one has ever seen or heard of such a slaughter of pagans, for they were burned on pyres like pyramids, and no-one save God alone knows how many there were. Count Raymond, however, caused the amir and those who were with him to be taken to Ascalon, safe and sound.

On the eighth day after the city was taken they chose Duke Godfrey[2] as its ruler, so that he might fight

---

brother and successor Baldwin, less devout and more practical, realised that a strict feudal organisation under a military ruler was the only chance of preserving the kingdom, and had himself crowned king (*P.L.*, CLV, Raymond of Agiles, coll. 660-2; Fulcher of Chartres, coll. 855-6 and 861-5).

paganos et custodiret Christianos. Similiter elegerunt patriarcham sapientissimum et honorabilem uirum nomine Arnulfum,[1] in die sancti Petri ad Vincula.[2] Haec ciuitas fuit capta a Christianis Dei XV die Iulii, in sexta feria.

Interea nuntius uenit Tancredo et comiti Eustachio, ut prepararent se et pergerent ad recipiendam Neopolitanam urbem.[3] Exierunt illi et duxerunt secum multos milites et pedones, et peruenerunt ad urbem. Habitatores uero illius reddiderunt se ilico. Denuo mandauit illis dux, ut cito uenirent ad bellum quod nobis[a] ammirauisus Babyloniae preparat urbi[b] Scalonae.[4] Illi autem festinando intrauerunt montaneam quaerentes Saracenorum bella, et uenerunt Caesaream. Itaque uenientes illi iuxta mare ad urbem Ramole, illic inuenerunt multos Arabes, qui precursores erant belli. Quos nostri persequentes, apprehenderunt plures ex eis, qui dixerunt omnia belli noua, ubi essent et quot essent, aut ubi bellare disponerent contra Christianos. Quod audiens Tancredus statim misit nuntium Hierusalem duci Godefrido et patriarchae, omnibusque principibus dicens: 'Sciatis quod nobis paratum est bellum Scalonae, uenite ergo festinanter cum omni uirtute quam habere poteritis!' Tunc iussit dux summoneri[c] omnes, ut fideliter irent preparati Scalonam, obuiam inimicis nostris. Ipse uero cum patriarcha et Rotberto Flandrensi comite exiuit de urbe in feria tertia,[5] et Marturanensis episcopus[6]

---

[a] DX *omit* nobis
[b] DX *omit* urbi
[c] summoueri DX

[1] Chaplain to Robert duke of Normandy. Raymond of Agiles, who disliked him, says he was the son of a priest, that he was not yet in major orders, and that his conduct on the crusade had been so scandalous that rude songs had been written about him (*P.L.*, CLV, 661). He was deposed a few months later.

against the pagans and protect the Christians. Like-
wise a most experienced and distinguished man called
Arnulf[1] was chosen as Patriarch, on the Feast of St
Peter's Chains.[2] (This city was captured by God's
Christians on the fifteenth of July, which was a Friday.)

While all this was happening, a messenger came to
Tancred and Count Eustace, asking them to make
ready and go to receive the surrender of the town of
Nablus[3]; so they set out, taking with them many
knights and foot-soldiers, and came to the city, the
inhabitants of which surrendered at once. Then Duke
Godfrey summoned them to come quickly, for the amir
of Cairo was getting ready to fight with us at Ascalon,[4]
so they went quickly into the mountains, looking for
Saracens to fight, and came to Caesarea, from whence
they came along the coast towards Ramleh, where they
found many Arabs who had been sent as scouts before
the main army. Our men chased them and captured
several, who gave us a full report as to where their
army was, and its numbers, and where it was planning
to fight with the Christians. When Tancred heard this,
he sent a messenger straight off to Jerusalem to Duke
Godfrey and the patriarch and all the other leaders,
saying, 'There is going to be a battle at Ascalon, so
come quickly with all the forces you can muster!'
Then the duke had everyone summoned so that they
might go faithfully prepared to fight our enemies at
Ascalon. He himself, with the patriarch, Robert
count of Flanders and the bishop of Martirano,[6] went
with them on Tuesday,[5] but the count of St Gilles and

---

[2] 1 August 1099   [3] The biblical Sichem
[4] This was the army of the Egyptians, under the command of al-Afdal
[5] 9 August 1099   [6] Arnulf, bishop of Martirano in southern Italy

cum eis. Comes uero Sancti Egidii ac Rotbertus Nortmannus[a] dixerunt se non exituros, nisi certum bellum
scirent. Iusserunt ergo militibus suis, ut pergerent
uidere si bellum uere esset; et reuerterentur quantocius,
qui ipsi mox essent parati ire.[b] Ierunt illi, uideruntque
bellum,[c] et cito renuntiauerunt se[d] uidisse oculis suis.
Continuo dux apprehenso Marturanensi episcopo, mandauit Hierusalem, quo milites qui ibi erant preparent[e]
se et ueniant ad bellum.

Quarta uero feria, illi principes exierunt, et milita-
uerunt ad bellum. Episcopus uero Marturanensis rediit,
reportans uerba missa patriarchae et duci, exieruntque
Saraceni obuiam ei, et apprehensum secum duxerunt.[1]
Petrus uero Heremita remansit[f] Hierusalem, ordinando
et precipiendo Grecis et Latinis atque clericis, ut fideliter
Deo processionem celebrarent, et orationes elemosinas-
que facerent, ut Deus populo suo uictoriam daret.
Clerici et presbyteri, induti sacris uestibus ad Templum
Domini[2] conduxere processionem, missas et orationes
decantantes, ut suum defenderet populum.

Denique patriarcha et episcopi aliique seniores congregati sunt ad flumen, quod est ex hac parte Scalonae.
Illic multa animalia, boum, camelorum, ouium, atque
omnium bonorum depredati sunt. Venerunt autem
Arabes fere trecenti irrueruntque nostri super illos, et
apprehenderunt duos ex eis, persequentes alios usque ad
eorum exercitum. Sero autem facto, patriarcha fecit
preconari per omnem hostem, ut in summo mane cras
essent omnes parati ad bellum, excommunicans ne ullus

[a] et Rotbertus Normannorum princeps DX   [b] uenire DX
[c] hostes DX   [d] DX *add* illos   [e] prepararent DX
[f] DX *add* in

[1] His fate is unknown.   [2] The Church of the Holy Sepulchre

Robert the Norman said that they would not go unless they knew for certain that there would be a battle, so they ordered their knights to go out and see whether the battle was really going to take place, and to come back as soon as possible, for they themselves were all ready to set out. The knights went out, saw the preparations for the battle and came straight back to report what they had seen with their own eyes. The duke at once summoned the bishop of Martirano and bade him go to Jerusalem to tell the knights there to get ready to come to the field of battle.

On Wednesday those lords went out and rode to battle. The bishop of Martirano was returning from Jerusalem, bearing messages to the duke and the patriarch, when the Saracens met him, and they captured him and took him away with them.[1] Peter the Hermit stayed in Jerusalem to admonish and encourage all the Greek and Latin priests and the clerks to go in procession devoutly to the honour of God, and to pray and give alms, so that God might grant his people victory. The clerks and priests put on their holy vestments and led the procession to the Temple of our Lord,[2] where they sang masses and orisons, praying that God would defend his people.

Meanwhile the patriarch and the bishops and the other leaders were assembled at the river which lies on this side of Ascalon. They carried off from thence many animals, oxen, camels and sheep, and other goods. About three hundred Arabs came up, and our men attacked them and captured two, driving the rest back to their own army. When evening came, the patriarch had it announced throughout all the host that every man should be ready for battle at dawn, and

homo intenderet ad ulla spolia donec bellum esset factum; sed eo facto reuerterentur cum felici gaudio ad capiendum quicquid eis predestinatum esset a Domino.

Summo uero diluculo in sexta feria[1] intrauerunt in uallem nimis pulchram secus litus maris, in qua suas ordinauerunt[a] acies. Dux instruxit suam aciem, et[b] comes Nortmanniae suam, comes Sancti Egidii suam, comes Flandrensis suam, comes Eustachius suam, Tancredus et Gaston suam. Ordinauerunt quoque pedites et sagittarios qui precederent milites; et sic ordinauerunt omnia, statimque coeperunt militare in nomine domini Iesu Christi. In sinistra uero parte fuit dux Godefridus cum sua acie; comesque[c] Sancti Egidii equitauit iuxta mare in dextera parte, comes Nortmanniae[d] et comes Flandrensis et Tancredus omnesque alii equitabant in medio. Tunc nostri[e] coeperunt paulatim ambulare. Pagani uero stabant parati ad bellum. Vnusquisque suum habebat uasculum pendens collo, ex quibus potarent persequentes nos; sed illis non licuit, gratia Dei.

Comes autem de Nortmannia[f] cernens ammirauissi stantarum habere[g] quoddam pomum aureum in summitate hastae, quae erat cooperta argento, ruit uehementer super illum,[h] eumque[i] uulnerauit usque ad mortem. Ex alia parte, comes Flandrensis nimis acriter illos inuasit. Tancredus igitur[j] impetum fecit per medium tentoriorum eorum. Quod uidentes pagani, continuo inierunt fugam. Paganorum[k] multitudo erat innumerabilis, numerumque eorum nemo scit nisi solus Deus.

[a] struxerunt DX

[b] DX *omit* aciem et, *and write* preclarus comes Normannorum

[c] comes DX (X *adds* uero)

[d] fuit (*om.* D) mitissimus comes (Rotbertus comes *add.* D) Normanniae DX   [e] nostri sic DX

[f] Incomparabilis itaque miles, scilicet domnus Rotbertus comes Normanniae DX   [g] habentem DX   [h] DX *add* qui hunc ferebat

[i] quem uiriliter (et X) prosternens DX   [j] uero DX   [k] quorum DX

that anyone who turned aside for plunder before the
battle was finished should be excommunicated, but that
thereafter they might return with great joy to take
whatever the Lord should grant.

At daybreak on Friday[1] our men entered into a
beautiful valley near the coast and drew up their lines
of battle. The duke, the count of Normandy, the
count of St Gilles, the count of Flanders, Count Eustace,
Tancred and Gaston each drew up his own men, and
foot-soldiers with archers were ordered to precede the
knights. All this was thus arranged, and they joined
battle at once in the Name of our Lord Jesus Christ.
Duke Godfrey with his men fought on the left wing,
the count of St Gilles on the right (near the sea), while
the counts of Normandy and Flanders, with Tancred
and all the rest, rode in the centre, and thus our men
began gradually to advance. The pagans, for their
part, stood ready for battle. Each of them had, hanging
round his neck, a bottle from which he could drink
while he was pursuing us, but by God's grace this was
not to be.

The count of Normandy, seeing that the amir's
standard had a golden apple on the top of the pole,
which was covered with silver, rushed straight at its
bearer and gave him a mortal wound. The count of
Flanders made a determined attack from the other side,
and Tancred charged straight into the middle of the
enemy camp. When the pagans saw this, they began
to flee at once. (There was an innumerable multitude
of pagans, and nobody knows how many there were

[1] 12 August 1099

Bella uero erant immensa; sed uirtus diuina comitabatur nobiscum tam magna, tam fortis, quod statim superauimus illos. Stabant autem inimici Dei excecati et stupefacti, ac uidentes Christi milites apertis oculis nil uidebant, et contra Christianos erigere se non audebant, uirtute Dei tremefacti. Pro nimio timore ascendebant in arbores, in quibus putabant se abscondere; at[a] nostri sagittando et cum lanceis et ensibus occidendo eos ad terram precipitabant. Alii autem iactabant se in terram, non audentes erigere se contra nos. Nostri igitur illos detruncabant, sicut aliquis detruncat animalia ad macellum. Comes Sancti Egidii iuxta mare occidit ex eis sine numero. Alii uero se precipitabant in mare, alii fugiebant huc illucque.

Veniens itaque ammirauissus ante ciuitatem,[b][1] dolens et maerens, lacrimando dixit: 'O deorum spiritus, quis unquam uidit uel audiuit talia? Tanta potestas, tanta uirtus, tanta militia quae nunquam ab ulla gente fuit superata, modo a tantilla gente Christianorum est deuicta! Heu mihi tristis ac dolens, quid amplius dicam? Superatus sum a gente mendica, inermi et pauperrima; quae non habet nisi saccum et peram. Ipsa modo persequitur gentem Aegiptiacam, quae illi plerumque suas largita est elemosinas, dum olim per omnem nostram patriam mendicarent.[c] Huc conduxi ad conuentionem ducenta milia militum, et uideo ipsos[d] laxis frenis fugientes per uiam Babylonicam, et non audent reuerti aduersus gentem Francigenam. Iuro per Machumet et per omnia deorum numina, quod ulterius non retinebo milites conuentione aliqua, quia expulsus sum a gente[e]

---

[a] sed DX   [b] DX *add* Ascalonam   [c] mendicaret DX
[d] illos DX   [e] DX *add* aliena et

[1] Ascalon

save God alone.) The battle was terrible, but the power of God was with us, so mighty and so strong that we gained the victory at once. The enemies of God stood about blinded and bewildered; although their eyes were open they could not see the knights of Christ and they dared not stand fast against them, for they were terror-stricken by the power of God. Some in their panic climbed up trees, hoping to hide, but our men killed them with arrows and spears and swords, and cast them down to the ground. Others threw themselves flat on the ground, not daring to stand up against us, so our men slaughtered them as one slaughters beasts in a shambles. The count of St Gilles, who was near the sea, killed any number of them. Some jumped into the sea and others fled hither and thither.

So the amir reached the city,[1] grieving and lamenting, and saying as he wept, 'O spirits of the gods! Who has ever seen or heard of such things as these? Such power, such courage, such an army as has never been overcome by anyone, to be defeated by such a wretched little force of Christians! Woe's me, sad and miserable man that I am! What more can I say? I have been beaten by a force of beggars, unarmed and poverty-stricken, who have nothing but a bag and a scrip. And this is the army which is now pursuing the Egyptians, who often used to give alms to these people when they went round our country begging. I led two hundred thousand soldiers hither to battle, and now I see them all fleeing with slack reins down the road to Cairo, and they have not the courage to rally against the Franks. I swear by Mohammed and by the glory of all the gods that I will never raise another army, because I have been defeated by a strange

aduena. Conduxi omnia armorum genera, et omnia machinamenta ut eos obsiderem in Hierusalem, et ipsi preuenerunt me ad bellum itinere dierum duorum. Heu michi, quid amplius dicam? Inhonoratus ero semper in terra Babilonica.'

Nostri autem acceperunt eius stantarum, quod comparauit comes de Nortmannia uiginti marchas argenti, et dedit[a] patriarchae in Dei honorem Sanctique Sepulchri. Ensem uero emit quidam sexaginta bisanteis. Superati sunt itaque inimici nostri Deo annuente. Omnes naues terrarum paganorum ibi aderant. Homines uero qui intus erant, uidentes ammirauisum fugientem cum suo exercitu, statim suspenderunt uela, et impulerunt se in alta maria. Reuersi sunt nostri ad tentoria eorum,[b] acceperuntque innumera spolia auri, argenti, omniumque bonorum; omniumque animalium genera, ac omnium[c] armorum instrumenta. Quae uoluerunt asportarunt, reliqua igne consumpserunt.[d]

Reuersi sunt[e] nostri cum gaudio Hierusalem, deferentes secum omnia bona, quae illis erant necessaria. Hoc bellum actum est pridie idus Augusti, largiente haec[f] domino nostro Iesu Christo, cui est honor et gloria nunc et semper et in secula seculorum.[g] Dicat omnis spiritus: Amen.[1]

---

[a] Nostri itaque admiralii eiusdem acceperunt standarum (stand. eiusdem adm. acc. X) quod (quem inclitus et ab omnibus X) honorandus miles Rotbertus Normannorum (X *adds* comes) nobilissimus perempto huius signifero prostrauerat, illud redimens (quem etiam ipse redemit X) x marcas (xx marcis X) argenti dedit (deditque X) DX   [b] illorum tentoria DX
[c] ac omnium anim. gen. omniumque DX   [d] combusserunt DX
[e] redieruntque DX
[f] DX *omit* haec
[g] per infinita seculorum secula DX

people. I brought all sorts of weapons and engines to besiege these men in Jerusalem, and it is they who have attacked me two days' march outside the city. Woe's me! What more can I say? I shall be held up to everlasting scorn in the land of Cairo.'

Our men captured the amir's standard, which the count of Normandy redeemed for twenty marks of silver and gave to the patriarch in honour of God and the Holy Sepulchre. The amir's sword was bought for sixty bezants. So by God's will our enemies were defeated. All the ships from the lands of the pagans were there, but when the crews saw the amir fleeing with his army they hoisted sail at once and made for the open sea. Our men went back to the enemy camp and found innumerable spoils of gold and silver, piles of riches, and all kinds of animals, weapons and tools. They took what they wanted and burnt the rest.

Then our men came back to Jerusalem rejoicing, bearing with them all sorts of provisions which they needed. This battle was fought on 12 August, by the mercy of our Lord Jesus Christ, to whom be honour and glory, now and for ever, world without end. May every soul say 'Amen'![1]

---

[1] The *Gesta Francorum* ends at this point. It is followed, in the two twelfth-century MSS Vatican Reginensis 572 and 641, by a 'Description of the Holy Places' written in the same hand as the *Gesta* itself. The style is terse, like that of the *Gesta*, but there is no direct evidence that the Author of the *Gesta* wrote it. It appears to be a brief guide-book to the Holy Places. Its inclusion suggests, although it does not prove, that the Author completed his pilgrimage. He certainly deserved to do so.

INCIPIT DESCRIPTIO SANCTORVM LOCORVM HIERVSALEM

Si quis ab occidentalibus partibus Hierusalem adire uoluerit, solis ortum semper teneat, et Hierosolimitani loci oratoria ita inueniet, sicut hic notatur. In Hierusalem est cubiculum uno lapide coopertum, ubi Salomon Sapientiam*a* scripsit. Et ibi inter templum et altare in marmore ante aram sanguis Zachariae fusus est. Inde non longe est lapis, ad quem per singulos annos Iudaei ueniunt, et unguentes eum lamentantur, et sic cum gemitu redeunt. Ibi est domus Ezechiae regis Iuda, cui ter quinos annos Deus addidit. Deinde est domus Caiphae, et columna ad quam Christus ligatus flagellis caesus fuit. Ad portam Neapolitanam est pretorium Pilati, ubi Christus a principibus sacerdotum iudicatus fuit. Inde non procul est Golgotha, id est caluariae locus, ubi Christus Dei filius crucifixus est,*b* et ibi primus Adam sepultus fuit, ibique Abraham Deo sacrificauit. Inde quasi ad magni lapidis iactum uersus occidentem locus est ubi Ioseph ab Arimathia domini Iesu corpus sanctum sepeliuit; ibique est ecclesia a Constantino rege[1] speciose fabricata. A monte Caluariae sunt XIII pedes usque ad medium mundum contra occidentem. A sinis-

---

a Sapientiae librum DX
b fuit DX

[1] *Recte* 'emperor'

HERE BEGINS A DESCRIPTION OF
THE HOLY PLACES OF JERUSALEM

If anyone, coming from the western lands, wishes to go to Jerusalem, let him direct his course due eastwards, and in this way he will find the stations for prayer in the lands in and around Jerusalem, as they are noted here. In Jerusalem is a little cell, roofed with one stone, where Solomon wrote the Book of Wisdom. And there, between the temple and the altar, on the marble pavement before the holy place, the blood of Zechariah was shed. Not far off is a stone, to which the Jews come every year, and they anoint it and make lamentation, and so go away wailing. There is the house of Hezekiah king of Judah, to whose span of life God added fifteen years. Next to it is the house of Caiaphas, and the pillar to which Christ was bound when he was scourged. At the Nablus gate is Pilate's judgement-seat, where Christ was judged by the chief priests. Not far off is Golgotha, that is 'The place of a skull', where Christ the Son of God was crucified, and where the first Adam was buried, and where Abraham offered his sacrifice to God. From thence, a stone's throw to the west, is the place where Joseph of Arimathea buried the holy Body of the Lord Jesus, and on this site there is a church, beautifully built by Constantine the king.[1] From Mount Calvary the navel of the world lies thirteen feet to the west. If you turn

tra parte est carcer, ubi Christus fuit carceratus.[a] In dextera parte sepulchri prope est monasterium Latinum in honore sanctae Mariae Virginis, ubi eiusdem domus fuit. Ibi altare est in eodem monasterio, ibique stabat Maria mater uirgo, et cum ea soror matris eius Maria Cleophe, et Maria Magdalene, flentes dolentesque in cruce positum Dominum uidentes. Ibi dixit Iesus matri: 'Mulier, ecce filius tuus'; discipulo: 'Ecce mater tua.'[1]

Ab hoc loco quantum potest arcus bis mittere sagittam, in orientali parte est Templum Domini a Salomone factum, in quo a iusto Symeone presentatus est Christus. In dextera parte huius templi, Salomon templum suum aedificauit, et inter utrumque templum porticum speciosam struxit columnis marmoreis. In sinistra parte probatica piscina est. Inde contra orientem quasi ad mille passus mons Oliueti conspicitur, ubi dominus Iesus ad patrem orauit dicens: 'Pater, si fieri potest,' et reliqua.[2] Et in lapide Pater Noster scripsit; et inde ascendit in celum, dicens discipulis: 'Ite docete omnes gentes,' et reliqua.[3] Inter Templum Domini et montem Oliueti est uallis Iosaphath, ubi uirgo Maria ab apostolis sepulta fuit. In qua ualle[4] mundum iudicaturus ueniet Dominus. Ibi prope est uilla quae dicitur Gethsemani, ibique prope est ortus trans torrentem Cedron, ubi Iudas Iesum tradidit. Inde prope est sepulchrum Isaiae prophetae. Inde ad mille passus Bethania, ubi Lazarus quatriduanus resuscitatus est. In eadem parte contra

---

[a] carceratus fuisse narratur DX

[1] John 19:26-27
[2] Matt. 26:39
[3] ibid. 28:19
[4] Prudent pilgrims used to mark stones on which they hoped to find seats at the Last Judgement (H. F. M. Prescott, *Jerusalem Journey*, p. 130).

north you will find the prison where Christ was imprisoned, and if south, near the Sepulchre, there lies the Latin monastery built in honour of St Mary the Virgin, whose house stood there. There is in that monastery an altar built on the spot where stood Mary the Virgin Mother, and with her Mary the wife of Cleophas, her mother's sister, and Mary Magdalen, weeping and mourning when they saw the Lord hanging on the cross. It was there that Christ said to his Mother, 'Woman, behold thy son,' and to the disciple, 'Behold thy Mother.'[1]

Two bowshots away from this place, going eastwards, is the Temple of the Lord built by Solomon, in which Christ was presented by the righteous Simeon. To the south of this temple Solomon built his own temple, and between them he set up a beautiful porch with marble columns. To the north is the Pool of Testing. About a thousand paces away eastward you can see the Mount of Olives, where the Lord Jesus prayed to the Father, saying, 'Father, if it be possible,' etc.[2] And he wrote the 'Our Father' upon a stone, and from that place he ascended into Heaven, saying to his disciples 'Go, and teach all nations,' etc.[3] Between the Lord's Temple and the Mount of Olives is the Valley of Jehoshaphat, where the Virgin Mary was buried by the disciples. This is the valley[4] in which the Lord will come to judge the world. Near to it is the village called Gethsemane, and close by, across the torrent of Kedron, is the garden where Judas betrayed Jesus. The tomb of Isaiah the prophet is quite near. A thousand paces away is Bethany, where Lazarus was restored to life on the fourth day. In the same direction,

Iericho ad milia XVIIII est arbor sicomorus, in quam
Zacheus ascendit, ut uideret Iesum. In alia parte ad
mille passus de Iericho est fons Helisei, ab ipso benedictus commixtione salis. Inde ad V milia est fluuius
Iordanis, in quo Dominus a Iohanne baptizatus est, ab
Hierusalem distans VIII leugis. Inde non longe est
mons unde Helias raptus est. A Iordane est uia XVIII
dierum usque ad montem Synai; ubi Deus Moysi in
igne rubi apparuit, eique legem dedit; ibique est ydria
magna, quae indeficiens oleum parturit. Mons Thabor
distat ab Hierusalem itinere trium dierum, ubi Dominus
transfiguratus est. In cuius montis pede dicitur esse
Galilea et mare Tyberiadis, quod non est mare sed
stagnum de quo Iordanis egreditur. In dextera parte
urbis Hierusalem contra meridiem extra murum[a] quantum potest arcus iacere, est mons Syon; ibique est
ecclesia a Salomone facta. Ibi[b] Iesus caenauit cum
discipulis ante passionem, ibique eos Spiritu Sancto
repleuit[c]; ibi etiam uirgo Maria migrauit a saeculo, et
spiritum reddidit, cuius corpus sanctissimum apostoli in
uallem Iosaphat transtulerunt. In cuius montis pede
contra meridiem est fons Syloa, subito egrediens e terra.
Inde non longe est Sychem, ubi Ioseph ueniens de ualle
Ebron quaesiuit fratres. Ibi est uilla quam dedit Iacob
Ioseph filio suo; ibique requiescit corpus eius. Inde ad
mille passus est Sychar, ubi Dominus mulieri Samari-
tanae locutus est. Inde non longe est locus ubi luctatus
est angelus cum Iacob. Ibi Bethleem est, ciuitas Dauid,

[a] DX *omit* contra . . . murum
[b] ibi Dominus DX
[c] eis Spiritum sanctum misit DX

nineteen miles out on the Jericho road, is the sycamore tree up which Zachaeus climbed so that he might see Jesus. In the other direction, a thousand paces from Jericho, is Elisha's spring, which he blessed by throwing in salt. Five miles further on is the river Jordan, in which the Lord was baptised by John, and it is eight leagues from Jerusalem. Not far off is the mountain where Elijah was carried up into Heaven. From the Jordan it is eighteen days' journey to Mount Sinai, where God appeared to Moses in the burning bush, and gave him the Law, and there is a great oil-jar, which never ceases to produce oil. Mount Tabor is three days' journey from Jerusalem, and there the Lord was transfigured. It is said that at the foot of this mountain lie Galilee and the Sea of Tiberias, which is not a sea at all, but a lake out of which the Jordan flows. To the south of Jerusalem, about a bowshot south of the wall, is Mount Sion, and there is a church which Solomon built. Our Lord ate the Last Supper there with his disciples before his Passion, and there he filled them with the Holy Ghost, and there the Virgin Mary departed from this world and gave up the ghost, and the apostles carried her most holy body into the Valley of Jehoshaphat. At the foot of this mountain, towards the south, is the Pool of Siloam, which bubbles straight up out of the earth. Not far off is Sychem, where Joseph came out of the valley of Hebron, looking for his brethren. There is the village which Jacob gave to Joseph his son, and there his body is buried. A thousand paces away is Sychar, where our Lord talked to the Samaritan woman, and not far off is the place where the Angel wrestled with Jacob. There too is Bethlehem, the City of David, where Christ was

ubi Christus natus est, distans ab Hierusalem quattuor
milibus contra meridiem; ibique est ecclesia marmoreis
columnis aedificata, in qua est locus ubi Christus natus
est. Non procul hinc in dextera parte est Domini pre-
sepe. Inde ad XII milia est castellum Abraham, quod
dicitur Tocor, ubi ipse Abraham et Isaac et Iacob
sepulti sunt cum uxoribus suis. In sinistra parte est
mons Dominus Vidit, ibique locus est ubi Abraham
immolare filium uoluit.

Explicit Itinerarium Hierosolimitanorum.

born, and it is four miles southwards from Jerusalem;
and there in the place where Christ was born is a
church built with marble columns. Not far from here,
to the south, is our Lord's manger. Twelve miles
further on is the castle of Abraham, called Tocor, where
Abraham and Isaac and Jacob are buried with their
wives. To the north is a mountain called 'the Lord
sees,' and there is the place where Abraham was willing
to sacrifice his son.

*This is the end of the tour of those who made the pilgrimage
to Jerusalem.*

INCIPIT MISSA IN VENERATIONE
SANCTI SEPVLCHRI[1]

Omnipotens sempiterne Deus, qui per passionem Vnigeniti tui humanum genus redimere dignatus es, et eius sepultura omnium fidelium sepulchra signasti, concede propitius, ut ad gloriam resurrectionis eiusdem pertingere mereamur, per eundem . . .

SECRETVM. Suscipe quaesumus omnipotens Deus hanc hostiam oblationis, quam tibi in illius commemoratione deferimus,[a] qui ad detergenda mundi facinora iniuriam crucis et sepulturae pro nobis clementer sustinuit, qui tecum uiuit . . .

PRAEFATIO. O aeterne Deus, qui oraculis prophetarum Vnigeniti tui gloriosum in quo caro illius non uideret corruptionem sepulchrum innotescere uoluisti; ut inde uictor mortis resurgens fidelibus spem resurgendi concederet; et ideo cum angelis etc.

POST COMMVNIONEM. Munera nostrae redemptionis quaesumus, omnipotens Deus, quae fideliter sumpsimus, et a uitiorum nos eruant sepulchris, et ad gloriam transferant beatae resurrectionis, per Dominum . . .

[a] offerimus DX

[1] The Proper Prayers only are given.

HERE BEGINS THE MASS IN HONOUR OF THE HOLY SEPULCHRE[1]

Almighty everlasting God, who hast vouchsafed to redeem mankind by the Passion of thine Only-begotten Son, and by his burial hast signified the burial of all thy faithful people, grant, we beseech thee, that we may be made worthy to be partakers of his resurrection, through him, etc.

SECRET. Receive, we beseech thee, Almighty God, this sacrifice which we present unto thee, in remembrance of him who graciously endured the cross and grave to blot out the sins of the world, who with thee liveth, etc.

PROPER PREFACE. O eternal God, who hast willed to declare to us by the mouth of the prophets that in the glorious sepulchre of thine Only-begotten Son his flesh should not see corruption, so that arising from it as Conqueror over death he should also give to his faithful people the hope of resurrection, therefore with angels, etc.

POST-COMMUNION. We beseech thee, O Almighty God, that the pledges or our redemption, which we have received by faith, may both deliver us from the tomb of our sins, and bring us to the glory of a blessed resurrection, through our Lord, etc.

[*Drawing of a line* 5¾ *inches* (129 mm.) *long, giving a total length of* 6 *ft.* 4 *in.* (1·935 *metres*).]

Haec linea quindecies ducta, et a sepulchro Domini Hierosolimis sumpta, longitudinem Christi designat. Die qua eam uideris, subitanea morte non morieris.

[*Drawing of a line* 4⅜ *inches* (98 mm.) *long, giving a total width of* 2 *ft.* 11 *in.* (0·882 *metres*).]

Haec secunda nouenario numero remensa, latitudinem Christi signat, eandemque salutem de morte subitanea dat, in die semel uisa.[1]

---

[1] This seems to be a talisman appropriate to a country in which sudden (i.e. unshriven) death was extremely likely to happen. It cannot be proved to have anything to do with the Author of the *Gesta*, but it seems to be in keeping with the character of a man who accepted, quite naturally, the intervention of the warrior saints at Antioch.

This line, copied from the sepulchre of the Lord at Jerusalem, and multiplied fifteen times, indicates the height of Christ. On the day on which you see it, you shall not suffer sudden death.

The second line multiplied nine times, indicates the breadth of Christ's Body, and it gives the same protection against sudden death on the day on which it has once been seen.[1]

INDEX

OF PERSONS AND PLACES

INDEX
OF PERSONS AND PLACES

Abbassid dynasty, xxi, xxii

Abraham, 98, 101

Achard of Montmerle (Mommellou), 5, 88–9

Acre (Acra), xxxvi, xxxvii, 86–7

Adam, 98

Adana. *See* Athena

Adela, daughter of William the Conqueror and wife of Stephen, count of Blois and Chartres, 15 *n*

Adhémar, bishop of Le Puy and papal legate, xxviii–xxix, xxxiv, 5, 15–16, 18–20, 32, 46, 58, 68, 74

Agiles, Rayond of. *See* Raymond

Agulani, 20 *and note*

Aix, Albert of. *See* Albert

al-Afdal, wazir of Cairo, xxxvii, 86, 88, 93, 96–7

al-Bara, 74–5, 77

— battle of, xxvii, xxxiii, 31

— bishop of. *See* Peter of Narbonne

al-Boukeia. *See* Sem

Albert of Aix, xi, xxvii

Aleppo (Aleph), xxii, 4, 30, 53, 55–6, 73

— amir of. *See* Rudwan

Alexandretta, 63

Alexius Comnenus, emperor, xii, xv–xvi, xviii, xxi, xxv, xxvii, xxix, xxxvi–xxxvii, 2, 3, 5–7, 8 *n*, 9–13, 16–17, 25 *n*, 34 *n*, 63, 65, 72

Ali ibn Munquidh, amir of Shaizar, 81 *and note*

— Usama, grandson of, 81 *n*

Amalfi (Malfi Scafardi Pontis), 7

Ammar, Fakhr-al-Mulk ibn. *See* Fakhr-al-Mulk

Andrew, St, 59–60

Andronopolis, 8

Anna Comnena, Byzantine princess and historian, xxvi, xxix, 5 *n*, 12 *n*, 18 *n*

Ansarieh mountains, 82

Anse (Ansa), Robert of. *See* Robert

Anselm of Ribemont, 85

Antioch, xiii, xvi, xxi–xxii, xxviii, xxxi–xxxviii, 4, 12, 26–30, 32, 39, 44, 46–8, 51–2, 57–9, 62–3, 65, 74–7, 80–1, 84

— battle of the Bridge of, xxxiii, 39, 42

— Bridge Gate of, 38, 41–2 *n*, 61 *n*, 76

— citadel of, 47, 50, 60–2, 68, 70–1

— great battle of, xxxiv, 54–5, 67–71

— lake of (Qara-su), 51

— — battle of the, xii, xxvii, xxxiii, 36–7

— monastery of St George at, 43

— mosque at, 39, 42

— rulers of. *See* Antiochus, Bohemond I, Bohemond II, Yaghi Siyan

— St George's gate of, 38, 43, 45

— St Mary's church in, 57, 61

— St Paul's gate of, 30, 38

— St Peter's cathedral in, 58–9, 61, 65, 75–6

— St Peter's chair in, 76

Antiochus (Soter), founder of Antioch, 77 *and note*

Anti-taurus mountains, xxxi, 27

Apulia, xi, xii, 52

Archae. *See* Arqa

Aregh (Harenc), castle of, 29, 35

Arnulf, bishop of Martirano, 93–4

— patriarch of Jerusalem, 93, 97

Arqa (Archae), xxxvi, 83–5

Ascalon (Scalonia), ix, xxxvii, 93, 96 *n*

Asia Minor. *See* Rum

Athena (Adana), 25

Aubré of Cagnano, 8

— of Grandmesnil (Grentamenilg), 56

Aubrée, mother of Bohemond, 5 *n*

Aups, Peter d'. *See* Peter

Aura, Abbot of. *See* Ekkehard

Azymites, 45, 49

Babylon. *See* Cairo
Bad-crown (Mala Corona), 46
Baghdad, xxi, xxvi, 37 *n*, 49 *n*
Bagrat, xxxi
Baldwin, count of Boulogne, later count of Edessa, finally king of Jerusalem, x, xiv, xvi, xxiv, xxviii, xxxi, xxxvi–xxxvii, 2, 6, 24–5, 86, 92 *n*
Baldwin, count of Mons, 2
Bardar. *See* Vardar
Bari, xxix, 5, 6
Barkyaruq, sultan, xxvi, 49, 66
Barlings Abbey, xl
Barneville, Roger of. *See* Roger
Baruth. *See* Beyrut
Batrun. *See* Bethelon
Baudri, archbishop of Dol, ix, xiv
Bearn, Gaston of. *See* Gaston
Beauvais, Rainald of. *See* Rainald
Beert. *See* Bearn
Bethany, 99
Bethelon (Batrun), 86
Bethlehem, xxi, 11, 100
Beyrut (Baruth), xxxvi, 86
Blois, Stephen, count of. *See* Stephen
Boel of Chartres, 8
Bohemond of Taranto, leader of the crusading forces from southern Italy, *passim*
— father of. *See* Robert Guiscard
— mother of. *See* Aubrée
— nephew of. *See* Tancred
Bohemond II, prince of Antioch, x
Bosphorus, xxvii, xxix
Botrenthrot, valley of, 24
Bouillon, Godfrey de. *See* Godfrey
Boulogne, counts of. *See* Baldwin; Eustace
— Guynemer of. *See* Guynemer
Brachium Sancti Georgii. *See* Bosphorus, Hellespont
Braym river (Nahr Ibrahim), 86
Brindisi, xxix, 5
Bulgaria, 52, 65. *See also* Macedonia
Byblos. *See* Gibelon
Byzantium. *See* Constantinople

Caen, Ralph of. *See* Ralph
Caesarea in Cappadocia. *See* Kaisarieh

Caesarea in Palestine, 87
Caesarea in Syria. *See* Shaizar
Cagnano, Aubré of. *See* Aubré
Caiaphas, 98
Cairo (Babylon), xxii, xxxvi, 37, 42, 93, 96–7
— wazir of. *See* al-afdal
Calvary, Mount, 98
Cambis, Jean-Louis-Dominique de, Marquis de Valleron, xxxix
Camden, William, xli
Camela. *See* Chamelle
Cannes (Cannae), Herman of. *See* Herman
Capharda. *See* Kafartab
Cassianus. *See* Yaghi Siyan
Castillon, Peter, seneschal of. *See* Peter
Castoria (Kastoria), 8
Cayphas. *See* Haifa
Cedron. *See* Kedron
Chamelle, La, (Camela, Hims, Homs), xix, xxxvi, 83
— amir of. *See* Janah-al-Dawla
Charlemagne, xxii, 2
Chartres, Boel of. *See* Boel
— Fulcher of. *See* Fulcher
— Stephen, count of. *See* Stephen
Clermont near Liège, 56 *n*
— Lambert, count of. *See* Lambert
Clermont, Council of, ix, xii, xxiv, xxviii, 1 *n*
Coëtivy, Cardinal Alain de, bishop of Avignon, xxxix
Cologne, *scholasticus* of. *See* Oliver
Constantine, emperor, 98
Constantinople (Byzantium, Istanbul), xix, xxii, xxiii, xxv, xxvii, xxix, 2, 4, 7, 10–11, 13, 16–17, 18, 65, 72
— emperor of. *See* Alexius Comnenus; Constantine; Heraclius; John Tzimisces; Nicephorus Phocas
Corosanum, Corrozanae, Corrozanum. *See* Khorasan
Coxon (Gueuk-su), 26–7
Cremona, Liutprand of. *See* Liudprand
Curbaram. *See* Karbuqa
Curti. *See* Kurds
Cyprus, 35
Cyvito, Cyvitot. *See* Kivotos

Dalmatia (Sclavinia), 5
Damascus, xxi, 30, 68 n
— amir of. See Duqaq
— — atabek of. See Tughtagin
Damietta, xxxviii
Danube river, xxix, 2 n
Daturre. See Geoffrey of Lastours
Demetrius, St, 69
Djebail. See Gibelon
Djibleh. See Gibel
Dog's river (Nahr al-Kalb), 86 n
Dol, archbishop of. See Baudri
Dorylaeum (Eski-Cheir), battle of,
  xii, xx, xxvii–xxix, 18–21
Drino (Drim) river, 8 n
Duqaq, amir of Damascus, xxvii,
  xxxii, xxxiv, 30 n, 47 n, 49
Durachium. See Durazzo
Durazzo, xiii, xxv, 6, 12 n

Edessa, xxvi, xxxi
— rulers of. See Baldwin; Thoros
Edgar Atheling, xxiii
Ekkehard, abbot of Aura, ix
Elijah, 100
Elisha, 100
Emma, sister of Bohemond, 5 n
Erachia. See Heraclea
Eregli. See Heraclea
Eski-Cheir. See Dorylaeum
Euphrates river, xxii, xxxi
Eustace, count of Boulogne, brother
  of Godfrey de Bouillon, 90, 93,
  95
Everard of Puiset, 5
— the Huntsman, 78
Exerogorgo. See Xerigordo

Fakhr-al-Mulk ibn Ammar, amir
  of Tripoli, 83–6
Far, Farfar. See Orontes river
Firuz (Pirus), 44–7
FitzGerald, Robert. See Robert
FitzRalph, Humphrey. See Hum-
  phrey
FitzToustan, Robert. See Robert
Flanders, Robert, count of. See
  Robert
Fleury, Hugh of. See Hugh
Fulcher of Chartres, x, xiii–xiv,
  xxi, xxx, xxxiv, 1 n, 59 n, 65 n,
  68 n, 86 n, 92 n
Fulco of Paris, xi

Galilee (Tiberias), sea of, xv, xxv,
  100
Gaston of Béarn (Beert), 92, 95
Genoa, fleet of, xxiii, xxxvi–xxxvii,
  88
Geoffrey of Lastours (Daturre), 79
George, St, 69, 87
Gethsemane, 99
Gibel (Djibleh, Gibellum), 84
Gibelon (Byblos, Djebail, Zebari),
  86
Gilo of Paris, xi
Godfrey de Bouillon, duke of
  Lower Lorraine, later advocate
  of the Holy Sepulchre, xii, xxi,
  xxviii, xxxvi–xxxvii, 2, 6, 11, 13–
  14, 18–20, 25, 46, 59, 61, 68–9,
  70, 72, 75–6, 80, 84–5, 87, 90,
  92–3, 95
— of Monte Scaglioso (Scabioso),
  21 and note, 61
Golgotha, 98
Grandmesnil. See Aubré; William
Gregory VII, pope, xxiv
Grentamenilg. See Aubré of Grand-
  mesnil; William of Grandmesnil
Gueuk-su. See Coxon
Guibert of Nogent, xi
Guiscard, Robert. See Robert
  Guiscard
Guy, half-brother of Bohemond,
  xvi n, 63–5
— Trousseau (Trursellus), 56
Guynemer of Boulogne, xxiii

Haifa (Cayphas), 87
Hamah, 73 n
Harenc. See Aregh
Hauteville, Tancred of. See
  Tancred
Hautpoul, Peter Raymond of. See
  Peter Raymond
Hellespont, (Bosphorus, Brachium
  Sancti Georgii), 3, 5, 7, 13
Henry IV, ruler of the Western
  Empire, xxiv
Heraclea (Erachia, Eregli), 23
Heraclius, emperor, xxi
Herluin, interpreter, 66–7
Herman of Cannes, 7
Hezekiah, 98
Hierosolem. See Jerusalem
Hims. See Chamelle

Historia Belli Sacri, x
Homs. *See* Chamelle
Hugh, count of Vermandois (Hugo
  Magnus), xii, xxiv, xxix, 5–6,
  18–20, 68, 70, 72
— of Fleury, xi
— the Berserk (Hugo Insanus), 61
Humphrey FitzRalph, 7–8
— of Monte Scaglioso, 8, 21 *n*
Iconium (Konieh, Yconium), xxvi,
  23, 63 *n*
Iron Bridge. *See* Orontes bridge
Isaac, 101
Isaiah, 99
Isard of Mouzon, 5
Istambul. *See* Constantinople

Jacob, 100–01
Jaffa (Japhia), xxxvi, 87 *n*, 88, 91 *n*
Janah-al-Dawla, amir of Homs, 30,
  83
Japhia. *See* Jaffa
Jehoshaphat, valley of, 99–100
Jericho, 100
Jerusalem (Hierosolem), ix, x, xiii,
  xvi, xxi–xxiv, xxvi–xxvii, xxxvi–
  xxxvii, 30, 73 *n*, 85–7, 90–4, 97.
  See also Description of the Holy
  Places, 98–101
— amir of. *See* Suqman-ibn-Ortuq
— David's Tower in, 91
— Holy Sepulchre in, *passim*
— —advocate of. *See* Godfrey de
  Bouillon
— king of. *See* Baldwin
— Mosque of Omar in. *See*
  Jerusalem, Solomon's Temple in
— patriarch of. *See* Arnulf
— St Mary's church near, 87
— St Stephen's church near, 87
— Solomon's Temple (Mosque of
  Omar) in, 91–2, 99
John the Baptist, 100
— Tzimisces, Emperor, 51 *n*
Jordan river, 100
Joseph of Arimathea, 98
— patriarch, 100
Judas, 99

Kafartab (Capharda), 81
Kaisarieh (Caesarea in Cappadocia), 25

Karbuqa (Curbaram, Kerboga),
  amir of Mosul, xi, xiv, xvi, xxvii,
  xxxi, xxxii–xxxiv, 49–56, 63, 65,
  66–70
Kastoria. *See* Castoria
Kedron (Cedron) valley, 87 *n*, 99
Kenilworth Priory, xl
Kephalia (Raphania), 82
Kerboga. *See* Karbuqa
Khorasan (Corosanum, Corrozanae,
  Corrozanum), 4, 5, 15, 39, 50–2,
  67
Kivotos (Cyvito, Cyvitot), 4, 5, 16
Komotini, 10 *n*
Konieh. *See* Iconium
Kurds (Curti), 49
Kyriopalatios, 10

Lambert the Poor, count of Cler-
  mont, 56
Laodicea (Latakieh, La Liche,
  Lichia), 84
Lastours, Geoffrey of. *See* Geoffrey
Latakieh. *See* Laodicea
Lazarus, 99
Lethold of Tournai, 91
Liche, La; Lichia. *See* Laodicea
Liudprand of Cremona, xviii *n*, xxii
Lorraine, Lower, Godfrey, duke of.
  See Godfrey de Bouillon

Ma'arat. *See* Marra
Macedonia (Bulgaria), 8, 10 *n*
Mala Corona. *See* Bad-crown
Malfi Scafardi Pontis. *See* Amalfi
Malikshah, Sultan, xxv–xxvi, 22 *n*
Malmesbury, William of. *See*
  William
Malregard (Maregart), castle of
  Mount, 30
Manichaeans, 8
Manustra (Missis, Mopsuestia), 25
Manzikert, battle of, xxv
Marakia (Maraclea), 84
Marash (Marasim), 27
Maregart. *See* Malregard
Maritza river, xxix, 2 *n*, 10 *n*
Marra (Ma'arat), xiii, xxxvi, 73,
  77–81
Martirano, bishop of. *See* Arnulf
Mary Cleophas, 99
Mary Magdalene, St, 99
Melfi, treaty of, xxv

Melun, lord of. *See* William the Carpenter
Mercurius, St, 69
Missis. *See* Manustra
Mommellou. *See* Achard of Montmerle
Monastir. *See* Palagonia
Mons, Count of. *See* Baldwin
Monte Scaglioso, Godfrey of. *See* Godfrey
— Humphrey of. *See* Humphrey
Montlhéry, 56 n
Montmerle, Achard of. *See* Achard
Mopsuestia. *See* Manustra
Morava river, 2 n
Moses, 100
Mount Pilgrim, castle of, xxxvii
Mouzon, Isard of. *See* Isard
Munquidh. *See* Ali

Nablus (Neopolis, Sichem, Sychem), 93, 98
Nahr al-Kalb. *See* Dog's River
Nahr Ibrahim. *See* Braym
Narbonne, Peter of. *See* Peter
Nazareth, xv
Neopolis. *See* Nablus
Nicea, xxix, 3, 4, 13–17, 22, 58
Nicephorus Phocas, emperor, xxii, 51 n
Nicomedia, 3, 13–14
Nicholas IV, pope, xxxix
Nogent, Guibert of. *See* Guibert
Normandy, Robert, duke of. *See* Robert

Oliver, *scholasticus* of Cologne, later bishop of Paderborn, xxxviii
Olives, Mount of, 99
Orange, bishop of, 80
Ordericus Vitalis, xi
Orontes, bridge over (Iron Bridge, Pons Farreus *or* Ferreus), 28 n, 29 n, 35, 37, 50, 70
Orontes river (Far, Farfar), 27 n, 28 m, 39 n, 51, 77, 81
Ortuqid dynasty, xxiii, xxvii, xxxvi, 86
Otranto, xxix, 5

Paderborn, bishop of. *See* Oliver
Palagonia (Monastir), 8

Paris, Fulco of. *See* Fulco
— Gilo of. *See* Gilo
Patzinaks (Pinzinaci), 6, 9
Paul of Samosata, heresiarch, 20 n
Paulicians (Publicani), 20 *and note*, 26, 49, 83
Persia, 4 n, 5
Petau, Paul, xxxix, xli
Peter Bartholomew, visionary, xxxiv, 59–60
Peter d'Aups, 25–6
— of Narbonne, bishop of al-Bara, 75
— Raymond of Hautpoul, 26
— St, 57–8, 66
— Seneschal of Castillon, 26
— the Hermit, xxiv, xxvi–xxviii, 2, 4, 33, 66–7, 94
— Tudebod of Civray, x, xxxviii n
Philip I, king of France, 3 n, 5 n
Philomelium (Philomena), 63
Piacenza, Council of, xxv
Pilet, Raymond. *See* Raymond
Pinzinaci. *See* Patzinaks
Pirus. *See* Firuz
Pisa, xxiii
Plastencia, 25 n
Poissi, Walter of. *See* Walter the Penniless
Pons Farreus *or* Ferreus. *See* Orontes bridge
Pontius Pilate, 98
Publicani. *See* Paulicians
Puiset, Everard of. *See* Everard
Puy, Bishop of Le. *See* Adhémar

Qara-su river. *See* Antioch, lake of
Qilij-Arslan I (Old Suleiman), ruler of Rum, xxvi, 22
Qilij-Arslan II (Suleiman), ruler of Rum, xxvii, xxix, xxx, 22

Rainald of Beauvais, 69
— the Italian, 3–4
Ralph of Caen, xi, 18 n
Ramleh (Ramola), xxxvi, 87, 93
— bishop of. *See* Robert of Rouen
Ranulf, brother of Richard of the Principality, 5, 7
— Richard, son of. *See* Richard
Ranyard, A. C., xl
Raphania. *See* Kephalia

Raymond, count of St Gilles and Toulouse, x, xii, xix, xxiv, xxviii–xxix, xxxiii, xxxvi–xxxvii, 5, 11, 13–16, 18–20, 25–6, 39, 46, 59, 61, 68, 71–8, 80–1, 83, 85–8, 90–6
— of Agiles, ix, x, xiii–xv, xx, xxxiv, xxxvi, 5 *n*, 13 *n*, 44 *n*, 57 *n*, 59 *n*, 60 *n*, 68 *n*, 81 *n*, 92 *n*
— Pilet, 73–4, 83, 87–9
— vicomte of Turenne, 83, 87
Rayy, battle of, xxvi, 47 *n*
Rheims, Robert of. *See* Robert
Riant, Paul, xlii
Ribemont (Riboatmont), 85 *n*
— Anselm of. *See* Anselm
Richard of the Principality, count of Salerno, 5, 7, 13, 20
— son of Count Ranulf, 8
Riha. *See* Rugia
Roaix, Peter of. *See* Peter
Robert, count of Flanders, xxix, xxxvii, 5, 13, 16, 18, 30–2, 46, 59, 68, 70, 72, 76, 80, 84–5, 87, 93, 95
— duke of Normandy (incorrectly called count of Normandy), xxiv, xxix, xxxvii, xxxix, xl, 5, 15–16, 18, 59, 68–9, 72, 76, 80–1, 85, 87, 94–5, 97
— FitzGerard, constable of Bohemond, xii, 36
— FitzToustan, 7
— Guiscard, father of Bohemond, xii, xxiv–xxv, 5, 12 *n*, 25 *n*
— of Anse, 7, 20
— of Rheims (Robert the Monk), ix, xxxvii *n*, xxxviii *n*
— of Rouen, bishop of Ramleh, 87
— of St Rémi, xi
— of Sourdeval, 7
— the Monk. *See* Robert of Rheims
Roger, count, uncle of Bohemond, 7
— of Barneville, 15–16
Romania. *See* Rum
Rouen, Robert of. *See* Robert
Rudwan, amir of Aleppo, xxvii xxxii–xxxiv, 35 *n*, 47 *n*, 83 *n*
Rugia (Riha), 77, 80
— valley of, 26
Rum (Asia Minor, Romania), 3, 11 *n*, 14, 22, 34–5, 50–2

Rusa, 27 *and note*
Russignolo, count of, 8–9

Sagitta (Saida, Sidon), 86
Saida. *See* Sagitta
St Gilles, Raymond, count of. *See* Raymond
St Mary of the Latins, monastery of, 99
St Rémi, Robert of. *See* Robert
St Simeon's Port, xxiii, 39, 42 *n*, 57, 76
Salerno, count of. *See* Richard of the Principality
Saljuqid (Seljuk) dynasty, xxiii, 27 n
Samosata, Paul of. *See* Paul
Scalonia. *See* Ascalon
Sclavinia. *See* Dalmatia
Seljuk. *See* Saljuqid
Sem, valley of (?al-Boukeia), 82
Sensadolus. *See* Shems-ed-Daula
Serres (Serra), 10
Shaizar (Caesarea in Syria), xxvi, xxxvi, 81
— amir of. *See* Ali ibn Munquidh
Shems-ed-Daula (Sensadolus), son of Yaghi Siyan, 50
Sichem. *See* Nablus
Sicily, 7
Sidon. *See* Sagitta
Siloam (Syloa), pool of, 88, 100
Silpius, Mount, 28 *n*
Simeon, 25
— the Just, 99
Sinai, Mount, 100
Sinehabere, Gualterius. *See* Walter the Penniless
Sion, Mount, 87–8, 100
Sourdeval, Robert of. *See* Robert
Spain, 34
Stephen, count of Blois and Chartres, xxix, xxxiii, 15, 63
— (Valentine), visionary, xxxiv, 57–9
Suleiman. *See* Qilij-Arslan
Suqman ibn Ortuq, amir of Jerusalem, 35 *n*, 49
Sur. *See* Tyre
Sychar, 100
Sychem. *See* Nablus
Syloa. *See* Siloam

Tabor, Mount, 100
Talamania. *See* Tell-Mannas
Tancred, nephew of Bohemond, xvi, xxix, xxxi, xxxvii, 7, 9–11, 13–14, 18, 20–1, 24–5, 32–4, 43–4, 55–6, 59, 64 *n*, 68, 70, 87, 92–3, 95
— of Hauteville, xii
Taranto, 7 *n*
— Bohemond of. *See* Bohemond
Tarsus, xxxi, 11 *n*, 24
Tatikios (Tetigus), envoy of the Emperor Alexius, 34–5
Taurina. *See* Turenne
Teheran, xxvi
Tell-Mannas (Talamania), 73
Tentoria. *See* Turenne
Tetigus. *See* Tatikios
Thoros, Armenian ruler of Edessa, xxxi
Tiberias. *See* Galilee
Tocor, 101
Tortosa, 83
Toulouse, count of. *See* Raymond
Tournai, Lethold of. *See* Lethold
Tripoli, xxvi–xxvii, xxxvi–xxxvii, 83–6
— amir of. *See* Fakhr-al-Mulk ibn Ammar
— castle of Mount Pilgrim near, xxxvii
Trousseau, Guy. *See* Guy
Trursellus. *See* Guy Trousseau
Tudebod, Peter. *See* Peter Tudebod
Tughtagin, atabek of Duqaq of Damascus. xxxii *and note*, 30 *n*
Turcopuli, 6, 9, 16
Turenne (Taurina, Tentoria), 83
— Raymond, vicomte of. *See* Raymond

Tutush, xxvi–xxvii, 22 *n*, 47 *n*
Tyre (Sur), 86
— William of. *See* William

Umayyad dynasty, xxi
Urban II, pope, xii, xxiv, 1 *n*

Vardar (Bardar) river, 8
Venice, xxiii
Vermandois, Hugh, count of. *See* Hugh
Via Egnatia, 5 *n*

Walter the Penniless (Gualterius Sinehabere, Walter of Poissi), 4
William I, king of England, 5 *n*, 15 *n*
— of Archis, 63 *n*
— of Grandmesnil, 56
— of Malmesbury, xi
— of Montpellier, 26, 78
— of Sabran, 88
— of Tyre, xi, 69 *n*
— son of the Marquis, 5–6, 21
— the Carpenter, lord of Melun, 33–4
— the Picard, 85

Xanthi, 10 *n*
Xerigordo, (Exerogorgo)

Yaghi Siyan (Cassianus), amir of Antioch, x, xxvii, xxxii–xxxiii, 47–50, 61, 76
Yconium. *See* Iconium

Zachaeus, 100
Zebari. *See* Gibelon
Zechariah, 98
Zion. *See* Sion